RELEASE THE SNYDER CUT

RELEASE THE SNYDER CUT

THE CRAZY TRUE STORY BEHIND THE FIGHT THAT SAVED ZACK SNYDER'S JUSTICE LEAGUE

SEAN O'CONNELL

APPLAUSE
THEATRE & CINEMA BOOKS
Guilford, Connecticut

Applause Theatre & Cinema Books
An imprint of The Rowman & Littlefield Publishing Group, Inc.
4501 Forbes Blvd., Ste. 200
Lanham, MD 20706
www.rowman.com

Distributed by NATIONAL BOOK NETWORK

Grateful acknowledgment is made to the following for permission to quote previously published and unpublished material:

Drew McWeeny, critic/publisher of *Formerly Dangerous* newsletter: Quotes from "Reading the Weather," January 10, 2020 (https://drewmcweeny.substack.com/p/reading-the-weather).

Mick Doyle: Quotes from "We Can Be Heroes" (https://afsp.org/story/we-can-be-heroes -superhero-fans-take-up-the-fight-for-suicide-prevention).

Sheraz Farooqi: Quotes from the Farooqi Brothers podcast on ComicBook Debate (https:// comicbookdebate.com/2018/05/09/joint-statement-on-behalf-of-the-dc-fandom/).

British Library Cataloguing in Publication Information Available

Library of Congress Cataloging-in-Publication Data

Names: O'Connell, Sean, 1974- author.
Title: Release the Snyder cut : the crazy true story behind the fight that save Zack Snyder's
    Justice League / Sean O'Connell.
Description: Guilford, Connecticut : Applause Theatre & Cinema Books, 2021. | Includes
    bibliographical references and index.
Identifiers: LCCN 2020046009 (print) | LCCN 2020046010 (ebook) | ISBN
    9781493059034 (paperback) | ISBN 9781493059041 (ebook)
Subjects: LCSH: Justice League (Motion picture) | Snyder, Zack, 1966-
Classification: LCC PN1997.2.J87 O38 2021 (print) | LCCN PN1997.2.J87 (ebook) |
    DDC 791.43/72—dc23
LC record available at https://lccn.loc.gov/2020046009
LC record available at https://lccn.loc.gov/2020046010

♾️™ The paper used in this publication meets the minimum requirements of American National Standard for Information Sciences—Permanence of Paper for Printed Library Materials, ANSI/NISO Z39.48-1992.

For Michele, P. J., and Brendan. Team O'Connell.
You three are my everything, always.

And for my mom, who set me down this comic book path
many, many Saturday mornings ago. Big Gulps,
hot dogs, and butter pretzels forever.

CONTENTS

CONTENTS

AUTHOR'S NOTE

Everything happens for a reason.

That has been a personal belief of mine for decades. Nothing quite as extreme as a *Jerry Maguire*-type "Mission Statement." Just a realization that I've encountered enough happy accidents over the course of my life to accept the fact that something else is guiding our path, and that even though we might not fully understand *why* at the time, everything happens for a reason.

One of those coincidences occurred at a pivotal moment for this particular book. In fact, I'm not exaggerating when I tell you that if this event didn't happen, you probably wouldn't be holding *Release the Snyder Cut* in your hands right now.

It's September 25, 2019. I'm in the earliest stages of this project, which means I've told a small band of trusted friends about my idea for a book about the failed *Justice League* movie, and the fight waged by Zack Snyder's fans to convince Warner Bros. Studios to eventually release his original version of the superhero blockbuster. I'd done just enough legwork to get a proposal in place to appeal to literary agents. After a handful of rejections (par for the course, I'm told), a literary agent emails me expressing interest.

Folks, an email of that sort legitimately feels like a life preserver being tossed to a drowning man. That sounds extreme, I know. But when you embark on the daunting task of attempting to write your first book, every step of the process is drenched in uncertainty. You are convinced that blind pitches sent to potential collaborators are being ignored or, worse, tossed in the trash. So to hear that even ONE person believes in your concept is a gift.

The aforementioned agent asked to read the first three chapters. Outstanding. However, I'd only written one.

Okay, I'd only written part of one.

Not a problem. I was flush with vacation days at CinemaBlend, the entertainment website for which I work, and was looking for a reason to use them. I carved out three weekdays in October and planned to hunker down to complete the requested pages. Writers love assignments, and thrive under deadlines, right? Also, someone actually wanted to read more of my work. That had to be interpreted as a positive sign.

Well, yes, but little did I know that an even bigger sign was heading my way, a "vote of confidence" from those aforementioned higher powers that are constantly waiting for the right moment to metaphorically tap you on the shoulder and say, "Pay attention, this is important."

As the vacation days approached, an email dropped into my inbox containing an invitation to a movie set. This happens regularly at CinemaBlend. We're lucky enough to spend time on film sets on a consistent basis, learning about the movie-making process from the artists we admire.

This invitation was different though. It was for Netflix's original production of *Army of the Dead*—directed by Zack Snyder.

The coincidence was too much to bear. I've been on a Snyder set before. As you'll read later, I was on the set of Snyder's *Justice League,* back when it was still Snyder's *Justice League,* so I've seen the filmmaker in action.

But to be invited to the set of the next Zack Snyder movie *while* I am plotting a book about an old Zack Snyder movie? What are the chances?

Slim. I'd have to say slim.

Additionally, I knew I'd eventually be asking Snyder for contributions to this book. Visiting his *Army of the Dead* set might not give me the chance to mention this project to him directly (film sets are consistently humming workspaces, and no one's busier than the director on an active set), but at least it would provide face time so that when I reached out to him later for his thoughts on the Snyder Cut of *Justice League,* he'd put two and two together and realize I was a legitimate film journalist who possesses an active interest in his work.

By the way, that worked. Shortly after announcing that Zack Snyder's *Justice League* would come to HBO Max, the director sat down for an exclusive interview for this book. I love it when a plan comes together.

The sheer coincidence of the timing of these events still boggles my mind. Everything happens for a reason. And the reason, this time, ends up being the book that I hope you are about to enjoy.

1

"I RECKON YOU SHOULD SHOW IT."

Zack Snyder didn't get out of bed the morning of May 20, 2020, expecting to invent a new holiday. But you better believe fans of the acclaimed film director will circle that date on the calendar and celebrate it with the reverence of a holy day. In their community, May 20 will forever be remembered as the day the Holy Grail of superhero movies was secured, the day Hollywood finally announced plans to release the Snyder Cut of the director's mythical *Justice League* movie.

I've seen my fair share of craziness while covering the film industry—from meteoric rises to devastating failures. At the 2017 Oscars, Warren Beatty announced the wrong movie as the Academy Awards Best Picture winner. That was crazy. Still, nothing I've encountered over the past three decades has been as fascinating, uplifting, and unpredictable as the story of the Release the Snyder Cut (or RTSC) movement.

Unified fronts in Hollywood fandom are few and far between. Fans, by definition, are fanatics who live to debate about the things they love. For that reason, it's rare to see a fandom accomplish any sort of stated goal. The RTSC movement formed over a shared belief in the existence of an alternate version of the 2017 superhero movie *Justice League*. Snyder walked away from the comic-book blockbuster for deeply personal reasons (though many still believe he was permitted to quit before the studio, Warner Bros., fired him). A replacement director was hired to complete postproduction, maintaining the movie's release date. Once *Justice League* opened, though, the fans who had waited years to see DC Comics' top heroes together on screen for the first time realized something had gone wrong. Snyder's footage was nowhere to be found in the theatrical cut. And Snyder, responding to his fanbase's inquiries, repeatedly whipped his followers into a frenzy by teasing the existence of his own cut, the Snyder Cut.

Snyder essentially laid down a gauntlet, and his dedicated fans picked it up. They bonded together as a team and worked tirelessly on behalf of his lost cut of *Justice League* until Warner Bros. agreed to let them see it. The members of the vocal, global RTSC community range from rabid social-media warriors to actual cast members of Snyder's DC films. And while this book will cover, in great detail, the behind-the-scenes Hollywood story of how the Snyder Cut of *Justice League* was ushered into the world faster than any other controversial director's cut of a botched movie, it's also about the individual members of the RTSC movement, and their impressive accomplishments. Snyder believes that the cut of *Justice League* that's currently heading to HBO Max wouldn't exist without the movement's persistence. He may have guided them along in key moments, but it was these fans who made this happen.

Snyder himself told me, "I owe them a huge debt of gratitude, because of course, there would be no director's cut, or Snyder Cut. It wouldn't exist in a way that anyone would ever see it if it weren't for them. And that's just a fact."[1]

The story begins with Zack Snyder signing on to shepherd the DC Extended Universe (DCEU) in 2010. Snyder is a visionary filmmaker whose resume includes such features as *300, Dawn of the Dead, Sucker Punch,* and the faithful adaptation of Alan Moore's controversial graphic novel, *Watchmen.* But he's best known in the comic book and pop culture community as the man who built a cinematic universe out of DC Comics' top assets for Warner Bros.—until he was ordered to stop.

Snyder was hand-picked by director Christopher Nolan (*Batman Begins, The Dark Knight*) and hired by Warner Bros. Studios to revive a dormant Superman film franchise, and potentially launch a DC shared cinematic universe on screen. The director tapped actors Henry Cavill, Amy Adams, Russell Crowe, Michael Shannon, Diane Lane, Kevin Costner, and more to bring DC's iconic blue Boy Scout, Superman, to the big screen in the 2013 origin story *Man of Steel.*

It was a fresh start for a character famously portrayed by the late Christopher Reeve in multiple Superman movies in the 1980s. It also marked a different, more aggressive tone for the Man of Steel, one that divided fans. The Superman who anchors *Man of Steel* isn't the pure beacon of hope that audiences have grown to love. Not yet anyway. His alien powers are new, and scary. Clark Kent (Cavill) questions his role as a God-like savior living amongst men and is even warned by his adoptive father against helping people in need (because, he's told, it might be more valuable to protect his identity). The repercussions of some of the creative choices made in *Man of Steel* are still being debated by dedicated DC fans. Parts of the online community, as an example, still vehemently disagree with Snyder's decision to have Superman kill his newfound nemesis, General Zod (Shannon), by snapping his neck at the conclusion of their destructive battle. Remember, fans love to debate about the things that they love.

Snyder continued telling Superman's updated origin story in the 2015 team-up adventure *Batman v Superman: Dawn of Justice* and approximately half of its sequel, *Justice League,* before his vision fell apart. The film studio—allegedly reacting to disappointing box office receipts and mainstream audience apathy for *Batman v Superman*—decided to change horses midstream. They hired a different director with a superhero pedigree, Marvel Studios veteran Joss Whedon, to complete the *Justice League* work that Snyder had started.

This was, to put it lightly, highly unusual. Whedon was a "Marvel guy," having helmed two high-profile *Avengers* movies for Disney and Marvel Studios. Several fans found it strange that Whedon was willing to jump ship and help the rival DC complete its first live-action *Justice League* movie. It was an unprecedented move. Also, it didn't work. Whedon's version of *Justice League* ended up becoming a critical and commercial failure, and Snyder's fans—still furious over his removal from the project—immediately began demanding retribution.

The problems extended beyond one film. Multiple Warner Bros. movies that were meant to follow Snyder's *Justice League* were altered by the studio's decision to replace him with Joss Whedon. Snyder, at the time, was the captain of the larger DCEU ship. This grand experiment would include individual films for multiple DC superheroes such as Wonder Woman, The Flash, and Green Lantern. But Snyder also had teased a five-film story arc of his own that would have been developed in his *Justice League* movie, and fans who had bought into his storytelling method felt like that potential had been ripped away.

In online conversations held after the theatrical release of Joss Whedon's *Justice League,* Snyder fans began to question how much of the film the director had managed to complete on his version of *Justice League* before he left the project. They speculated how different the structure and tone of the lost *Justice League* movie was going to be from the final version Warner Bros. eventually released to theaters. And perhaps most importantly, they asked themselves—and anyone else who would listen—if Snyder's original cut of *Justice League* could ever be salvaged.

THE MOTHER OF ALL OUR QUESTIONS

On May 20, 2020, concrete answers to a number of those inquiries finally started to form. In truth, this happened much quicker than even Snyder expected.

"I never would've thought, I've got be honest, that it would work out like this," the director said. "Well, I never thought it was going to work out on this timetable, let's put it that way."

On the morning of May 20, Snyder hosted a *Man of Steel* viewing party from his home theater in Southern California. Online attendees were able to sync their own copies of the 2013 movie to the director's and watch along with him on the social media platform Vero while he provided a live audio commentary track. Snyder had promised to field a few questions afterward, which created mild buzz in the RTSC community. They wondered if this finally would be the event for which they had been waiting, an announcement of a potential release of the *Justice League* cut they'd been demanding to see.

As the *Man of Steel* screening drew to a close, and Snyder started preparing for the question-and-answer session, fans understood that something extraordinary was about to happen because the movie's star, Henry Cavill, suddenly joined Zack and his wife, Deborah, for a very special announcement.

"I think the second Henry showed up, my heart just knew it was happening," said Giovanni Torres, a thirty-one-year-old product manager from

New York City, and a die-hard RTSC member. Torres joined the RTSC family during the earliest stages of the movement and fought daily alongside fans who wanted to see Snyder's vision for *Justice League* restored. It was a three-year wait to hear Snyder say the words confirming his plan to release the Snyder Cut, and Torres admits that, in the moment, he could hardly believe it was happening.

"Honestly," he said, "the whole time watching the Q-and-A stream, I was so nervous. I heard nothing that was happening in the film, or what Zack was saying. When Henry showed up, I knew."[2]

That's not to say they rushed to the announcement. In hindsight, it's borderline cruel that Snyder put his historic Snyder Cut reveal at the end of a full screening of *Man of Steel*. Like Torres, all of Snyder's fans endured the screening and director's commentary, praying that they'd be rewarded with breaking Snyder Cut news. But Snyder's a born showman, and he knew that in this moment he had his audience eating out of the palm of his hand. So, Cavill and the Snyders leisurely reminisced about the filming of *Man of Steel* and the massive impact the role had on the actor's career. Their stroll down memory lane eventually expanded into a spirited conversation, as hand-picked fans joined the Zoom call with prearranged inquiries. The group covered a wide range of topics, dancing around the only question every audience member wanted to hear. Finally, Snyder fan Daniella Cares from Chile, South America, cut through the nonsense.

"I have a question that is the mother of all of our questions, as a fandom," she said. "When will you release the Snyder Cut?"

Even through cyberspace, you could feel the air get sucked out of the room. Cares admits she barely slept the night before, wrestling with the right way to phrase the question. She didn't want Snyder to misinterpret it or weasel out of answering.

"I really thought it was the longest shot ever," Cares told me after the fact, "but the chance was unique."[3]

Snyder playfully tried to deflect. He told viewers that he wasn't fully in control of the distribution situation for the Snyder Cut, and even if he could show it, what would his version of *Justice League* even look like? But no one intended to let Snyder off the hook. Not after years of waiting.

"I reckon you should show it," Cavill said. The fanbase held its collective breath.

"I mean, I can't show the movie right now," Snyder replied. "Because there's still a little bit to do. But, I mean, there is this. I do have this. I don't know if *this* is helpful."

At that point, Snyder turned his own laptop to face the camera so everyone tuned into the feed could see the black-and-white image of his *Justice League* cast. The photo had a "JL" logo and the title *Zack Snyder's Justice League*. Beneath the title was the confirmation fans fought three long years to secure: "2021. Only On HBO Max."

"So *that's* coming," Snyder concluded, as the gathered fans gasped and cheered. Victory, finally, was theirs.

A VOCAL MINORITY

Weeks after the Snyder Cut reveal, when the fever pitch surrounding the anticipated HBO Max announcement had cooled to a simmer, Snyder reflected on the impact of the day. He still was feeling the emotional reverberations of the RTSC movement's hard-fought win.

"I wanted to honor what the fans had created by trying to do this [announcement] in a way that would be dramatic or cool," he said. "Our intent was just to try and honor what everyone had done by giving them a reveal that was worth the effort. If that was possible! And the truth is, I don't even know if that, as a concept, was possible."

Snyder understood, better than anyone, how much time and energy was spent raising (and maintaining) awareness for the Snyder Cut of *Justice League*. He had tracked every step of the fierce battle waged by the RTSC family to convince Warner Bros. to allow him to finish his incomplete vision. He supported their efforts to educate naysayers by posting exclusive behind-the-scenes imagery to social media. He backed the charitable fundraising campaigns that often were associated with the RTSC movement.

And he shared what would have been his dream-scenario plan for the celebratory Snyder Cut reveal, if the world had not been drastically affected by the COVID-19 pandemic in 2020.

"Ideally, on this timetable, I would have tried to hold it [until] Comic-Con. That was my dream," he said. "If Comic-Con existed, in another world. That's the Holy Grail. It would have been the Holy Grail of reveals. They would've gone completely nuts."

He's not wrong. And now that he has said it, we can lament the fact that it didn't happen. Imagine a Warner Bros. Studios panel in Hall H at the San Diego Convention Center, where Zack Snyder struts on stage in front of 6,500 rabid attendees to surprise reveal the Snyder Cut of *Justice League*. It would have blown the building's roof off.

"But short of that," he continued, "I just felt like there's so much love out there for *Man of Steel* in the community. There's so much, in my opinion, just a great amount of good will around Henry [Cavill] and around that movie that I just felt like [the viewing party] was a great way to do it."

He also explained why Gal Gadot, Ezra Miller, Jason Momoa, Ben Affleck, and Ray Fisher—the other members of Snyder's *Justice League* cast—didn't end up being part of the historic May 20 announcement, despite their support over the years for the Release the Snyder Cut campaign.

"I talked to Henry about it because he and I started the journey together, and this felt . . . it was appropriate to just have it be Henry," Snyder said.

Never in his wildest dreams did Snyder imagine he'd be returning to his cut of *Justice League* so soon after having to leave it in 2017. Nor did he allow himself to ever fully believe that the studio would permit fans to see the director's complete vision of this epic story, and that he'd be given the chance to suitably prepare it for an HBO Max release.

"I was kind of expecting, 'Oh, one day, maybe. . . .' Because I had the cut, I was mostly thinking that when they do the documentary [someday], it would be good to have a couple of scenes that they could cut to," he said.

Snyder knows that his fanbase's constant support for the Snyder Cut of *Justice League* convinced HBO Max to collaborate on this passion project. The director expressed complete awe at the RTSC movement's persistence, and their unshakable resolve.

"I just felt like, as with anything, we would just be, 'Sure, it's fine to be mad about it, or feel like there was something more to see or something happened,' or whatever. But in the end, it's a movie, so I guess part of me just always thought that they would just, not *give up* so much as the next thing would come along," Snyder said. "There's a lot of noise in the world. There are a lot of noisy things to keep you occupied."

But the movement itself generated more than enough noise. In the press release confirming Zack Snyder's *Justice League* on HBO Max, Warner Media Entertainment chairman Robert Greenblatt singled out the nonstop requests by the RTSC community as a factor in the company's decision to back Snyder's cut.

"Since I got here 14 months ago, the chant to #ReleaseTheSnyderCut has been a daily drumbeat in our offices and inboxes," Greenblatt said. "Well, the fans have asked, and we are thrilled to finally deliver. At the end of the day, it really is all about them and we are beyond excited to be able to release Zack's ultimate vision for this film in 2021."[4]

Snyder couldn't help but laugh while discussing the omnipresent social media presence of the RTSC family, especially when it came to anything posted online by Warner Bros., Warner Media, or HBO Max. "Their websites, their Twitter, their *everything* . . . they were paralyzed. They were literally paralyzed," he said. "They could make no release. They could talk about nothing. I was talking to an unnamed executive who said that [HBO Max] would tweet something about *Sesame Street,* and people would be like, 'Fuck Elmo! Release the Snyder Cut!' That was the world they lived in. And they were like, 'Jesus Christ, what are we supposed to do? We can't function!' That's pretty rad."

Show business is a business. And the supportive RTSC movement, through all its global Release the Snyder Cut activities, gave the filmmaker the bargaining chips that he needed when he returned to the negotiating table with the studio.

"It was during, I think, [2019's] Comic-Con where there was an article written that said, 'The biggest Warner Bros. and DC presence at Comic-Con this year is for a movie they'd never released.' Which I was like, 'Holy shit, that's amazing,'" Snyder said. "We did all these analytics. And when we went in to talk to Warner Bros. about possibly releasing the movie, I said to them in the boardroom, 'You realize, I don't know if you're aware of it, but the biggest, the most volume for any social media campaign for any movie Warner Bros has ever done is for a movie that you guys never released. The most tweets, the most social media noise in the history of Warner Bros. is for a film that you guys don't have out.' And at that stage in time, had no *intention* of releasing. In what world is that okay? In what world does the business model support this point of view? It just seems insane. And you know, apparently that didn't fall on deaf ears.

"But it's just a hard thing to argue with," Snyder continued. "They would say things like, 'Well, it's just a vocal minority. It's just a small amount of people.' I'm like, 'Okay, fair enough. If that's what you want to say. But *if* that's true, and it's not that big of a deal, how come you guys, a giant media corporation, cannot generate the same number of social media impressions as this vocal, grassroots minority that aren't that big of a deal? How come you wish, in your best-case scenario, you could volumize one of your products in the same way that this handful of people, so you say, can do it? And if it is [just] a handful of people, you should have them working for you because they are unbelievable at their jobs. At their hobby, actually! Because none of them are getting paid for it."

How did we get to this point? Why did Zack Snyder walk away from the DCEU before *Justice League* was finished? Who let Joss Whedon butcher the existing *Justice League* footage and deliver what critics and fans dismissed as a mediocre film? How did the ceaseless demand for an incomplete movie get so loud that the studio, which altered it, could no longer ignore the calls? In short, how did Zack Snyder and his fans release the Snyder Cut of *Justice League*? We know this journey reached its official end on May 20, 2020. Now, let's trace it all the way back to its beginning.

② WHY THEY FIGHT

Why on earth did so many people care about an alternate cut of *Justice League*?

The 2017 comic book blockbuster was an unmitigated disaster, the byproduct of too many cooks interfering in the superpowered kitchen. In an attempt to add humor to Zack Snyder's existing footage, replacement director Joss Whedon showed a complete lack of understanding for what makes the Justice League work. The usually somber Batman (Ben Affleck) cracked jokes. The Flash (Ezra Miller) was painted as a coward. The villain, Steppenwolf, looked like a video game character. The theatrical cut of *Justice League* bombed so emphatically, on every conceivable level, that it single-handedly torpedoed Warner Bros. and DC's ambitious dreams of an interconnected on-screen universe that would have paired Superman (Henry Cavill), Batman, and Wonder Woman (Gal Gadot) with the remaining members of DC's planet-protecting armada.

So, who actually fought to see the rumored 214-minute version of that movie?

For one, there were the Nerd Queens. Self-described as two girls who met on a Harry Potter website and now use the pseudonym the Nerd Queens online, Nana and Cole run a YouTube channel that celebrates their shared interests: travel, books, cosplay, comics, and Zack Snyder's contributions to the DCEU. The Nerd Queens first became actively involved with the RTSC movement during San Diego Comic-Con 2018, when they agreed to help distribute "I [Heart] ZS" T-shirts for attendees to wear, spreading the Snyder Cut gospel to the uninitiated.

"The entire experience that summer was unlike anything," Cole said. "The moment we started handing out those shirts, it was like the crowd woke up around us and were discussing Zack and his work and mutual love for him. People who had spent the last few hours in line together but had not spoken were suddenly talking like best friends. I think it was in that moment, it hit us just what this movement could be."[1]

A communal bond shared by strangers, and an appreciation for Snyder that brings people together, formed. These fans weren't even swayed by the knowledge that the Snyder Cut wasn't complete. Snyder himself clarified on the social media platform Vero on December 24, 2019, that his version at the time was "not 100 percent finished" and that there is "still some stuff I want to do, as with every film I've made."[2] Snyder went on to emphasize that he's "not sure what difference it makes as to the finished level of the film," but seemed to suggest that the hard creative decisions had been completed.

But the movement wasn't about that . . . or, completely about that. There's a lot more going on beneath the surface of the RTSC movement. And it's time that side of the story was told.

MIGHTY MOTIVATIONS

Members of the RTSC movement will tell you that they primarily fought for the concept of artistic integrity, to restore and defend Snyder's right to deliver his intended version of the *Justice League* story, because of the ramifications that its release could potentially have on the film industry, at large.

"To me, the Snyder Cut movement represents creative freedom and artistic integrity," said Lindsey Staton, a twenty-one-year-old author and devoted Snyder Cut supporter from West Virginia. In Staton's words, the movement even reaches beyond Zack Snyder and his specific *Justice League* film. "It's a constant, unrelenting voice for *all* directors who aren't allowed to express themselves in blockbuster superhero films. Just look at Scott Derrickson with the [planned] *Doctor Strange* sequel. He wanted to make a horror-esqe film, but Disney and [Marvel Studios] wouldn't have it. So what happened? They parted ways, and now Scott Derrickson isn't making a *Doctor Strange* sequel. This is exactly what we're fighting against."[3]

Similar sentiments are shared by thirty-four-year-old RTSC member Joseph Todd, from Illinois. "This isn't just about Zack Snyder," said Todd, the codirector of a local transportation service for senior citizens and disabled individuals. "This is a stand for every creative that was mistreated by a big studio. This is representative of standing up for the filmmaker and fighting for the creator's vision as a whole. Every filmmaker deserves for his or her vision to be seen, regardless of feelings on the content itself."[4]

Fighting for the artist is noble, but the RTSC movement ultimately caught my eye, and touched my soul, with its charitable efforts.

In March 2017, the Snyders lost their twenty-year-old daughter Autumn, who died by suicide. As a result, the members of the movement—with Zack's support—regularly campaigned to raise awareness for suicide prevention, a cause they know is near and dear to the hearts of Zack Snyder and his wife Deborah. As of July 2020, the RTSC movement reportedly raised more than $200,000 in charitable contributions for the American Foundation for Suicide Prevention (AFSP), a charity singled out by the Snyders. Almost all the marketing efforts staged on behalf of the RTSC movement come with a built-in charity component that immediately benefits AFSP.

"The topic of suicide and mental health is very close to our hearts," said Nana, one-half of the Nerd Queens. "And Zack Snyder's movies helped me personally through the darkest time of my life."

"Personally, as someone who has struggled with mental illness for a very long time, the charity aspect has just made the movement so much more unique and amazing," added Cole. "Being fans of Zack and wanting to advocate for suicide prevention just made this the perfect marriage of passions."

Perhaps most importantly, Release the Snyder Cut efforts created a community united in pursuit of one shared goal—a family that consistently found support and strength in each other.

Megan Loucks, twenty-five years old, lives in Michigan, where she works as a store manager and a freelance writer. She enjoys films, comics, and has a self-diagnosed "obsession" with Funko Pops. She's also a member of an all-female group of dedicated Zack Snyder podcasters known as Snyder's Amazons.

"We speak of our love for Zack's films, and give a female perspective on the themes and characters within his films," she said.[5]

Loucks first learned about the RTSC movement online in March 2018, as she became more active on Twitter and kept seeing the #ReleaseTheSny derCut hashtag trending. At first, her interest centered on the film. "After rewatching the first Comic-Con trailer and seeing how a lot of the film wasn't in the [theatrical] movie, I wanted to fight for Zack's vision."

Over time, though, Loucks found greater personal inspiration by serving as a devoted member of the Release the Snyder Cut family.

"I wanted to be a part of [this] because I wanted Zack to get his art out into the world, as it was intended," she said. "I wanted to be a part of something bigger than myself and do it in a positive way. I've never been involved in anything like this before, and it's been life changing. [The movement] means everything to me: friendship; artistic freedom; and hope. I have met so many great people through this movement, many of these people that I probably would've never had the chance to meet if this movement didn't exist. It means helping those who need help, whether that's through the AFSP charity work, or being a listening ear.

"It has changed my life in tremendous ways," Loucks continues. "Growing up, I never really felt like I was someone that fit in anywhere. I am twenty-five now, and this is the first time I've felt that I belonged. I found a group of people who all have a common interest as me. I found a charity that resonates with me. I was able to connect with my favorite director. I started writing for one of my favorite blogs. I have met some amazing people who I get to call my friends."

These friendships, forged by a dedication to Zack and Debbie Snyder, often lead to fruitful collaborations. Loucks and the Nerd Queens, for example, joined forces in July 2020 to host the first-ever fan event dedicated to Zack Snyder's *Justice League*. Dubbed Justice Con, the two-day celebration featured informative panels hosted by actor Ray Fisher (Cyborg in *Batman v Superman: Dawn of Justice*), *Justice League* cinematographer Fabian Wagner, a gaggle of Snyder-themed YouTube hosts, and Snyder himself. Justice Con is one of many fantastic examples of Snyder's fans wanting to pay the director back, in some way, and continue to shine a light on his body of work.

Other fans claim to have formed deep familial bonds thanks to their involvement in the campaign to release the Snyder Cut of *Justice League*. A group self-dubbed as TPZ, which stands for "Team Pro Zack," has been extremely active behind the scenes for many of the movement's marketing and fundraising campaigns. Their names and accomplishments will resurface as this story unfurls.

"I do not use the term 'brothers' lightly. These men are family to me," stated Darren Benson, a forty-five-year-old IT program manager and TPZ member who lives in Norman, Oklahoma. "Although we have only known each other a short few years, it feels like we have known each other for decades. We talk daily, we help each other with problems, we celebrate our differences. It is a true brotherhood."[6]

"[This movement] gave me the opportunity to connect with so many amazing people from all over the world, some that I now consider family," Geraldo Cortes added about the TPZ group. Cortes, thirty-seven years old, lives in Rio de Janeiro. He's a lifelong DC Comics fan who joined the RTSC movement because of how badly he felt Snyder had been treated by the studio. "I firmly believe that it is important for everyone to make connections like these with people from different cultures and countries. You learn more and more how people are (although different in their respective environments, languages, beliefs, and customs) essentially very much alike. Life becomes better because of these connections."[7]

Chris Wong-Swenson, a thirty-seven-year-old entrepreneur who hails from Honolulu, Hawaii, confirms that the movement has permanently changed him because his involvement in it has made him feel less lonely. Like most members of the Snyder Cut family, he has followed DC Comics his whole life, and fully supported Zack Snyder's interpretations of these cherished characters. He routinely creates videos on his YouTube channel, Ping Pong Flix, which analyzes the DC Cinematic Universe. He pays extreme attention to the contributions of Snyder and helped lead the three-year quest to unearth the Snyder Cut of *Justice League*. Wong-Swenson's love of Superman goes deeper than passionate fandom, though. He says that because of his adoration since childhood of Christopher Reeve's Superman, his parents legally changed his name to "Chris" to reflect that dedication. So yeah, he's a fan.

"Before *BvS*, I felt alone, constantly berated, bullied [and] beaten down by local friends because I enjoyed [Zack Snyder's] *Man of Steel*. I started my videos talking about *BvS* and have found others like me that enjoy the Snyderverse," he said. "With the movement, I've found friends all over the world who share the same love for Snyder and his work. I even found out how much *BvS* or *MoS* has affected many lives in so many ways, curing depression, inspiring artistic tendencies, motivating few to create their own businesses, etc. I am forever grateful for how much this movement has opened my eyes to the world. It's helping people connect and band together for what I believe is a just cause."[8]

SALVATION, WHEN ALL HOPE WAS LOST

For some, the formation of the RTSC movement occurred when they least expected it, but needed it the most.

Take Jeff Purdy, a structural engineering manager from Missouri, and a vocal supporter of the Release the Snyder Cut push. Purdy was enamored with Zack Snyder's work in the DC on-screen universe, even if he admits it took him "a couple of viewings to really grasp what Zack was going for" in the 2013 Superman origin movie, *Man of Steel*.

"I think these characters are unique and have depth," Purdy said. "We can dig into their mythos and find ourselves."[9]

The theatrical cut of *Justice League,* however, arrived at a particularly brutal moment in Purdy's personal life. For starters, his mother received a devastating cancer diagnosis in February 2017. Meanwhile, at work, Purdy says his boss replaced him, filling the position with one of the boss's close friends. Purdy remembers that, at the time, he desperately wanted to escape his real-life hardships by celebrating his beloved on-screen DC heroes. But the butchered *Justice League* released by Warner Bros. provided no respite.

"This film series going from exceptional to embarrassing deserves some of the burden for my two-year state of depression," Purdy said. "I was catatonic. Superman is supposed to be about hope. But I lost all hope after watching this [movie]."

Casual filmgoers oftentimes forget the healing power of cinema, and how movies can boost an audience member's spirits when they are down in the dumps. Uplifting and inspirational films possess the ability to change our lives. On the flip side, disastrous versions of highly anticipated movies can leave us feeling disappointed, even devastated. A handful of outside forces, coupled with the nightmare that was *Justice League*'s theatrical cut in 2017, overwhelmed Purdy.

"I had nowhere to turn without feeling hopeless," he said. "Ultimately, my mother passed away at the age of sixty-five, my generation lost its voice [in Zack Snyder], and my career was, essentially, over. I thought to take the easy way out."

You hear heartbreaking stories like this from a number of members of the Release the Snyder Cut community as they open up about the reasons why they joined the fight to restore Zack's vision. And it's tied, directly, to Autumn Snyder's suicide, a devastating tragedy that affected Snyder's involvements in the DC Cinematic Universe.

Essentially, though, the RTSC movement threw Jeff Purdy a lifeline when he needed help the most.

"I found the people on Twitter," he said. "They fought for artistic integrity and suicide prevention. I found my new home. At the lowest point in my life, I found salvation."

When asked how the RTSC movement has changed him, Purdy simply replies, "It saved my life."

A REAL-LIFE MARTHA MOMENT

There's a popular Batman quote that often comes to mind when writing about the Snyder Cut community: "It's not who I am underneath," the Caped Crusader once said on screen, "but what I *do* that defines me."[10]

Sure, that's a quote from Christopher Nolan's Batman origin story, *Batman Begins,* and not from any of Snyder's DC films. But the message aptly fits the mantra of the RTSC movement, so I'm co-opting it for Snyder's fanbase.

Underneath, they are amazingly different people from wildly different walks of life. They're global citizens who found commonality in their appreciation for Zack Snyder and the work he did on the DC movies for Warner Bros. And they want to be defined by their successful efforts to release the director's cut of a flawed movie while also raising awareness for a charitable cause that is important to the Snyders.

Hamad Al-Mansouri, for example, is a husband and father from the Middle Eastern country of Qatar. He works as a senior manager of human capital at the Qatar Financial Center. He's also a die-hard DC fan who has been a leader and contributor to the RTSC movement from day one.

"There are two main reasons [why I joined]," Al-Mansouri explained. "One is my emotional investment [in the] DCEU. And the other is the injustice that happened to Zack."[11]

Al-Mansouri remembers the disappointment that set in following his screening of the theatrical cut of *Justice League*. His memories sync up with many other DC fans who dreamed of seeing Snyder's vision preserved and continued by Joss Whedon and his team.

And with good reason. When Warner Bros. approached Whedon to replace Snyder on the work-in-progress *Justice League* (for reasons I'll explain later), Warner Bros. Pictures president Toby Emmerich tried to assuage the concerns of fans by claiming the amount of new direction on the production would be minimal, and that the studio was doing everything it could to maintain Snyder's approach to the material.

Most of that ended up being false.

"After *Man of Steel*, I was 100 percent onboard this cinematic universe, and I was ready for all the grittiness and darkness it would bring," Al-Mansouri continued. "When I first left [*Justice League*] after watching it, I thought it was fun and entertaining. Slowly, despair came raining down after realizing what happened. This isn't Zack's movie.

"Precisely a week after its release, I went on Twitter and saw that there were other people who shared my suspicion," Al-Mansouri said. "I didn't need evidence at that time. The only thing I needed was *Man of Steel* and *Batman v Superman*. Both these movies were enough to tell me that *Justice League* theatrical was not Zack's movie, and knowing Zack and his director's cuts, a different version definitely exists. From then on, the evidence came, reaffirming what we have always believed."

Loyalty to and sympathy for Zack Snyder led Al-Mansouri to the RTSC movement. But that sense of community and the shared bond of family is what kept him in the fight. In his own words, his main goal initially was to pressure Warner Bros. to release Zack Snyder's version of *Justice League*.

But after being immersed in the movement for the better part of three years, Al-Mansouri celebrates the fact that the RTSC efforts have connected him with unexpected, like-minded comic book supporters from all corners of the planet.

Ironically, one of the closest friends Al-Mansouri has made through the RTSC family is Jeff Purdy from Missouri.

"My favorite connection, which is the reason the fandom is so passionate with the Snyder DCEU, is with a guy called Jeff Purdy," Al-Mansouri told me. "One day I saw him talk about his mother who passed away recently. My mother had also passed away, almost two years ago. I decided to message him to see if he wanted to talk about it. So we started to talk about our mothers, and how the world is so different to us without them. We both came to the conclusion that our mothers are both great human beings."

That, alone, is a beautiful and worthwhile connection. A shared passion for a cinematic universe brought together a financial manager in Qatar and a structural engineering manager from the United States. What happened next, though, is borderline impossible.

"[It] dawned on me," recalls Al-Mansouri, "that our mothers *have the same name*. The infamous Martha scene, which a lot of people joke about [from Zack Snyder's *Batman v Superman: Dawn of Justice*], has connected this Qatari guy to this other American guy from Missouri in the most deep way."

It remains a running joke. During a pivotal moment in Snyder's superhero standoff *Batman v Superman: Dawn of Justice,* the Dark Knight (Ben Affleck) finally gets the upper hand on Kal-El (Henry Cavill). Right before Batman delivers a death blow, Superman pleads, "Save Martha!" He's begging Batman to save his mother, who has been kidnapped by Lex Luthor's goons. Only, Superman doesn't realize that Martha also happens to be the name of Batman's murdered mother, and the emotional connection reminds Bruce Wayne that Superman is, in fact, a man. He recognizes a bond, and it (conveniently) removes the perceived differences that drove the superpowered heroes apart. From there on, they are united.

As are the dedicated members of the RTSC community.

"This is what the Snyder Cut movement means to me," Al-Mansouri said. "We are family now."

FIONA JOINS (AND LEADS) THE FIGHT

If the Snyder Cut family was a tree, its roots would be found in Fiona Zheng.

Zheng lives in the city of Harbin, which is the capital of Heilongjiang, China's northernmost province, and owns a small medical clinic. She's always been an avid moviegoer, and particularly loved the Marvel superhero films. Then she learned about Zack Snyder by screening *Batman v Superman: Dawn of Justice.*

"I was blown away by the film," Zheng said. "I had never seen such a powerful, relatable, visually stunning, smart, witty and fun-to-watch superhero film ever before. I loved how Snyder considered himself as making a great film first, rather than a comic book movie film. *BvS* was a Greek tragedy, plus a political thriller. Snyder was ambitious and brave, to raise issues few other blockbuster filmmakers dared to touch."[12]

Zheng immediately headed online to find similar fans who shared the same passion for Snyder's films. She spread the "Gospel of Zack" on Twitter and became a very active member of the director's fan community, even forming a friendship with Snyder behind the scenes. And she says she knew instantly that the version of *Justice League* that was released into theaters in November 2017 was not the version Snyder intended.

"We just knew there must be a completely different film out there," Zheng said.

She decided to do something about it. Something major. As a result, Fiona Zheng is recognized by members of the RTSC as the founding mother of the movement. Her impact traces back to a November 21, 2017, tweet, where Zheng implored, "Guys, I have to say, I am sure, deadly sure, there's a director's cut of *Justice League.* . . . It exists. It's not just a longer or better version of the film. There's a real final chapter of the trilogy out there. We have to fight for it."[13]

Nearly two years later, almost to the day, on a November 16, 2019, podcast celebrating the anniversary of the release of the *Justice League* theatrical cut, two rabid Snyder fans who call themselves The Film Exiles spoke of Zheng's early work on behalf of the RTSC movement. Cohost Tolu Walker praised, "Fiona is about the most powerful force that started this movement. . . . In terms of organizing the fandom, and just being a voice, she carried the torch, pretty much solo-dolo, for so long."[14]

"There are so many people that I consider leaders in the movement because there are so many different ways that people lead," TPZ member Darren Benson concludes. "Some have brilliant ideas for campaigns, some are great at leading events and gathering support, some spend loads of their own free time pushing the #ReleaseTheSnyderCut hashtag, and that lights a fire under others. There are many more examples, but I think the strength of the movement is the diverse and multitalented makeup of the people within it."

In order to decipher how DC fans even got to the point where they had a cinematic universe to cheer for—and to lament when it abruptly disintegrated—let's dive into Warner Bros.' rocky history with its superhero world-building, and the hasty way they tried to catch up to Marvel Studios, its closest competitor.

3

A (JUSTICE) LEAGUE OF THEIR OWN

If you threw a rock at a random movie theater marquee in the year 2019, you were all but guaranteed to hit a comic book blockbuster.

Every major movie studio—from Walt Disney Studios and Warner Bros. to Lionsgate and 20th Century Fox—had a comic book franchise in its stable. The most prestigious comic book publishers, Marvel and DC, also happened to produce the biggest superhero film franchises at Disney and Warner Bros., respectively. Yet even studios like Universal Pictures figured out alternative ways to mine the superhero movie craze, like when they deconstructed the traditional comic book genre with M. Night Shyamalan's *Glass,* the sequel to his 2000 cult hit *Unbreakable.*

It's one thing for a smaller studio like Lionsgate to hold the rights to a standalone character like Mike Mignola's Hellboy, however, and another thing for a studio to possess its own cinematic universe.

By 2019, pop culture influencers had firmly established that movie-going audiences liked their recognizable properties to share space. Team ups weren't just appreciated in the superhero movies of this era, they were expected—no matter how difficult, logistically, they might have been to pull off. For example, fans would actively lobby for Wolverine (Hugh Jackman) or the X-Men to show up in a movie like 20th Century Fox's *Deadpool 2* simply because they knew that the characters all were owned by the same studio. Who cares if it didn't make sense storywise? Crossover events are cool, so give the people what they want!

This line of thinking even led a legitimate industry player like Sony Pictures, which owned the lucrative character rights to Spider-Man (and supporting characters like Venom or Carnage), to enter into an unprecedented rights-sharing agreement with rival studio Disney. This historic partnership allowed the wall-crawler to join Iron Man (Robert Downey Jr.), Captain America (Chris Evans), Thor (Chris Hemsworth), and virtually every major Marvel character on screen in the mega-sized blockbusters *Avengers: Infinity War* and *Avengers: Endgame.*

This is just how things were done at the time. And to a die-hard comic book fan who had grown up on these legendary stories, it was admittedly awesome.

How dominant are superhero movies in this modern era? By the end of 2019, three of the five highest-grossing films for the year were superhero movies: Joe and Anthony Russo's *Avengers: Endgame;* Anna Boden and Ryan Fleck's *Captain Marvel;* and Jon Watts's *Spider-Man: Far From Home.* All three of these films topped the $1 billion mark at the worldwide box office, with *Avengers: Endgame* successfully knocking off James Cameron's *Avatar* as the highest-grossing film of all time—a record *that* movie held for just under a decade. In fact, if you surveyed the entire release calendar for 2019, there were only two months out of the entire frame (September and December) that didn't have at least one comic book movie dropping into multiplexes.

This was a tremendous time for fans of superhero blockbusters. But that wasn't always the case.

HERE THEY COME TO SAVE THE DAY

Hollywood has been making movies adapted from comic book source materials since the 1930s, though back then, Dick Tracy and The Shadow were the heroic equivalents of our Iron Man and Batman. Classic comic book characters like The Lone Ranger and Barbarella gradually expanded the types of stories that got silver-screen treatment, and by the 1970s, superheroes and the entertainment industry were working hand in hand.

Feature-length stories pulled from these comic book worlds were few and far between in those days, however. Forget about monthly comic book movies like we see nowadays. In these early stages of the genre, fans often waited *years* between wide releases and never knew when the next comic book movie might arrive.

Ironically, it was Warner Bros.' creative partnership with DC Comics that helped this particular film genre take flight, both literally and figuratively.

The DC Universe, as we now know it, began on the pages of DC's comic books in 1938, when *Action Comics* No. 1 introduced the world to an orphaned alien named Kal-El. Shortly after Superman established himself in Metropolis, Batman and Wonder Woman joined the company's ranks in 1939 and 1941, respectively, forming a holy trinity that would carry DC Comics for generations. It wasn't until DC's parent company, Kinney National Company, acquired Warner Bros.-Seven Arts in 1969 and rebranded it as Warner Bros. Picture, though, that the merger between the comic publisher and the movie studio solidified, giving Hollywood a stable foundation upon which they would create numerous memorable superhero films.

Just as Superman helped introduce the DC Universe in comic books in 1939, the "Big Blue Boy Scout" also gave Hollywood its initial template for transitioning heroes to movie theaters. Richard Donner's 1978 crowd-pleaser, *Superman,* convinced audiences that a man could fly—and proved to skeptical studio heads that comic books were lucrative source materials for film productions.

The groundbreaking origin story benefitted from perfect casting across the board. Relative newcomer Christopher Reeve so seamlessly embodied the Man of Steel on screen that it became impossible for the actor to separate himself from Superman for the rest of his professional career. Additionally, Donner hit grand slam home runs by luring Oscar winner Gene Hackman (*The French Connection*) to play Superman's conniving nemesis Lex Luthor, and casting Margot Kidder as the spunky ace *Daily Planet* reporter Lois Lane. Couple these casting coups with a heartwarming script, John Williams's iconic film score, and some Oscar-winning visual effects, and Hollywood finally had the ingredients for its first major superhero franchise.

"*Superman* was so important to me growing up," said Geraldo Cortes, a thirty-eight-year-old musician and video producer from Rio de Janeiro, Brazil. "Mainly because of the heart of that specific interpretation of the character, and because of one point of that particular story: The father and son relationship. That always moved me so much because I could relate perfectly, being as close as I am to my own dad. So much so that it's hard to put in words. It was because of [Richard Donner's] movie that I dove deeply into comic books, and Superman became my favorite comic book character of all."[1]

Crossovers in the superhero genre, though, were still decades away. That sort of forward-thinking, cross-pollination of comic book franchises wouldn't rear its ambitious head for at least another thirty years. Coincidentally, DC and Marvel might have arrived at the decision to team up their iconic heroes in blockbuster movies around the same time. The Hollywood trade paper *Variety* notes in a February 22, 2007, news article that Warner Bros. had hired co-screenwriters Kiernan and Michele Mulroney to pen a treatment for a Justice League of America movie, proving that the idea was on the table a full decade before Joss Whedon's *Justice League* would ever open.

"The Justice League of America has been a perennial favorite for generations of fans, and we believe their appeal to film audiences will be as strong and diverse as the characters themselves," Warner Bros. president of production Jeff Robinov said at the time of the announcement of the hiring of the Mulroneys,[2] which made a ton of sense, according to die-hard DC fans who had been patiently waiting for an on-screen universe shared by their favorite comic book characters for years . . . even for a lifetime.

"These are characters that are timeless and universal," said Carlos Orbegozo. Known online as "Carlos Digital," Orbegozo is a forty-year-old resident of Toronto, Canada. He works as an engineering department manager for an international tech company. And he loved what Zack Snyder was doing with his beloved DC superheroes, until the studio interfered.

"[These characters have been] an anchor for the medium, and the brand, for more than eighty years. If we are going to make a universe, these characters have to be right in the middle of it," Orbegozo said. "There are many people I come across who recognize the characters, and know the actors related to each character, with ease and acceptance. It's not easy to get that type of recognition."[3]

Meanwhile, across the street at Marvel Studios, they, too, were capitalizing on celebrity and recognition as they constructed their on-screen world. Perennial partier Robert Downey Jr. rehabbed his career by stepping into the role of billionaire playboy philanthropist Tony Stark in the *Iron Man* movies. Chris Evans ended up being perfectly cast as Captain America, the head of Marvel's Avengers team. We'll dig deeper into Marvel Studios' significant contributions to the evolution of the superhero movie genre in our next chapter, so stick a pin in that thought because it's relevant to the path that the DCEU took under Zack Snyder's watch.

Instead of seeking ambitious team-ups, Hollywood studios throughout the 1980s, 1990s, and 2000s rifled through comic book properties looking for anything with standalone franchise potential. Warner Bros. and DC, who already had a seat at the proverbial table, milked the potential of the *Superman* franchise for one good sequel, Richard Lester's *Superman II*, before running the whole endeavor into the ground with two more disastrous chapters and an uneven spinoff, Jeannot Szwac's 1984 adventure *Supergirl*.

Ironically, it was original *Superman* director Richard Donner's experience with comic book movies that actually set a precedent for what Snyder would encounter decades later. Prior to the fight for the Snyder Cut of *Justice League,* the most significant unreleased DC superhero sequel to get its director's cut restored would be *Superman II: The Richard Donner Cut.* As the story goes, Donner shot footage for Warner and DC's 1978 origin story *Superman: The Movie,* as well as its planned follow-up, simultaneously. But the director was only partially finished with what would become *Superman II* when he paused production to wrap work on *Superman.* While on this hiatus, Donner's relationship with his producers reportedly deteriorated, leading to him being replaced by director Richard Lester, who completed the shoot, and the post-production process.

Sound familiar?

Fans were aware of Donner's existing footage; however, calls for a "Donner Cut" of *Superman II* didn't really swell until 2001. That year, *Superman: The Movie* received a DVD restoration, so Warner Bros. opted to kill two birds with one stone. A team was assembled to reconstruct Donner's *Superman II* from original camera negatives and restore the director's true vision for his supersequel.

Superman II: The Richard Donner Cut held a world premiere event at the Director's Guild of America building in Hollywood on November 2, 2006. That's more than twenty-five years after the theatrical cut of *Superman II* opened in the United States on June 19, 1981. Snyder Cut fans should thank their lucky stars they didn't have to wait that long.

There was hardly a shortage of superhero stories in those decades, yet very little consistency in terms of studios developing a series around a recognizable or marketable brand. There would be standalone hits at different studios from time to time, though none of them led to larger arcs of continued storytelling.

Director Mike Hodges and producer Dino De Laurentiis, for example, collaborated on a campy *Flash Gordon* picture for Universal Studios in December 1980. Starring Sam J. Jones in the title role and the iconic Max von Sydow as Ming the Merciless, *Flash Gordon* proved to be a modest hit for Universal (thanks, in large part, to its catchy soundtrack composed and performed by the legendary rock outfit Queen), opening the door even wider to future film adaptations of comic book properties. If *Flash Gordon* had come out in 1990, only ten years later, a sequel likely would have been guaranteed, but studio heads and executive producers weren't thinking in terms of franchise potential just yet. Five years after *Flash Gordon,* De Laurentiis instead went back to the well for a different feature film based on the Marvel Comics character Red Sonja, assisted by the appearances of both Brigitte Nielsen and Arnold Schwarzenegger in the lead roles. Reviews for *Red Sonja* were terrible, and the box office haul was even worse. But between these single-serving comic stories and the established wins Warner Bros. and DC were enjoying with Superman and Batman, a brand new genre of storytelling had been introduced to the film industry, and the landscape hasn't been the same since.

By 2008, however, the rules of the game started to change. Up to that point, numerous characters from several disconnected comic book series got a shot at silver screen stardom, with bankable A-list talents taking bold career chances by playing popular heroes such as Daredevil (Ben Affleck), Judge Dredd (Sylvester Stallone), Blade (Wesley Snipes), Spider-Man (Tobey Maguire), Catwoman (Halle Berry), Ghost Rider (Nicolas Cage), and the Hulk (Eric Bana). Some of these movies worked. Many of them did not. For every winning *X-Men* saga, there was a creative and financial failure like Keanu Reeves's *Constantine* or the discombobulated *The League of Extraordinary Gentlemen* serving as a cautionary tale for studios that bet big on the wrong comic book properties. Just ask Dolph Lundgren, who parlayed his star-making turn in *Rocky IV* into an ill-fated feature centered around Marvel Comics' spirit of vengeance, The Punisher.

Jon Favreau's *Iron Man* movie changed everything. Literally. Released in 2008 and fitted around the boozy charms of Downey Jr., *Iron Man* launched what has become known as the Marvel Cinematic Universe, and the superhero genre was forever altered. Marvel Studios' impact was felt in every corner of the film industry—though no stronger than at their perceived rival, DC, and its creative partner, Warner Bros. While both companies are often quick to downplay any concept of a competition between their films, it's easy in hindsight to step back and recognize DC's creative decisions following the release of *Iron Man, Thor, Iron Man 2*, and *Captain America: The First Avenger* as a hasty reaction to the world that Marvel Studios was building on screen.

Simply put, DC wanted that.

MAN OF STEEL

The 2013 Superman origin story *Man of Steel* was meant to launch a connected universe of superhero films for DC and Warner Bros. that would challenge the Marvel Cinematic Universe. Emboldened by the overwhelming success of Christopher Nolan's Batman trilogy—consisting of 2005's *Batman Begins,* 2008's *The Dark Knight,* and 2012's *The Dark Knight Rises*—Warner Bros. intended to capitalize on fan goodwill and revive a classic character so that Superman could serve as the centerpiece of a new, expanded DC Cinematic Universe. And they believed they had just the right people in place behind the scenes to help them pull this off.

Two significant creative titans transitioned from the Christian Bale-led Batman trilogy to *Man of Steel*: Christopher Nolan and David S. Goyer. Nolan agreed to produce the film, still basking in the glow of praise for successfully rescuing DC's Caped Crusader from the neon-glow nightmare of the Joel Schumacher sequels *Batman Forever* and *Batman & Robin.* Nolan believed in a story pitch by his frequent collaborator Goyer, the screenwriter for Nolan's esteemed *Dark Knight* trilogy, and the duo sold Warner Bros. on their idea of a Superman reboot. It would be a traditional origin story, covering the expected bases of Krypton, Kansas, the *Daily Planet*, and the emergence of the Man of Steel into our world. Goyer agreed to pen the script, but Nolan had no intention of directing, so Warner Bros. needed a strong voice to step in.

Several prestigious names were considered for the *Man of Steel* directing gig. Tony Scott, Matt Reeves (who would eventually land a gig directing a Batman reboot for Warner), Guillermo del Toro, Matthew Vaughn, Jonathan Liebesman, and Duncan Jones were all reported to be on the studio's shortlist. *Back to the Future* director Robert Zemeckis also admitted to MTV News that he was in the running, but the project didn't interest him in the slightest.

"I passed on that faster than a speeding bullet," Zemeckis told the news outlet. "When they asked if I wanted to make the, what is it, seventeenth version of *Superman,* I said, 'No, I don't think so.'"[4]

Zack Snyder was interested. The award-winning director was already a company man at WB thanks to collaborations on *300, Legend of the Guardians: The Owls of Ga'Hoole,* and *Sucker Punch.* Snyder even had experience playing in the DC Comics sandbox, having adapted Alan Moore's controversial (and reportedly unfilmable) graphic novel *Watchmen* to general acclaim in 2009. Snyder was both a visionary choice and a safe choice to take over the reins on Superman, and the studio made the hire official in October 2010.

It was an assignment that would consume roughly the next seven years of Snyder's professional career.

Snyder fan Geraldo Cortes from Brazil admits to being slightly skeptical of the hire at first. "I'd seen almost all of his previous films and thought they were incredible but had a huge question mark in my mind when I tried to envision what he would do with Kal-El and Clark Kent," Cortes said. "*Man of Steel* came out, and to say my mind was blown is an understatement. I can't praise the movie enough. To me, it's a masterpiece. It's the greatest Superman movie ever made. . . . What *really* touched me deep down was that Zack managed to not only maintain the beauty of the father-son relationship that meant so much to me when I was a little boy, but he expanded and enriched it beyond my greatest expectations. The bond that exists between Kal-El and Jor-El, between Clark Kent and Jonathan, that unconditional love that is so hard to put into words. To see that being taken seriously, to see the story even I didn't know I was waiting for make it to the screen, was more than I could ever hope for."

Snyder had to realize that he wasn't just rebooting Superman in *Man of Steel.* He was also establishing the framework for a larger cinematic universe that in time would involve the assorted heroes of the DC Comics roster. When Warner Bros. head of production Jeff Robinov sat down with *Entertainment Weekly* in 2013 to discuss both *Man of Steel* and the long-term strategies of the DC film division, he made this point crystal clear.

"It's setting the tone for what the movies are going to be like going forward," Robinov said. "It's definitely a first step. . . . I think you'll see that, going forward, anything can live in this world. [Christopher Nolan's] Batman was deliberately and smartly positioned as a stand-alone. The world they lived in was very isolated without any knowledge of any other superheroes. What Zack and Chris have done with this film is allow you to really introduce other characters into the same world."[5]

Warner Bros. and DC had designs on building a cinematic universe of their own. The seeds would be planted in 2013's *Man of Steel,* but they'd grow over the course of several films until they had enough assets in place to tell a proper Justice League story. The full extent of the studio's grandiose plan finally was revealed, to overall shock and awe, on October 15, 2014. Then-Warner Bros. CEO Kevin Tsujihara unveiled an ambitious slate of ten DC titles that would reach theaters between 2016 and 2020. This would include a two-part *Justice League* story directed by Zack Snyder, as well as solo films for The Flash (Ezra Miller), Aquaman (Jason Momoa), Shazam, Cyborg (Ray Fisher), and Green Lantern.

"Clearly, the opportunity is enormous," Tsujihara told Warner Bros. shareholders following this announcement, according to a report in the *Los Angeles Times.* "DC will be a key engine for growth across all of Warner Bros."[6]

Of course, "announcing" ten movies and "delivering" ten movies are two totally different things. And at the time of this book's publication, only six of the announced DC movies on Tsujihara's slate ever opened: *Batman v Superman: Dawn of Justice; Suicide Squad; Wonder Woman; Justice League; Aquaman;* and *Shazam.* The others, meanwhile, have been shelved in favor of new projects under the DC film banner. Also, Tsujihara resigned as chairman and CEO of Warner Bros. on March 18, 2019.

Time moves quickly and things change fast in Hollywood, but the journey started by Zack Snyder and his team on *Man of Steel* continued in what would be viewed as the most significant step toward the realization of an anticipated *Justice League* movie—the release of *Batman v Superman: Dawn of Justice.*

RELEASE THE SNYDER CUT

BATMAN V SUPERMAN: DAWN OF JUSTICE

Too often with Warner Bros. and its burgeoning DC cinematic universe—the DCEU—the creatives put their cart before the horse as they raced to meet the perceived need of a passionate fanbase. Sensing the desire of DC fans to finally see Superman, Batman, Wonder Woman, and the core members of the Justice League together on the big screen (as an answer to Marvel Studios' *Avengers* movie), Warner and DC skipped most of the steps needed to fully establish a comic book world on screen and rushed to cram everyone together in one epic film.

Case in point: plans for a *Man of Steel* sequel surfaced in the Hollywood trades on June 10, 2013—four days before Snyder's Superman origin story even opened in theaters. That shows how confident the studio seemed in Snyder's vision, but also how adamant they were in maintaining the course toward building and launching the DCEU on screen.

It wasn't until July 2013 though, during an appearance at the annual fan extravaganza San Diego Comic-Con, that Snyder, DC, and Warner Bros. would officially confirm that the *Man of Steel* sequel would actually be a Superman-Batman team up film. And in true Snyder fashion, he announced it from the stage of Hall H at Comic-Con (his self-proclaimed "holy grail" scenario) to the roar of a satisfied crowd.

Snyder's an incredible storyteller, and also a confident public speaker (as opposed to similar intelligent filmmakers who shun press and detest public appearances). Knowing full well that he was preaching to his own choir in Hall H, Snyder affected the buoyant tone of a carnival barker as he teased the gathered masses with his historic reveal. It really was something to behold.

"I wanted to take a second personally, I know there has been a lot of speculation about what we're doing. And I just wanted to . . . have it come from me that it is *official* that we are going to make another Superman movie," Snyder told the Hall H fans with an enthusiasm that, in hindsight, is downright tragic once you know how this story ends. "And so I know what happens next with you guys. You go, 'Zack, what is the movie about? What is it going to be about?' And the truth is, you don't *want* me to tell you what the movie is about. That's like . . . right? You love the movies, so you want to go and see the movie.

"But, but . . . I can say that, maybe there's a single element that's in the film, that will be in the film, that we could—I don't know, that I could help you out with," Snyder continued, as the excitement in the room reached a fever pitch. "And so, I was thinking about how to do that. How could I do that? And I sort of pored through the DC Universe to look for a way to tell this [news]. And so what happened was, I came across the thing that I feel like sort of sums up . . . but of course, we're writing the thing now, so it doesn't exist. But there is a thing that I found that helped me understand what it is. So, I have a friend, Harry Lennix, who was in *Man of Steel*. And the reason I brought him out is because his voice is just way better than mine. . . . He's going to read you a little thing. He's going to read a little thing. And, some of you will recognize it. It's not . . . we're not adapting this thing. But it is the thing that will help tell that story."[7]

At this point in the Hall H presentation, Snyder asked for a lone spotlight to shine down on the lectern, and he turned the microphone over to *Man of Steel* costar Harry Lennix. A hush fell over the crowd (impressive, as the hall holds up to 6,500 attendees), allowing Lennix to read a legendary passage from Frank Miller's seminal Batman graphic novel, *The Dark Knight Returns*. In that book, an older and far-more-grizzled Bruce Wayne confronts Superman using a high-tech exoframe suit. The two DC titans battle to a near-death conclusion, answering the age-old question of who would win in a fight between the Man of Steel and the Caped Crusader.

Standing on stage in Hall H, Lennix understood that he held the massive crowd of DC fanatics in the palm of his hand. He gracefully paused, slipped on his reading glasses, then made comic-book-movie history by delivering this passage:

> I want you to remember, Clark, in all the years to come. In all your most private moments. I want you to remember my hand at your throat. I want you to remember the one man who beat you.

With that, the lights in the exhibit hall turned off. The classic Superman "S" logo appeared on the large screen behind the dais. And the pitch-black shadow of Batman's insignia appeared behind it.

In the years that followed *Man of Steel,* when Snyder was in production on *Batman v Superman: Dawn of Justice,* the director would swear he never considered the inclusion of Batman into Superman's world until they started kicking around ideas for a sequel. Snyder first brought up the possibility of the team using Batman as an antagonist during an interview with *Forbes* magazine in 2014. "In the first meeting, it was like, 'Maybe Batman?' . . . The problem is, once you say it out loud, then it's kind of hard to go back, right? Once you say, 'What about Batman?' then you realize, 'Okay, that's a cool idea. What else?' I mean, what do you say after that?"[8]

Whether you believe Snyder or not is a different story. That could be a spin, in 2014, to get audiences to believe that Warner Bros. and DC's efforts to finally construct their own shared universe were organic, and story-driven. Or you could choose to believe that DC was chasing a model they saw at Marvel Studios, in hopes of replicating that success for themselves.

Either way, the stage was set for an unprecedented on-screen confrontation between the biggest heroes in the DC universe. *Batman v Superman: Dawn of Justice* was coming. It would include the introduction of Wonder Woman (played by Israeli actress and model Gal Gadot) in her very first theatrical feature, but also signify the debut appearances of Ezra Miller's The Flash, Jason Momoa's Aquaman, and Ray Fisher's Cyborg, albeit in brief cameos.

Snyder recognized exactly how much he had bitten off with the project. In preparation for the release of the highly anticipated *Batman v Superman*, the director told *Entertainment Weekly* in a July 2015 cover story, "It's a marathon. No, it's a marathon within a marathon. Do you know that race from Death Valley to the top of Mount Whitney? It's, like, 100 miles and it's from the lowest point in the continental United States to the highest. It's crazy. Anyway, it's like that."[9]

Daunting. No, even that's an understatement. A marathon within a marathon. Perfect analogy. With the announcement of *Batman v Superman: Dawn of Justice*, Warner Bros. was well on its way. The studio was carving a path that they believed would finally lead them to the first appearance of the Justice League together in one blockbuster feature, an idea that had been brewing behind the scenes since 2007.

If only they knew then how horribly wrong things would go.

4

A MARVEL-OUS RIVALRY

In order to fully understand the shared universe Warner Bros. and DC Entertainment were trying to construct through the launch of *Man of Steel, Batman v Superman: Dawn of Justice,* David Ayer's *Suicide Squad,* and Patty Jenkins's *Wonder Woman,* you also have to acknowledge everything Marvel Studios accomplished in terms of cinematic superhero world-building with their stable of iconic comic book characters.

You see, our pop culture landscape has always been littered with heated rivalries. Coke versus Pepsi. *Star Wars* versus *Star Trek.* Backstreet Boys pitted against 'N Sync. You get my point. And depending on your tastes, you tend to side with one or the other.

The same holds true for Marvel versus DC. The vicious rivalry between the publishing giants extends back to the earliest days of comic books, with Superman making his debut for DC in 1938, followed by Marvel (then known as Timely Comics) introducing The Human Torch in 1939. Avid readers over the years have usually chosen a "side" in the Marvel-DC war, favoring either the mythical stories of Superman, Batman, Aquaman, and Wonder Woman or the heroic tales of Spider-Man, Captain America, the Hulk, and Captain Marvel. Naturally, you are *allowed* to like both universes, but few fans actually do.

Author Reed Tucker documents the decades-long competition between the comic powerhouses in his own book, *Slugfest.* And in a 2018 interview with the website OkayPlayer, Tucker explains that Marvel was, in essence, created as a direct response to Superman. They weren't DC's lone competitor at the time. But they grew, through a series of successes and failures, to become the yin to DC's yang.

"[Marvel] started releasing superhero comics back then, but they weren't all that successful," Tucker explained to OkayPlayer. "So they were dormant for a couple of decades in the superhero world. They published a lot of other stuff—romance comics, western comics, war comics. But it wasn't until the '60s when Stan Lee and Jack Kirby decided to launch *The Fantastic Four* that Marvel Comics became a force in the superhero world. The battle has been raging for years, but it really got heated starting in 1961 with the release of *Fantastic Four* #1 and it's been going ever since."[1]

Mostly, that "battle" was contained to the pages of monthly comic books. Beginning around 2010, the combat lines between Marvel and DC finally crossed over into our local multiplexes in massive fashion.

The work being done behind the scenes at Warner Bros. and DC Entertainment to establish a shared cinematic universe for their iconic DC characters around that time was neither original nor groundbreaking. Everyone outside the situation understood exactly what was happening. DC Entertainment was chasing Marvel Studios. And so, by looking at what Marvel Studios and Walt Disney Studios built around the same time, you can see exactly how Warner Bros. and DC tried to emulate it.

THE AVENGERS INITIATIVE

The Marvel Cinematic Universe (MCU), as we now know it, began in 2008 with Jon Favreau's origin film, *Iron Man*. The film's production history has been documented repeatedly and isn't as important to our discussion, though there's one pivotal scene from the film that requires dissection here because of its significance regarding the groundbreaking idea of a "cinematic universe."

It's a midcredits scene—which, alone, was a novel concept that has now become commonplace thanks to their inclusion in virtually every Marvel Studios film released since *Iron Man* in 2008. Having defeated his adversary, Obadiah Stane (Jeff Bridges), Tony Stark (Robert Downey Jr.) returns home and addresses his personalized AI, Jarvis. Before he can get comfortable in his Malibu mansion, Stark sees a shadowy figure standing near his window.

"'I am Iron Man.' You think you are the only superhero in the world?" this stranger asks before turning to reveal himself as Colonel Nick Fury (Samuel L. Jackson), director of the covert government agency S.H.I.E.L.D. "Mr. Stark, you've become part of a bigger universe. You just don't know it yet."

The audience didn't know it yet, either. Fury concludes with the bombshell, "I'm here to talk to you about The Avenger Initiative."[2]

The entire passage—but specifically that one sentence—changed everything with regard to comic book movie franchises and continues to shape creative decisions made by major studios to this day.

You likely know what happened next. Marvel Studios followed up *Iron Man* with Louis Leterrier's *The Incredible Hulk* exactly one month later. The superhero drama starred Edward Norton and Liv Tyler, and expanded the role of General Thaddeus "Thunderbolt" Ross (William Hurt), a character who would resurface in MCU films like Joe and Anthony Russo's *Captain America: Civil War*, as well as the prequel film, *Black Widow,* serving as connective tissue for the larger on-screen Marvel universe. And yes, *The Incredible Hulk* is mainly remembered for the unexpected Downey Jr. cameo as Tony Stark in its midcredits scene, which established a shared bond between *Hulk* and *Iron Man,* and furthered the promise of a much larger Marvel story to be told down the line.

Marvel called its initial slate of films "Phase One," which included Favreau's successful sequel, *Iron Man 2,* and standalone origin-story features for Thor (Chris Hemsworth) and Captain America (Chris Evans) before concluding with Joss Whedon's blockbuster team-up ensemble *Marvel's The Avengers* in 2012.

The accomplishment was unprecedented. Hollywood had delivered superhero franchises before. But no studio had attempted to launch new characters in individual films, then team them up as part of an encompassing effort to create a shared on-screen universe.

"For us, every movie is about expanding the Marvel Universe and the idea of the Marvel Universe," said Marvel president Kevin Feige, the forward-thinking architect of the MCU, in a 2010 interview with MovieWeb meant to promote *Iron Man 2.* "My goal is that moviegoers have that same experience comic book readers had, that when you turn the page, anybody can pop up and any other character can come into it. . . . With *The*

Avengers coming down the line, we really look at each film as being more of expanding that mythology."[3]

Forget the fact that, logistically, this should be a nightmare to pull off. Anyone who understands how hard it is to make ONE successful movie would scoff at the idea of trying to produce several films that end up being connected parts of a developing whole. Such a juggling act was believed to be impossible, until Feige and his Marvel Studios team showed the industry how possible it could be.

PLAYING CATCH-UP

That's not to say Marvel Studios was immune to production hiccups. In fact, the superhero factory suffered a string of high-profile divorces from some key directors, foreshadowing some of the issues Snyder reportedly ran into when he attempted to maintain his singular voice in a studio environment driven by opinionated producers.

The most intriguing "what if?" in MCU history has to be Edgar Wright's *Ant-Man*. Wright is a kinetic visual director known for marrying musical cues and sharp comedic dialogue to his airtight edits. His collaborations with British comedians Simon Pegg and Nick Frost on the sarcastic features *Shaun of the Dead* and *Hot Fuzz* put him on Marvel's radar, and Wright got deep into the development for Marvel's first Ant-Man movie before "creative differences" forced him off the project. Wright hadn't filmed the bulk of a feature film, the way that Snyder did on *Justice League*. But I can tell you that he did splice together an insanely entertaining action sequence involving the insect-sized Avenger, which he brought to Hall H at San Diego Comic-Con in 2012. That footage brought the house down.

But Wright wasn't the only director to lose a gig at Marvel Studios. Patty Jenkins was hired, then fired, from the 2013 sequel *Thor: The Dark World* before *Game of Thrones* veteran Alan Taylor took the job. That might have been a mistake. Jenkins would go on to find enormous success at DC with the origin story *Wonder Woman* and its sequel, *Wonder Woman 1984*. Meanwhile, *Thor: The Dark World* regularly gets singled out by discerning fans as one of the weakest chapters in the MCU.

In January 2020, Scott Derrickson also walked away from the Doctor Strange sequel, *Doctor Strange in the Multiverse of Madness* (also due to "creative differences") and was replaced by one-time *Spider-Man* helmer Sam Raimi. And Disney temporarily removed James Gunn from the *Guardians of the Galaxy* franchise in July 2018 due to insensitive Tweets found on his social media feed from years prior. Gunn eventually was rehired by Disney in 2019, showing that Marvel Studios can reverse course if it feels it's making the right creative decision for a comic book franchise.

Even with these behind-the-scenes production wrinkles, Marvel had chartered a steady course for its superhero blockbusters. By the time that Warner Bros. and DC Entertainment finally decided to attempt to follow in Marvel Studios' footsteps by creating a cinematic universe of their own, they were very far behind the MCU and hurriedly scurried to catch up.

Before *Man of Steel* opened on June 14, 2013, Marvel Studios was already seven films deep into its on-screen experiment. The MCU spent its first four years establishing different corners of its cinematic universe with five films, from Thor's celestial palace in Asgard to the World War I-era trench-warfare adventures of Captain America. They crafted well-rounded movie versions of their beloved comic book characters, and methodically built up to the combined Avengers movie, educating casual moviegoers while also pleasing the dedicated Marvel fan by paying close attention to storytelling details.

Marvel Studios had completed its Phase One and had taken the first significant step—in the form of Shane Black's *Iron Man 3*—through its announced Phase Two before Warner delivered *Man of Steel*. Marvel's Phase Two would include lucrative Thor and Captain America sequels, a second Avengers film that used Ultron (James Spader) as its villain, the introduction of a rag-tag band of space misfits known as The Guardians of the Galaxy, and an Ant-Man (Paul Rudd) origin story. Audiences packed theaters around the globe to keep up with the latest adventures in the Marvel Cinematic Universe, while Kevin Feige continuously dangled "bait" in the form of new production updates on MCU films for second- and third-tier superheroes like Black Panther, Captain Marvel, The Eternals, Shang-Chi, and more.

"The MCU certainly gives creatives some sense of freedom and has brought in a number of big-name directors, but there's an underlying flavor in every project—for better or worse—that doesn't stray too far from the mold," said Stephen M. Colbert, an editor for the entertainment website ScreenRant who has been covering the Snyder Cut movement from its earliest days. "On one hand, that helps guarantee consistency so audiences know what to expect, but on the other hand, it constrains the potential, so you know Marvel will never do something quite like *Batman v Superman, Joker,* or *Birds of Prey.*"[4]

Needless to say, things were going swimmingly at Marvel Studios, and DC—fueled, I'm sure, by its decades-long rivalry with "The House that Stan Lee Built"—wanted a piece of the superhero-blockbuster action.

As the final straw, when Zack Snyder's *Man of Steel* finally opened in theaters in 2014, Marvel Studios was basking in the glow of its first *Avengers* film earning a staggering $1.5 billion in worldwide ticket grosses. And *Iron Man 3* kicked off the 2014 summer blockbuster season with a whopping $174.1 million opening weekend, putting it on the path to its eventual global haul of $1.2 billion in tickets sold. The Marvel machine was printing money. And DC had to believe that a *Justice League* movie, their equivalent of a superhero team-up, possessed the same potential earning power.

But how could DC catch up to Marvel Studios?

The short answer was, they couldn't. At least not overnight. It would take years to properly establish a series of individual DC films that, if they worked, might lead to a Justice League movie. So, as we noted, *Man of Steel* was meant to establish this world, then *Batman v Superman: Dawn of Justice* and *Suicide Squad* would immediately expand it.

"It's more than just a franchise for us," said Dan Fellman, Warner's president of domestic distribution, in a June 2013 *Wall Street Journal* article about *Man of Steel* and its enlarged sequel. "It really opens up the door to do combinations of the DC Comics characters. We can build them up like Marvel did, and benefit from the history of DC."[5]

This became the company line. When discussing *Batman v Superman* with MTV News in 2015, star Henry Cavill was also beating the "shared universe" drum for DC by telling the outlet, "I wouldn't call this a Superman sequel. This is Batman versus Superman. It's a separate entity altogether. It's introducing the Batman character and expanding upon the universe. . . . It's an introduction of the [Batman] character. And ultimately, the introduction of Justice League."[6]

Now, for fun, try to imagine Marvel rushing through its introductions and hastily establishing its universe. What would have happened if Joss Whedon's first megateam-up *Avengers* movie had followed on the heels of *The Incredible Hulk*, the second film in the nascent MCU? Or if *Hulk* director Louis Leterrier had been tasked by Marvel Studios to somehow work Thor and Captain America into his story? It likely would have been a disaster. What if Jon Favreau had been ordered to establish the entire foundation of the MCU in his lone *Iron Man* movie? It wouldn't work. It couldn't.

That's not to say all DC fans wanted Warner Bros. to follow the model established by Marvel Studios and Walt Disney.

"The last thing DC should have done was follow the step-by-step formula of the MCU," swears Matthew Criscuolo, a dedicated Zack Snyder fan from Rockland County, New York, who goes by the name "Leonidas" on social media. "Snyder was doing something on par cinematically, but at the same time doing something so fresh, unique and bold, giving DC its own path to walk."[7]

Criscuolo believes it would have been unwise for Warner Bros. and DC to patiently lay out its universe the way that Marvel did because as we've explained, they were playing catch up. He surmises that if DC took the time needed to properly build up the Justice League team, teasing the antagonist Darkseid and introducing complicated narrative elements like time travel, the MCU would have established like-minded stories first, effectively beating them to the punch.

"Cinematically, DC would be forever trailing the MCU if they took that road," he said. "Also, by the time DC got around to killing off Superman and introducing Darkseid, the mainstream would have already experienced these similar stories with Marvel. So Snyder brilliantly put DC in the driver's seat cinematically and allowed WB to maintain equal footing with Disney in terms of storytelling opportunities."

Other fans viewed that approach through a different lens. Justin M. Lesniewski, thirty-seven years old, teaches high school English in Central Florida. He's dedicated to Zack Snyder and has been analyzing the director's films since 2009. He compares the MCU to McDonald's, without meaning that as a slight.

"There's nothing wrong with McDonald's," Lesniewski told me. "It's a certain type of product. It's mass produced to sell to as many people as possible, and high-quality culinary art is not a primary value for the company. You know what you're getting, and it can be enjoyable every once in a while. However, a steady diet of it will kill you."[8]

Extending the metaphor, Lesniewski posits that food is fuel for the body, but art is fuel for the soul. And Zack Snyder, in Lesniewski's opinion, makes art.

Criscuolo and Lesniewski's valuable opinions prove that every fan brings a unique perspective to the speed and scope of on-screen world building. And as it turns out, studios *can* build a cinematic universe. Sustaining it, though, is harder than Warner Bros. and DC realized. Zack Snyder found himself behind the eight ball while building the DCEU from the ground up in a rapid fashion. And Warner Bros., in my opinion, hired Snyder to turn *Man of Steel* and, by extension, the full slate of DCEU films into the anti-Marvel franchise. They wanted dark and gritty, akin to what Christopher Nolan achieved in his Dark Knight trilogy, to serve as a juxtaposition to the perceived light, soft and audience-friendly tone of the early MCU movies. This mature approach, by all accounts, would define Snyder's overall vision for the DCEU.

It also would be his downfall.

5

WHY SO SERIOUS?

I've established why DC was destined to struggle when attempting to catch up to their rivals at Marvel Studios. By 2013, Marvel had already solidified its cinematic universe over the course of seven films and was well on its way to delivering a full slate of exciting new features in the company's Phase Two. The best way for DC and Warner Bros to compete on this comic book battlefield was to offer audiences something totally different than what they were finding in the MCU.

To do that, DC chose to be *tonally* different. They opted for darker, grittier, and more mature approaches to their superhero properties. At one point, it was even argued by prominent film blogger Drew McWeeny of *Formerly Dangerous* that there was a "no jokes" mandate in effect at Warner Bros. for their DC superhero projects (though actor Seth Rogen, of all people, shot this down by Tweeting this theory was "bullshit"[1] and "not true"[2]).

This tonal shift actually took its cues from DC's darker source materials. "From the moment *Swamp Thing* relaunched in the '80s to *The Dark Knight* and several other [works] in the '90s, the DCEU firmly established itself as adult books with mature stories," said Jonita Davis, a film and culture critic and prolific freelance writer. "They got gory, gritty, and bleak, but were damn good narratives and spectacular artwork. It redefined them for us, and we loved them for it."[3]

There was no denying that the DC movies were more adult-oriented than the Marvel fare being released at that same time, and more than likely, the shift to more serious tones was an attempt by Warner Bros. to reclaim some of the magic spun by Christopher Nolan for his Oscar-winning Batman trilogy.

This conscious push-back toward more mature storytelling started with Zack Snyder's *Man of Steel,* released into theaters on June 14, 2013. To understand how *Man of Steel* embraced its adult side, it's important to understand what executive producer Christopher Nolan and Snyder were thinking during preproduction.

In preparation for the launch of its new Superman series, Warner Bros. started soliciting pitches from noted comic book writers (Grant Morrison, Mark Waid, and Geoff Johns all participated, according to reports) and seasoned filmmakers (including *Charlie's Angels'* McG and *Layer Cake's* Matthew Vaughn) as far back as 2008.

Speaking with MTV in August of that year, Morrison opened up about *how* to bring Superman back to the big screen in the wake of Bryan Singer's pious, humdrum 2006 effort, *Superman Returns.* That movie wanted to mimic Richard Donner's noble tone and wore those intentions on its skin-tight blue sleeves. In fact, the running joke about the extended fight between Superman (Henry Cavill) and Zod (Michael Shannon) at the end of *Man of Steel*—the one that devastated large swaths of Metropolis and concluded with Kal-El snapping his adversary's neck—is that it was a direct response to Singer's gentle, nostalgic (but ultimately unsuccessful) *Superman Returns.* Brandon Routh's version of the Blue Boy Scout hardly even threw one punch in that standalone movie. Cavill's Superman was destined to fight.

Morrison told MTV that every choice made in Singer's *Superman Returns* was "wrong," focusing on the bizarre decision screenwriters Michael Dougherty and Dan Harris made to give Superman and Lois Lane a child.

"If you're making the movie in a vacuum, and there will be no other Superman movies ever again, go ahead and give him a son," Morrison surmised. "But otherwise, that's a staggeringly awful idea. . . . The idea [in that movie] was to make an American Christ figure, but what they centered on was his weakness. They made him more a lamb of God, rather than give us a real powerful Superman. They had too many scenes where he's being kicked to the floor, and that's not Superman. Superman would get up and fight."[4]

That reaction, stated by Morrison but shared by many, helped fuel a lot of the decisions that would lead to the production of *Man of Steel.* Snyder undoubtedly followed his own path, but part of what we see in *Man of Steel* comes across as a reaction to what we didn't see in *Superman Returns*, and that would be super-powered action.

SUPERMAN BEGINS

Man of Steel also came from a direction conceived by Christopher Nolan and David S. Goyer as they were figuring out how to conclude their own Batman trilogy. Nolan's Batman films were widely praised for the grounded approach they took to the comic book source material. But *Batman Begins* was never meant to start a franchise.

Nolan confirmed in a 2018 interview with *Variety*, conducted at the Cannes Film Festival, that sequels weren't part of his plan when he started his origin story *Batman Begins*. He took each movie one story at a time. So when he was coaxed back to the director's chair for not one but two subsequent Batman films, he viewed them as different opportunities to explore new and unexpected genres, with tones driven by the villains he selected. *The Dark Knight,* for example, focused both on the Joker (Oscar winner Heath Ledger) and Two-Face (Aaron Eckhart), which allowed Nolan the freedom to make a neo-noir crime thriller that happened to have DC characters in it.

"Shifting genres and the nature of the antagonist felt [like] the way to take the audience on a journey and tell them something different about Bruce Wayne," the auteur told *Variety*. "Yes, it's a superhero, but it's based on ideas of guilt, fear, these strong impulses that the character has."[5]

That focus on character would dictate a number of the choices made behind the scenes on *Man of Steel*. In the back of his mind, Nolan knew that this new Superman could not fit into the same blueprint that was being used by Marvel Studios. During a 2010 interview with *Empire* (via SuperHero-Hype), Nolan spoke of the distinct differences between the two comic studio giants, explaining, "Marvel characters are very different to DC characters. . . . You've got to go back to that element of, 'What do I see when I close my eyes and think of Batman? What do I see when I close my eyes and think of Superman?' And for me a big part of that is their individuality. They are extraordinary beings in an ordinary world. And the reason I think the two are fascinating is because Superman is very specifically superpowered and obviously otherworldly; Batman is very human and flawed."[6]

"Extraordinary beings in an ordinary world." That sums up Nolan, Goyer, and Snyder's approach to the alien origin story presented in *Man of Steel*. And those themes immediately connected with an audience who had always recognized the immigrant story at the heart of Superman's origin.

Nana, one-half of the Nerd Queens, revealed that the immigrant angle in *Man of Steel* finally helped her relate to and better understand Superman as a character because she was barely a casual fan of the character before her online partner, Cole, made her watch Snyder's DC movie.

"It was multiple factors that helped to form this opinion," Nana said. "At that point in my life, I was on the road. Living in the US and working in the US, I was an immigrant, even if not a permanent one. And the portrayal of Superman in *Man of Steel* and then *Batman v Superman* made the character really important to me in that aspect. Seeing both films tackle the issue [of immigration] on the big screen in a very real way was important for me back then. And it's even more important to the world right now. Ultimately, it's only one of many things that those movies captured perfectly. Zack managed to take these powerful heroes from the pages of comic books and place them in a very real world. Not a movie world. A real one. He made them face reality as if it was happening right here, right now.

"What would we do today if aliens came?" Nana continued. "If we found out Superman existed? *Man of Steel* and *Batman v Superman* showed a mirror to our society. The films didn't back away from the ugly parts. They showed them as they are. And from all perspectives. It made me think. To look at things not just as an immigrant in my story, but as that person on the other side, who seemingly dislikes me too. What Zack was doing with his story was asking the tough questions. He wasn't asking just his characters, but the audience as well. And that's what makes his art so special to me. That's why I fight for his vision."[7]

But the specific buzzword used by Snyder in a November 2012 interview with the *Los Angeles Times* was "serious," and that term became the core foundation for Snyder's DC Comics projects.

"It's a more serious version of Superman," the director said about *Man of Steel*. "It's not like a heart attack. We took the mythology seriously. We take him as a character seriously. I believe the movie would appeal to anyone. I think that you're going to see a Superman you've never seen before. We approached it as though no other films had been made. He's the king-daddy. Honestly, that's why I wanted to do it. I'm interested in Superman because he's the father of all superheroes. He's this amazing ambassador for all superheroes."[8]

Say what you will about *Man of Steel*. Detractors have to at least admit that the movie treats the hero's origin and mythology respectfully. Opening on the alien planet of Krypton during a time of open rebellion, the movie immediately drives a wedge between political leaders Zod (Michael Shannon) and Jor-El (Russell Crowe), forcing the latter to send his newborn baby, Kal-El, into the safety of exile.

From there, Snyder and *Man of Steel* screenwriter David S. Goyer play around with the traditional narrative of the Superman origin story. They start with a grown Superman (Henry Cavill), a drastic departure to the early Kansas days showcased in Richard Donner's 1978 classic, where a lanky, prepubescent Clark lifts the Kent's rustic red truck over his head. In Snyder's revamped and contemporary adaptation, a conflicted Clark Kent walks this earth and performs heroic acts of kindness while also wrestling with his midwestern upbringing, which we are eventually treated to in flashbacks. He's called to be a hero, but he's haunted by the pivotal warning passed down by his adopted father, Jonathan Kent (Kevin Costner), that the world might not be ready for an alien being as powerful as Clark.

The solemn approach to these mythical characters definitely connected with die-hard DC and Zack Snyder fans. It helped that the titular hero actually punched his enemies, in the process.

"I've always wanted to see a live action Superman that had the same action as we see in the animated attempts, or in the comics," said Chris Wong-Swenson of Honolulu, Hawaii. "Zack Snyder did exactly that, and more. Zack brought in the sci-fi elements into a cinematic Superman. He also brought that character into the ugliness of our world and challenged that character in our modern society."[9]

Matthew Criscuolo, a rabid comic book movie lover from Rockland County, New York, echoed Wong-Swenson's sentiments when discussing Snyder's work on *Man of Steel*. Criscuolo, who fought daily in the online war to get the Snyder Cut of *Justice League* released, recalls how "ground-breaking" *Man of Steel* felt at the time, especially when compared to previous superhero films centered around other comic characters.

"I think Snyder fused arthouse with blockbuster in a way that has never been done quite like that before," he said. "He took the realism, the grittiness, the stakes of Chris Nolan's Batman films, and introduced Superman into that type of aesthetic as he worked toward *Justice League*. . . . I consider *Man of Steel* to be the greatest origin superhero film ever made.

"He is my favorite fictional character of all time," Criscuolo continued. "I remember being opposed to seeing Snyder's *Man of Steel* in the first place due to finding out the classic John Williams theme would not be included. Looking back at my initial hesitation, due to a lack of perceived nostalgia, I realized many people had similar issues when dealing with Snyder's depictions of Superman. Thankfully, I gave *Man of Steel* a chance. It sparked an awakening in me, and I realized [that] this is the Superman we need in the modern world."[10]

Man of Steel truly was a complete departure from the Superman movies delivered by Warner Bros. over the years. Snyder wasn't just competing with the seminal Donner take on Superman. He was washing away the bad taste left by Singer's too-safe *Superman Returns* from 2006 and educating fans on how a principled hero like Superman could fit into our cynical, distrustful contemporary era.

"I always liked Superman, my dad being a huge part of [the reason why]. But *Man of Steel* made me love Superman," said Megan Loucks, twenty-five years old, from Michigan. "The way that Kal was portrayed as an outsider, he wasn't perfect, and he struggled with being himself. This is something that resonated with me tremendously. . . . I loved the direction Zack Snyder was going in, I enjoyed the darker, more story-driven superhero films. At the time, the market was so consumed in lighter, more audience-friendly films. I was yearning to see these heroes again, and in the same style."[11]

At first, Snyder's DCEU launch worked like a charm. *Man of Steel* has its critical detractors (the movie has a 56 percent Fresh grade on the review aggregate Rotten Tomatoes, but boasts a 75 percent Audience Score), but the movie banked $668 million in worldwide tickets sold. That nearly doubled the $391 million earned by its predecessor, Bryan Singer's

Superman Returns, signifying to Warner Bros. that Snyder's attempt to reboot Superman was on the right track.

Several prominent film critics isolated the immigrant conflict told by Snyder through Clark Kent's struggle to assimilate to his new world. He is cautioned by his adopted father, Jonathan, that the world might never accept him, yet encouraged by his birth father to become the hero that these people need. It's a human conflict that grounds the alien Superman in a deeply relatable parable that speaks to audiences from all corners of the globe.

Those themes, so prevalent in Snyder's approach to Superman's origin, touched the heart of thirty-one-year-old Giovanni Torres, a product manager based in the Washington Heights neighborhood of Manhattan.

"It's a neighborhood predominantly composed of people from the Dominican Republic, and this culture is a strong part of me," said Torres, who couldn't wait to see *Man of Steel* because Superman was, and is, his favorite comic book character. "As the son of immigrant parents, I saw a lot of my personal struggles in Supes. It was always strange to grow up feeling different than the people around you."[12]

To Torres, the approach that Zack Snyder took, and the way he captured Clark Kent's struggles to fit in, struck an emotional chord. "The challenges of this superhuman existing in a modern world, [and] his relationship with [his adoptive father] Jonathan [Kent] was just so perfect. I loved the film so much."

Warner Bros. and Snyder could have continued to explore Superman's hopeful expeditions on his adopted planet in a traditional Superman sequel. By the end of *Man of Steel,* Clark is telling the suspicious lieutenant general Calvin Swanwick (Harry Lennix) that he "grew up in Kansas" and is "about as American as it gets."[13]

But the seeds of distrust between our planet's leaders and this alien visitor were planted, so Snyder and coscreenwriters Chris Terrio and David Goyer committed to that path for their follow-up story. They zeroed in on the alien-immigrant identity that's part of Superman's myth, then dug deep into the fear and paranoia too many in contemporary America often bring to the contentious, divisive immigration discussion. In that argument, they found the narrative backbone for what would become *Batman v Superman: Dawn of Justice.*

GOD VERSUS MAN

Carlos Orbegozo, an engineering department manager from Toronto, Canada, summed it up best when he was asked about Snyder's early efforts in the DCEU and how they were meant to flourish.

"I think that Snyder had a clear plan and path for a very large story and was planting the seeds very early on," Orbegozo said. "*Justice League* was meant to be a different film than *BvS,* just like *BvS* was different from *Man of Steel.* I was fully supportive and interested in seeing the plan of a large story develop."[14]

Orbegozo, who goes by "Carlos Digital" online, is another dedicated member of the RTSC family who championed Snyder's vision for a sophisticated and mature take on DC's well-established heroes. He's actually credited as being the first person to use the phrase "Release the Snyder Cut" on social media, though not the first to apply the famous hashtag.

"These movies also almost feel like they are taking place in the actual comics universe," Orbegozo summarized, defending the approach adopted by Snyder, Chris Terrio, and David Goyer. Orbegozo says that he loves finding references to classic DC Comics curators such as John Byrne, Frank Miller, Dan Jurgens, and Gerry Conway in the visuals and narrative nods worked into Snyder's films. Orbegozo adds, "As a fan that wants to see comics seen from a motion picture lens, there was no better way to approach [these stories] than this one."

Based on his films, Snyder seemed to agree. Tasked with the responsibility of bringing Batman into the fold for his *Man of Steel* follow-up, Snyder leaned into the paranoia and fear that make Bruce Wayne a powerful crime fighter. He brilliantly opened *Batman v Superman: Dawn of Justice* during the climactic battle of *Man of Steel,* only he showed it to us from the point of view of a grounded human being who was looking up at gods. And instead of teaming up his two leads, as might have been the case over at Marvel Studios, Snyder pit a distrustful Batman against the mysterious Superman in what Lex Luthor (Jesse Eisenberg) devilishly described on screen as "the greatest gladiator match in the history of the world. God versus man. Day versus night. Son of Krypton versus Bat of Gotham."[15]

It doesn't get much more serious than that.

This approach was actually instilled in Snyder during his formative years as an artist. He admits that fact in a 2016 interview with *Forbes,* where he confesses how impactful Alan Moore's *Watchmen* graphic novel and Frank Miller's *The Dark Knight Returns* were to understanding how the DNA of an iconic superhero could (and should) be deconstructed to make them less mythological and more relatable. And once you accept that truth, you understand why *Man of Steel* and *Batman v Superman,* under Snyder's watch, were destined to go against the grain of a more traditional superhero story.

"I saw my comic book heroes get shot down by *Watchmen* and by *The Dark Knight Returns,* and that's ringing in me still. And the deconstructivist nature, and the sort of longing I have to make the mythology mean something, comes from those experiences," Snyder said. "[Miller] basically did the same thing with story and tone that Alan Moore did with mythology. He did it with story and tone, in the sense of the idea that a comic book grew up in that one singular moment, or that I grew up as I read it, and it said basically, 'Put away your bullshit.'"[16]

Snyder credits his *Man of Steel* producer, Christopher Nolan, as being another storyteller who managed to walk the thin line between a man trying to be a hero, but also being okay with flirting with the possibility of danger if it means getting the job done. Naturally, this applies better to Batman than Superman, but Snyder confesses that these comic book characters can't ever evolve or move forward if their steadfast morality isn't somehow challenged by otherworldly complications.

At the time, though, Snyder also understood, from a filmmaker's perspective, that it doesn't get much bigger than Batman versus Superman, in terms of superhero blockbuster staging.

"You can talk all you want about other superhero movies, but it's Batman and Superman, let's just be honest," Snyder said when speaking with *USA Today* in a July 2014 interview. "I don't know how you get bigger than that."[17]

He was right. Of course, the bigger you are . . .

6

DAWN OF OBSTACLES

The way I see it, two events from 2016 damaged Zack Snyder's reputation and led to his temporary departure from Warner Bros. and the DCEU.

First, his anticipated superhero blockbuster *Batman v Superman: Dawn of Justice* failed to cross the $1 billion mark at the global box office. Crazy as it sounds, "$1 billion" had become the measuring stick of success for big-ticket superhero adventures. Snyder's massive DC tentpole fell short. It opened to $166 million domestically during its debut weekend of March 25–27 and tallied an impressive $420 million worldwide in that same frame. *BvS* instantly notched Hollywood's largest March opening (beating *The Hunger Games'* pull of $152.5 million) and nearly topped *Harry Potter and the Deathly Hallows—Part Two* as the highest opening weekend total in Warner Bros. history at the time.

Things looked promising for Snyder's second DCEU installment, until the movie suffered a larger-than-expected 69 percent drop in box office totals in its second weekend, signifying issues. (A 50 percent drop is standard for blockbusters, and analysts suggested *BvS* might drop 60 percent heading into its second weekend at the time.) By April 10, *Batman v Superman: Dawn of Justice* was knocked out of the No. 1 slot on the box office Top 10 list (a position it only held for two consecutive weeks), and the film's financial momentum noticeably slowed.

Don't get me wrong: *BvS* made plenty of money—$873.6 million worldwide, to be exact—when all was said and done. Most producers would sell a body part for receipts like that.

It just didn't make enough.

Still, box office experts weren't necessarily ringing the death knell for the DCEU. Longtime box office analyst Paul Dergarabedian declared *Batman v Superman* to be an "unqualified box office hit"[1] when speaking to the trade website The Wrap in May 2016. Dergarabedian pointed out that comic book movies usually avoid the month of March, favoring the summer season when teenagers can pack area multiplexes, and concluded that the industry only had roughly twenty films in that billion-dollar club, so it would be foolish and premature to write off Snyder's accomplishment.

Backing up that statement, Exhibitor Relations analyst Jeff Bock also told The Wrap, "Nobody's touching Disney right now. If it was Disney coming in less than $1 billion, then there'd be cause for concern. . . . *Batman v Superman* will still wind up being one of the top 10 films of the year."[2]

And it was. But Bock dropped the "D" word with good reason because the second 2016 occurrence that further hindered Snyder's DCEU happened when Disney and Marvel Studios' *Captain America: Civil War* (which opened in May) sailed past $1 billion at the international box, becoming the fourth movie in the MCU to achieve such a lofty goal.

From a box office standpoint, the Marvel model of superhero storytelling was setting the standard. Even the third *Iron Man* film, released in 2013, grossed $1.2 billion worldwide. The *third* Iron Man movie! Meanwhile, the historic on-screen team up of Batman and Superman couldn't gain entrance into that esteemed billion dollar club. No one from Warner Bros. has said this on record, but anyone paying attention to the race between Marvel and DC had to understand how much that stung.

"I don't think the box office or Rotten Tomatoes score of *BvS* was the *reason* for [Snyder's] vision being changed, it was merely the excuse," said Stephen Colbert of ScreenRant. "We know from interviews . . . that Geoff Johns and others weren't fully behind Snyder's take on the characters, and a billion-dollar box office wouldn't have changed that. It just would have given them less leverage to intervene.

"Warner Bros. wanted something more like the MCU, and even if Snyder wasn't making that for them, they wanted to market things that way," he continued. "So audience expectations are a major factor. Being up-front about what it actually was that Snyder was doing may have helped ease many of those expectations."[3]

It also didn't help Warner Bros. and DC's case that David Ayers's super-villain thriller *Suicide Squad*—a movie that willingly embraced the dark and serious tone of Snyder's DCEU—struggled critically and financially in 2016 amidst rumors and reports of drastic reshoots and significant behind-the-scenes studio tinkering. Though blessed with one of the best movie trailers in recent memories, Ayer's finished film was a mess of false starts and empty storytelling promises that squandered decent performances by the likes of Margot Robbie, Will Smith, and Viola Davis.

Suicide Squad somehow feels like a movie that's being rewritten as you watch it. Reviewing *Squad* for CinemaBlend, senior movie critic Eric Eisenberg writes: "The film almost entirely exists as a showcase for char-acter work, whether it's the deadly assassin Deadshot (Will Smith) trying to reconnect with his daughter any way he can; the flame-generating El Diablo (Jay Hernandez) repenting for his past sins; or the aforementioned crazy-in-love Harley Quinn and Joker hoping to reunite and raise hell in Gotham City. It's the opportunity to play with these typical antagonists as protagonists that clearly drives Ayer's passion for the property, but this pre-dilection for big personalities also draws focus from actual plot, leaving the blockbuster to be shockingly simple and predictable. . . . When combined with the fact that the larger narrative is excessively straightforward—with nary a single interesting or complex twist to be found in the story—you get the sense that the writer/director spent the bulk of his time individually de-signing all the puzzle pieces that make up the script, and then rushed at the end to find a way to make them all stick together."[4]

Ayer himself might agree. The director is no cheerleader for the fin-ished film, complaining often on social media about how the movie he dreamed of making is not the one that Warner Bros. released in theaters. In a Tweet shared on January 21, 2017, Ayer admits that he made "a controversial film" that "took inspiration from the insanity of the original comics." But he also adds, "Would I do a lot of things different? Yep, for sure. Wish I had a time machine. I'd make Joker the main villain and engineer a more grounded story."[5]

Taking a page from Snyder, Ayer occasionally shares photos online of *Suicide Squad* scenes that he shot that didn't make it into his theatrical cut. This led to the formation of a smaller yet no less passionate #Releas-eTheAyerCut movement on social media. In the summer of 2020, that movie's fanbase capitalized on the success of HBO Max's *Justice League* decision by rekindling their campaign to secure Ayer's cut. Ayer encouraged it, talking about how the ability to reassemble his true vision would be cathartic, and even quite simple. As this book went to press, though, no progress on the release of an Ayer Cut of *Suicide Squad* had been announced.

The director, instead, seemed more reflective than defensive in his recent social media posts regarding *Suicide Squad*. "Movies are fragile. They are like dreams, haunting moments that run from your vision. They have their own logic and truth," Ayer posted on Instagram in November 2019. The text accompanied a photo of Jared Leto in character as Joker from a scene that didn't appear in the theatrical cut. "If you change the destination after the trip is complete is it still the same journey? The spine of *Suicide Squad* was Harley's journey. In many ways it was her movie, her escaping her relationship with Joker was the major emotional through line. A director holds an invisible compass in their hands. It guides every shot, every performance. That compass points to the destination. . . . If the desintation [*sic*] changes, did the journey even happen?"[6]

Well, yes. The journey did happen. And it was very bumpy. *Suicide Squad* earned $746 million in global ticket sales but posted a putrid 27 percent Fresh grade on Rotten Tomatoes. (*BvS* didn't fare much better with critics, scoring a 28 percent Fresh grade with 413 reviews filed.)

The takeaway seemed to be that both directors who had DC blockbusters opening in theaters in 2016 faced alleged studio interference that led to disappointing (and incomplete) versions of their movies playing to fans. You can blame a lot of people not named Zack Snyder for the reception of these DCEU movies. But the buck stopped with Zack and Debbie Snyder in 2016, since they served as producers on these collective projects, and not enough bucks were flowing into WB's vaults.

In fact, in a March 2016 profile, The Hollywood Reporter straight up asked the Snyders how much money *Batman v Superman: Dawn of Justice* would have to earn to make Warner Bros. happy. Zack candidly replied, "I don't know. The more people see it, the better. The business is very important to us, and in the end, it is a business. . . . [But] pop culture is a liquid and amorphous thing that's hard to judge and/or predict. You try and just supply all the things that I get excited about as a movie fan, comic book fan, fan of drama. If we've done our jobs, then the pressure is a little bit less because it becomes about the storm outside these walls and how it gobbles it up or rejects it."[7]

As one might expect, dedicated Snyder fans gobbled up *Batman v Superman: Dawn of Justice,* though they all, almost unanimously, prefer the longer and R-rated Ultimate Edition over the theatrical cut.

"The Ultimate Edition of *Batman v Superman* is my favorite movie," said Benjamin Hunt, a twenty-seven-year-old graduate school student studying communications at Grand Valley State in Michigan. Hunt's favorite character of all time is Batman, and he was "ecstatic" when he first learned of Snyder's plans to drop the Caped Crusader into the *Man of Steel* universe.

"Although it sounds ridiculous, it was a truly transcendent experience for me when the second trailer for *Batman v Superman* dropped," Hunt admits. "Batman in a desert with a jacket and goggles, the armor suit, seeing Bruce Wayne run into post 9/11-esque danger. No one else could have pulled this off other than Zack Snyder, and it was pure bliss knowing that someone like him who really 'got it' was at the helm of DC on film.

"At the time, most notably in the years leading up to *BvS* and *Justice League,* I was working toward my undergrad, and on campus in a city that was far from my hometown," Hunt continued. "I lived alone, was uninterested in a lot of the social activities on campus and was therefore somewhat isolated from the rest of my environment. The future of Zack Snyder's DC movies was what kept my energy high, day in and day out, especially after *Batman v Superman* released. I saw it on opening night with my mother and brother, and then I took friends to see it multiple times."[8]

Hunt echoes the sentiments of several loyal DC and Snyder fans when he says he was "completely on board" with Warner Bros.' plan to launch its own cinematic universe around the iconic DC characters.

"What made this idea unique was that WB was marketing this plan as director-driven," Hunt said. "Meaning that WB would allow their directors to steer the ship in regard to what that universe of movies would be by their own collaboration. It gave [fans] something different, something interesting and compelling in ways that were different than what Marvel was doing. But unfortunately, those in charge of WB at the time, that being Geoff Johns, Diane Nelson, Jon Berg, Kevin Tsujihara, and Toby Emmerich, went back on their director-driven word very early on in an attempt to cash in on Marvel's success. This plan backfired, and the rest is history."

Even fans like Hunt could read the tea leaves. There was more than enough growing concern in the industry at large, and likely in the board-rooms on the Warner Bros. studio lot, that the general public was rejecting the darker vibe that drove the DCEU. Critical reaction to the studio's two 2016 efforts was brutal, and the movies—while profitable by definition—were not showing the same promising trajectory enjoyed by the rivals over at Marvel Studios.

When asked point blank if Snyder fans believe Warner Bros. would have kept Zack Snyder at the helm of the DCEU had *Batman v Superman* crossed the $1 billion mark, their opinions vary wildly.

"I think the old regime of WB's management was misled by biased enter-tainment journalists and chose the wrong way to develop the franchise," said pivotal Release the Snyder Cut leader Fiona Zheng. "So even if *BvS* crossed the $1 billion mark, it would still be polarizing in the critics' eyes. WB got the wrong impression that if they changed the future films to something more akin to the MCU formula that critics had been pestering them for, they would get the financial success of Snyder's version, with added critical success. But they obviously were very wrong. They managed to upset their own fans and didn't win over critics or Marvel fans."[9]

Chris Wong-Swenson of Honolulu, Hawaii, argues that the *Batman v Superman: Ultimate Edition,* which reflected Snyder's proper version of that story, would have crossed $1 billion if it got a theatrical release. While Hamad Al-Mansouri of Qatar backed up the sentiment, stating, "I don't think *BvS* reaching a billion would have changed anything. Warner Bros. was mostly affected by the overall perception of the theatrical cut. Seeing all these YouTubers screaming at the camera about Superman not smiling or Batman being too mean is probably what made WB panic. Racking over $800 million from a theatrical cut that had been edited down by thirty min-utes is still successful by every standard."[10]

It's hard to argue with that logic.

Meanwhile, Carlos Orbegozo lays out what appeared to be the real-ity of the situation when he explained, "I think that if the movie had met *Avengers*-type money, the executive team would have been hands-off and many things would have continued, as well as many people would have kept their jobs. Unfortunately, that does not speak well of the management team's logic, as only the absolute best outcome would have kept things growing according to plan.

"The problem goes beyond the box office result and falls significantly on the misplaced and exaggerated expectations of an executive team that perhaps wasn't fit to manage, and was likely subject to be influenced by others to maintain their idea of success," he continued. "If you think about it, you can see an incremental level of anxiety in the postproduction changes for *BvS, Suicide Squad,* and then ultimately in a complete film change with *Justice League.* Not to mention the mistreatment of many, including Snyder and Ayer.

"It is my belief that the executive structure governing DC Films . . . promised immediate results to their superiors in direct comparison to the financial results of the Marvel brand, a Disney-backed exercise that had been developing and growing their hype with multiple films and marketing almost five years before," said Orbegozo. "As ridiculous as it sounds, not surpassing or even meeting these numbers immediately, I'm certain, made a lot of exaggerated promises to investors difficult to back up. The most natural result was to try to modify the product (which had a clear differentiator) to mimic the other brand. I'm certain some within the company identified and used that obvious weakness for personal gain, adding to the chaos. This misguided mindset results in an irresponsible lack of appreciation for what they did have, and what they had achieved: A group of films which were performing quite well for being such early entries, an alternative competing brand with a market differentiator, and a growing online follower base. *BvS* is only the second film in a franchise (and the highest grossing Superman film in history). I feel that the expectation was that a home run must be achieved, only for swinging without putting any context or having any consideration of what was being built. Say what you want about Snyder, but he had vision, and, more importantly, he took on the competition head on, maintaining DC as a prestigious player in a multi-million dollar market."[11]

Beautifully said.

The irony of the situation, however, is that Snyder falling out of favor with the studio executives running the DCEU machine only benefits the *Justice League* movie that he's now able to make. The drastic changes made to the theatrical cut of *Justice League* might have altered the course of the

DCEU as a whole, but according to Snyder, it also means that he's no longer beholden to any larger storytelling effort. Nor does his resuscitated *Justice League* movie exist under the thumb of corporate bean counters who would second-guess his every creative decision.

"I had a pretty complex universe that I was working on," Snyder said in an interview for this book that took place after the HBO Max announcement. "And so for me, what the movie has become . . . what *Justice League* is now, is this Elseworld *Justice League*. I think that's what it's become. And I don't begrudge that, by the way. I think finally people will be able to watch the movie, and where we were going to go, in a way that has less pressure on it. Because DC has gone on another path with the DCEU. Sort of the *Birds of Prey* or *Aquaman 2* [direction]. . . . I think that all just points in a different direction than where I was going. Not to say it's not valid and cool. It certainly can be. But it's just not what I had in mind."[12]

Snyder describing his current *Justice League* cut as an "Elseworld" story is groundbreaking. In the DC Comics, Elseworld stories were created by the publisher to exist outside the canon of the DC Universe. It provided creators immense freedom to explore any type of storytelling environment with popular DC characters, without drastically disrupting ongoing DC narratives. One such example of a popular Elseworld book, Brian Augustyn's *Gotham By Gaslight,* found Batman investigating Jack the Ripper in 1889.

Back in 2015, however, the "business" aspect of show business overwhelmed Snyder's process, so analysts spent time writing obituaries for *Batman v Superman* that touched on its creative ambitions, its industry expectations, and yes, its box office performance.

"[*Batman v Superman*] was a conundrum, and you can't evaluate it without wondering what might have happened financially had the picture been more pleasurable to watch and not so dour," wrote Deadline's Mike Fleming in a March 2017 article analyzing monies left on the table by major studios. "It is hard to evaluate the movie without wondering how much larger its $873 million global gross might have been had the film just worked in some humor and not been so relentlessly bleak."[13]

The industry's report card on Snyder's DCEU contributions wasn't great. It felt, at the time, like something drastic needed to happen to shake things up. And on June 9, 2016, something drastic did.

7

CHANGE THE (NARRATIVE) TIDE

Having spent years running an entertainment website, I can tell you that when a publicist texts, emails, or calls after hours, it means something is wrong. You've misquoted a client in an article. You published a scoop that wasn't supposed to go live. One of your writers tweeted something inappropriate. The usual communication breakdowns.

As the managing director of CinemaBlend, I've received my fair share of those messages from trusted studio contacts—more than I'd probably care to admit. Never, though, had I received an email like the one that arrived in my inbox on Thursday, June 9, 2016, at 9:02 pm.

"Around for a fast call? If so, best number?" inquired this publicist, whose name I'll choose to protect. My stomach twisted like a pretzel. What was so urgent that it couldn't wait? Like I said, late-evening requests like this usually led to being chewed out over the phone because someone, somewhere, was upset about something.

This wasn't the case. The publicist was checking my availability for a set visit that was going to happen just a few days later. In London. To watch Zack Snyder film *Justice League*.

Oh, that's all?

The invitation to see Snyder work on one of the most anticipated superhero blockbusters in history wasn't the only bombshell. There was a delicious caveat. There was no embargo on press coverage, meaning we could start publishing stories the day we returned from set.

I can't emphasize this enough: This never happens. Ever.

Traditionally, when one attends a studio-sanctioned set visit, the knowledge obtained is kept under lock and key by airtight embargoes, and editors can only publish details of what they learned when the inviting studio decides they want to get the information out. We absorb significant plot details on set visits because we visit while the movies are early in production. But for *Justice League*, we were told—in complete contrast to the way things normally are done—that we could start sharing details immediately. In fact, we were all but begged to run our stories from the set as soon as was physically possible.

The reasoning behind the decision was crystal clear.

A MAJOR SHAKEUP

By June 9, 2016, when that fateful set visit invitation arrived, the verdict on Zack Snyder's *Batman v Superman: Dawn of Justice* was in. The film had crossed $330 million domestically, but was days away from concluding its theatrical run (the website BoxOfficeMojo.com has its final day in theaters as June 16), and the hard truth had sunk in that the movie was going to fall short of $1 billion worldwide. The ramifications had the potential to be enormous . . . and disastrous.

In a blog post published on January 10, 2019—years after the dust had settled on Zack Snyder's contributions to the DCEU—Drew McWeeny, formerly of HitFix and current publisher of the *Formerly Dangerous* newsletter, reminisced about the hand-wringing that reportedly was going on at Warner Bros. between the release of *Batman v Superman* and the start of production on *Justice League*. According to his sources, there was an apprehensive mood at Warner Bros. in the wake of *BvS* because the Snyders already were "deeply embedded" in the DCEU as a director and as executive producers on multiple upcoming titles.

"When I was hearing bad things about *Batman v Superman*, it was from every direction, and it kept getting louder," McWeeny recalled in this blog post. "One day, one of those conversations was with a person working directly for Team Snyder, and that person vented some very real anxiety about what might happen if the film didn't work. They explained just how deeply embedded the Snyders were at that point in the future of the DC Films 'big plan,' and how much it would throw a wrench in things if they couldn't make a crossover film between their two biggest characters into a hit, and how much stress there was on figuring out the interconnected franchise somehow.

"The thing they said that stood out most was how they were already far enough down the road on *Justice League* that it was happening no matter what," McWeeny continued. "But the fear was that a stumble on *BvS* would start a domino effect that would screw up all the other plans, including the films that were connected to *Justice League*."[1]

None of this could be considered a shock to anyone paying attention to the situation that was slowly unfolding in the DCEU. Zack Snyder's *Justice League* train left the station long before *Batman v Superman* opened in theaters, with screenwriter Chris Terrio reportedly completing his version of the script as early as July 2015. The Snyders also admitted to feeling that pressure in the wake of *Batman v Superman: Dawn of Justice* because they, too, understood its role as a foundation for the DC movies that had been announced.

"*Batman v. Superman* was always a stepping stone for *Justice League*, and it was a way to bring the worlds together without being too jarring," Zack Snyder told *The Hollywood Reporter* in a March 17, 2016, profile. "Our philosophy, though, is it's filmmaker-driven. . . . To understand that, there is a bigger storyline, and let's all support that and not blow up the entire universe because you have an idea that you think is awesome but doesn't make sense with the bigger thing."[2]

Great point. Ironic, when you consider what happened to Snyder (and other directors in the WB/DC system). But a great point nonetheless. There were multiple branches stemming off the tree that was planted by the Snyders in both *Man of Steel* and *Batman v Superman*. The burgeoning DCEU needed to support announced movies such as *Suicide Squad, Wonder Woman,* and *Aquaman*. Also, when *Justice League* was first announced by Warner Bros. in 2014, it was conceived as a two-part epic. And yet, if audiences rejected the foundation established by the Snyders, the entire "house" would crumble.

The studio needed more buy-in. From my perspective, they'd processed the less-than-stellar performance of *Batman v Superman* at the international box office and surmised that the majority of audience members paying to see superhero blockbusters in theaters preferred the jokey, mainstream approach of the MCU over the bold, aggressive tone of Snyder's DC movies, to date.

This led to a major shake-up behind the scenes at Warner Bros. that many point to as the beginning of the end for Zack Snyder's role in the DCEU.

"HOPE AND OPTIMISM."

In May 2016, Warner Bros. streamlined its chain of command for its DCEU films. Under a newly created banner dubbed DC Films, Executive Vice President Jon Berg and DC's chief content officer Geoff Johns were given complete oversight over the theatrical plans of upcoming DC movies. The studio's move wasn't meant to solely target the work being done on DC movies. Other executives at Warner Bros. shifted their own roles to better focus on movies being made in the *LEGO* and *Fantastic Beasts* franchises, for example. But a massive changing of the guard was happening at the Burbank movie studio, and the DCEU was getting swept up in the transition.

Berg had already been working on all the DCEU properties at the time. After serving as a producer on films including *Out of Time, Elf, Meet Dave,* and the Tom Cruise thriller *Edge of Tomorrow,* Berg transitioned to the DC feature films, producing *Wonder Woman, Justice League,* and *Aquaman.*

Geoff Johns, meanwhile, was the rock star comic book writer who'd steadily climbed the ranks at DC Comics by shepherding well-received books focused on the Green Lantern, Superman, and The Flash. In 2010, Johns was named chief creative officer of DC Entertainment, a subsidiary of Warner Bros. that was meant to spread DC content across several different media platforms. By July 27, 2016, Johns was confirmed by *The Hollywood Reporter* as being named president of DC Entertainment, putting him in charge of DC's numerous film and television projects.[3]

Needless to say, Johns's fingerprints were about to be all over the DC Cinematic Universe. And his approach to these characters fundamentally differed from the one Snyder had taken for the bulk of two movies.

Writing about Johns's ascension to the top of DC Entertainment and the DC Films banner in May 2016, Vulture reporter Abraham Riesman spelled out the obvious. "One phrase came out of [Johns's] mouth over and over again as he talked about DC's comics: 'hope and optimism.' Though Johns would never speak ill of *Batman v Superman: Dawn of Justice* or its director, Zack Snyder—Johns is nothing if not loyal to the company that made him a star—it's crystal clear that his vision for DC looks a lot brighter than the much-maligned grimness Snyder provided earlier this year."[4]

A few months later, in a *Wall Street Journal* interview, Johns finally confirmed, on record, that his goal was to alter the direction of DC's films.

"Mistakenly in the past I think the studio has said, 'Oh, DC films are gritty and dark and that's what makes them different.' That couldn't be more wrong," Johns said. "It's a hopeful and optimistic view of life. Even Batman has a glimmer of that in him. If he didn't think he'd make tomorrow better, he'd stop."[5]

The invitation to the set of *Justice League* in June 2016 was meant to sell that point. It was meant to turn the narrative tide, to let fans know (through the pieces written by the invited journalists) that *Justice League* was going to be different than *Man of Steel* and *Batman v Superman*.

In the same *Wall Street Journal* article, Berg copped to *Justice League* rewrites with Snyder and Chris Terrio that implemented changes following fan reaction to *Batman v Superman*.

"We accelerated the story to get to the hope and optimism a little faster," said Berg.[6]

It was official. Under the guidance of Berg and Johns, the DC films were going to be Fun, with a capital F.

IN ALL THEIR GLORY

The thing is, everyone we spoke with on the set of Zack Snyder's *Justice League* seemed to agree with this shift in focus. Starting at the top, with Zack himself. In fact, the way that Snyder told it to us, this lighter tone was a natural progression toward where he'd intended to go with his DC movies the entire time. It's now what we expect to see weaved into Snyder's *Justice League* on HBO Max.

"It's fun for me to finally get to this point now, in sort of the progression of the three movies, where we are building a team and making the Justice League, if you will," Snyder told us while we were on the set. "Inherently, you've got to remember that the whole thread of [*Batman v Superman*] was to draw those two into conflict. I wanted to make sure that each of them was—and I felt like they were both—evolving. In my mind, anyway.

"But I guess my point is . . . the idea of drawing Superman and Batman in conflict meant that you really had to dig down on the darker parts of them to make them fight each other," Snyder continued. "And I really do believe that with this movie, with *Justice League*, they both have been freed of the shackles of that responsibility to be in a place where they would fight each other. And I think that is liberating for us in some ways in making the movie. Because now we have a single enemy with a single objective, and it's really about uniting the team. And that, to me . . . it really is a fun, fun activity."[7]

"Fun." He even made sure to say it twice. Possibly not the word that DC fans and dedicated Snyder enthusiasts want to hear, given their stated preference to the darker, serious tone of the movies that preceded *Justice League*. But Deborah Snyder, who serves as a producer on the film, made it clear in her conversations with us on the *Justice League* set that it was always their intention to make "a totally different movie" than *Man of Steel* and *Batman v Superman*.

"I think that [*Man of Steel*] and *Batman v Superman* were origin stories," Debbie said "We kind of saw them at points in their life that they were challenged. . . . But this is a movie about coming together. It's a movie about building them up."[8]

A lot of faithful Snyder fans continue to argue that the changes made to Snyder's DC vision were forced on him from executives on high. And I would agree that, to a certain extent, there were conversations held on various levels at the studio to pivot the DCEU in a lighter, more audience-friendly direction. Yet during this fascinating and informative set visit, Snyder admitted to us that the overall fan reaction to *Batman v Superman* surprised him, and made him rethink his approach to *Justice League,* leading to more positive swings.

"When *Batman v Superman* came out, I was like, 'Wow, okay, woof.' It did catch me off guard," Snyder candidly admitted to us on set that day. "I have had to, in my mind, make an adjustment just because of . . . maybe it is my hardcore take on the characters? As far as, I love them, and I love the material. And I do, I take it really deep. And so, I think that the nice thing about now working on *Justice League* is that it is an opportunity to really blow the doors off of the scale and the bad guys and team building and all this stuff that I think could justify it as [a] big, modern comic book movie."

It's informative to look back on these quotes to see what Snyder's mindset was in 2016 regarding the tone and construction of the universe. Building on the director's self-reflective criticism, Debbie Snyder opened up about the main lesson she thought their team learned from *Batman v Superman*, stating, "I think the main thing we learned [is that] people don't like to see their heroes deconstructed. I think that's hard because it's people that we've grown up with, and that we care about. [Fans] like seeing them, I think, in all their glory."

To that end, Zack Snyder chose a scene to screen for the gathered journalists that day to show off the tone he was aiming for in his feature. It was a scene that still exists in the theatrical cut of *Justice League,* though one that suffers from obvious reshoots. It's the moment that Ezra Miller's Barry Allen, aka The Flash, first meets Ben Affleck's Bruce Wayne in the speedster's stripped-down apartment. And the humor that Snyder wanted to bring to *Justice League* was evident even here.

"I do think that [this scene] shows a little bit about what Ezra brings to the movie," Snyder told us. "You know, Batman is Batman. Bruce Wayne has this kind of 'Batman humor,' that's not the same. As you could see, he's the straight guy. It's what he's good at. When I saw the scene—and we just cut it together the other day—I was like, 'Oh God, this is fun.' It's an interesting way of understanding how the movies have gone in a progression."

Everything Zack Snyder was telling us on the *Justice League* set that day proved that a lighter tone was part of his design, just as the dour mood of *Batman v Superman* was part of the design of that particular story. But the team-building aspect of *Justice League,* and the cast additions that included Ezra Miller, Ray Fisher, and Jason Momoa, would lead—he hoped—to a more audience-friendly adventure.

Snyder also pushed back on the notion that any changes being made to the overall vision on *Justice League* were mandated by the studio in any way. And he poured cold water on the idea that, at the time, he wasn't getting along with new creative collaborator Geoff Johns.

"Geoff and I have had a great working relationship, even on *Batman v Superman*. On *Wonder Woman*, we worked together really closely," Snyder said. "He's just a really . . . his knowledge of comics is crazy. He's like an ency-clopedia of comic books. I'll be like, 'Hey, is there, like, a weird Lantern from whatever?' And he'll be like, 'You know . . . ' He's really amazing with just keeping everything in canon that I'd be like, 'I had never even heard of that.'"

In hindsight, this could be viewed as spin. And while Snyder refuses to name names, he admitted to me in a June 2020 interview that even though "every movie is a fight," *Justice League* was marked by an abnormal number of behind-the-scenes arguments.[9] The director, though, seemed sincere when he explained to us back in 2016 how cooperative Warner Bros. had been with him on every step of this daunting undertaking.

"I think there is a slight misconception about . . . how much pressure there was on us, and the pressure on [*Batman v Superman*] to perform in a certain way," Snyder clarified. "From my point of view, and maybe because I just don't know how to do it any other way, we make really personal mov-ies. I love the characters. I love comic books. And maybe to a fault some-times. Like, I dork out on the hardcore aspects of the comic books. Because I'm a grownup, and I love that part of it.

"I have had a great time making the movie, and I don't think that War-ner Brothers, when we were shooting the movie, that there was some sort of corporate mandate to get Batman and Superman in the movie," Snyder continued. "That [just] happened. Chris [Terrio] and I had that idea. And then it just so happened that that was a way toward *Justice League*. And it came along at a great time for us, and as the studio was moving forward with the other DC titles and getting the DCEU to exist. But I don't think the birth of Batman versus Superman was some corporate conspiracy to sell tickets or do whatever. I think it just became this great vehicle that had a lot of focus put on it because of where it ended up in the timeline."

But the takeaway from our visit to the set of Zack Snyder's *Justice League*—and make no mistake, it very much was still Zack Snyder's *Justice League* at that time—is that the creative force behind *Man of Steel* and *Bat-man v Superman* was intending to shift away from the darkness as he fol-lowed the progression of this new story. Some of that was by design of the team-building nature of the narrative he was establishing in *Justice League*. And some of it was a reaction to the criticisms leveled at *BvS*, which the Snyders admitted they heard.

But in Snyder's own words, the tone of *Justice League* was always going to be different than its predecessors, even if he'd likely stop short of the more funny nature of the Marvel Studios movies to which his DC films always were going to be compared.

"I'm obsessed with tone in the movies," Snyder told us as the set visit was drawing to a close. "Tone has always been the main thing that I go after with a movie. And I really wanted the tone of the three movies to be different chapters, and not be the same note that you strike and [be] like, 'Okay there's this again.' I really did. I really wanted that. And I do believe that since *Batman v Superman* came out and we've really wrapped our heads around what *Justice League* would be, I do think that the tone has—because of what the fans have said, and how the movie was received by some is that, you know, we have really put the screws to what we thought the tone would be and, I feel, just crushed it even that little bit further."

Zack Snyder would not be allowed to cross the finish line with his version of *Justice League* until approximately three years later, and only after his fans fought to correct a perceived injustice. Instead, Snyder's superhero journey was about to be sidetracked. A tragedy would rock the Snyders' world, leading to his departure from the DCEU. But the end for Zack would also be the beginning of a significant chapter in the growth and development of the Release the Snyder Cut family.

8

A DEATH IN THE FAMILY

In March 2017, the unthinkable happened. Autumn Snyder, the adopted daughter of Zack Snyder and his first wife Denise Weber, died by suicide. Autumn was twenty years old.

The Snyders have eight children, half of whom are adopted. Autumn and her sister Willow were adopted from China by Zack and Denise Weber. Zack and Debbie Snyder later adopted two additional children, Sage and Cash, while Zack has four biological kids in Olivia, Eli, Ezekiel, and Jett.

To be completely transparent, I've struggled with how to approach this chapter of the story. Unspeakable personal tragedy trumps film, on every level. Even attempting to discuss something as frivolous as a superhero movie in the same conversation as the loss of a child feels wrong. It instantly makes a blockbuster thriller seem insignificant and small. Nothing we could say about either version of *Justice League* matters in light of the Snyders' immeasurable loss.

But Autumn's story actually is woven deeply into the fabric of Zack Snyder's history with Warner Bros. and DC's film slate. Autumn's death directly impacted Zack's involvement in the DCEU, prompting his official departure from *Justice League* in 2017. That led to the hiring of Joss Whedon to finish the film, and the domino effect of Whedon's overall contributions marks the beginning of the fight to unearth the alternate cut of the comic book film in the first place.

Finally, the Snyders' tragic loss provided the RTSC movement with an emotional reason to exist beyond the film, a justifiable cause they continue to rally behind, even after achieving the release of the Snyder Cut. And it's those inspirational campaigns, held on behalf of the American Foundation for Suicide Prevention (AFSP) and often backed by the Snyders, that deserve all the recognition and celebration in the world.

"THE GOAL ISN'T TO LIVE FOREVER, THE GOAL IS TO CREATE SOMETHING THAT WILL."

The pop culture world largely learned about Autumn Snyder's death when Zack Snyder revealed it as his reason to step down from *Justice League* on May 22, 2017. In an interview conducted by *The Hollywood Reporter*, the director explained that he hoped it would be "cathartic" to return to *Justice League* and use it as a distraction.[1] He describes the filmmaking process as "all-consuming," but eventually had to admit that try as he might, he wasn't able to balance the workload on the superhero sequel with the overwhelming desire to be home with his family, where they could properly mourn.

Looking back on that difficult time period, Snyder confirmed to me in a 2020 interview that he was emotionally prepared to leave the DCEU in 2017, and harbored no expectation that he'd ever return to the stories he had started in *Man of Steel*.

"I just was kind of done with it," Snyder said as we spoke for this book. "I was in this place of [knowing] my family needs me more than this bullshit, and I just need to honor them and do the best I can to heal that world. I had no energy to fight [the studio], and fight for [the movie]. Literally, zero energy for that. I really think that's the main thing. I think there's a different world where I stayed and kind of tried. And I'm sure I could have . . . because every movie is a fight, right? I was used to that. But I just did not have the [energy]. There was no fight in me. I had been beaten by what was going on in my life and I just didn't want to, I didn't care to . . . that was kind of where I was."[2]

This is the first time Snyder had admitted, on record, that the constant fighting with the studio over his approach to *Justice League* also contributed to his departure from the film. Fans assumed this, but the official reason for leaving the sequel was always Autumn's death. And at least one dedicated Release the Snyder Cut family member sympathizes with the heartache the

Snyders were enduring during this difficult phase, and how it could lead to him walking away.

John Aaron Garza, thirty-three years old, lives in Austin, Texas. His full-time gig is in the auto industry, though he edits for the ReelAnarchy website and cohosts *The Reel In Motion* podcast in his free time. In 2014, Garza lost a child—a devastating tragedy that helped him better understand Zack Snyder's headspace when it came to juggling work and personal loss.

"Knowing Zack loved all of these [DC] characters, and was even working through it all, I understood," Garza said. "His work was helping him—at least, it was, shortly after the incident. Speaking from experience, work is how I healed, and was how he was healing. That's how creative minds get through tough times, I feel."[3]

But at the same time, Garza could understand the push and pull of the job being too much for Snyder because a similar situation happened during his mourning period.

"I know the place I was working at during that time for me was changing so many things I didn't agree with, that I simply left," he said. "It wasn't important to me because what was helping me continue on with life became a burden. So him leaving [*Justice League*] was understandable."

The Snyders said they never planned to make Autumn's suicide a news item. Their intent was to keep it private, an internal grief they'd handle together. But Snyder told *The Hollywood Reporter* at the time that he also understood how the internet would create narratives once it became known that he was leaving *Justice League,* so he opened up about Autumn and the family's loss in an effort to get ahead of the rumor tsunami.

"The truth is . . . I'm past caring about that kind of thing now. . . . I want the movie to be amazing, and I'm a fan, but that all pales pretty quickly in comparison," he said.[4]

As Snyder correctly predicted, the fans were devastated. And worried. But they were also deeply sympathetic to what Zack and Debbie were going through.

Graduate school student Benjamin Hunt from Detroit, Michigan, recalls seeing the headline of Snyder's departure from *Justice League* on Twitter, but claims the fate of the movie never crossed his mind.

"It was mostly just the hope that he was doing okay," Hunt said. "The loss of his daughter was far more important than him having to step away from the production of a movie. My response was the fandom's response, which was really nice. Everyone coming together for Zack. The most important thing at the time, within the fandom, was us being there for him, and that meant showing him that his fans fully supported him stepping away from *Justice League* if that was what he thought was best for him and his family."[5]

Giovanni Torres of New York City also says his thoughts went immediately to Zack Snyder and his family on that fateful day. Torres distinctly remembers ordering Chinese food for lunch when his phone blew up with text messages from friends asking if he'd heard the news. As he sat down to eat, and process what had happened, Torres thought of the Snyders and not of his anticipated *Justice League* movie.

"I was heartbroken," Torres recalls. "I knew how important his family was to him. I simply could not imagine what it would feel like to lose a daughter. And the worst part is that the hate [online] didn't stop. People didn't stop and think this is bigger than some comic book movie. The man is hurting [with] a pain you don't want anyone to ever go through."[6]

A TPZ member, Darren Benson of Norman, Oklahoma, was just home from the hospital himself when he learned of Snyder's departure. "I can still see myself sitting at my desk at work when I saw the news. It took the energy out of me," he recalls. "I watched the trailer repeatedly in the hospital. I was probably more hyped for *Justice League* than any other film, ever. To all of the *Star Wars* fans that were pumped and excited for *Star Wars* that year, I would tell them 'This is my *Star Wars*.'"[7]

Hamad Al-Mansouri, a senior manager of human capital at the Qatar Financial Center, also recalls seeing a portion of the comic book fanbase celebrating Snyder's departure from *Justice League* because they didn't agree with the darker direction he was taking the DC franchise after *Man of Steel* and *Batman v Superman: Dawn of Justice*.

"It came from verified film bloggers and journalists, and they got away with it without scrutiny," Al-Mansouri said. "It hurts seeing all this to this day."[8]

But even in his departure interview with *The Hollywood Reporter,* Zack Snyder tried to put things into perspective, reminding audiences that *Justice League,* no matter who directed it, would always be just a movie. And one that he hoped would continue his vision and have a lasting impression on the culture at large.

To that end, the Snyders shared a Chuck Palahniuk quote in *The Hollywood Reporter* interview that they said Autumn, a writer herself, included in *everything* that she wrote. "We all die. The goal isn't to live forever, the goal is to create something that will."

Justice League was supposed to be that thing. And at the time of Snyder's departure from the movie, the studio tried to assure fans that Whedon's contributions would be nominal and delivered in service of Zack's ultimate vision for these characters, and for the DCEU.

"The directing is minimal and it has to adhere to the style and tone and the template that Zack set," Warner Bros. Pictures president Toby Emmerich told *The Hollywood Reporter* at the time. "He's handing the baton to Joss, but the course has really been set by Zack. I still believe that despite this tragedy, we'll still end up with a great movie."[9]

Spoiler alert: They didn't.

FROM RTSC TO AFSP

If there is one point to be made in this book, it's that the RTSC movement is about so much more than the movie in question. It's about defending artistic integrity. It's about forming lasting bonds with like-minded fans from all corners of the globe. But it's largely about raising awareness for suicide prevention and generating contributions to AFSP, an offshoot of the RTSC efforts that traces back to Autumn's death. In the darkest hour of this difficult journey, the RTSC family found a light of hope, and it has been boosted over the years by Zack and Debbie Snyder.

We will dig deeper into the relationship between the AFSP and the publicity campaigns launched by the Release the Snyder Cut family later in the book. The compassionate efforts of the RTSC movement have helped raise an impressive amount of funds for this vital cause.

Snyder himself helped forge that link between his fanbase and the AFSP. "Why We Fight" was the title of a Vero post the director shared on November 27, 2018. It was a photograph of Autumn. Accompanying the image Snyder wrote, "I want to say thank you to all of the amazing people who have given their thoughts, kindness, and support to me and my family throughout this difficult chapter and acknowledge the noble work that has been done raising money for the American Foundation for Suicide Prevention."[10]

That "noble work" completed by the RTSC movement has included fan art T-shirt and merchandise drives, social media pledge drives, walks that raise awareness and charitable contributions, and the impressive "Project Comic-Con" effort, which led to numerous #ReleaseTheSny derCut billboards being purchased around San Diego during the 2019 Comic-Con celebration.

Matthew Criscuolo has been deeply involved in the movement from its earliest days, when Fiona Zheng organized the fanbase and launched the campaigns that would raise awareness for the existence of a Snyder Cut of *Justice League*. He remains amazed at what he calls the "volcanic eruption of emotion" that has poured out of passionate DC and Zack Snyder fans over the years as they have shifted from trying to release a cut of a movie to changing lives by supporting organizations like the AFSP.

"At the infancy, the movement was about one film, but has branched out to bring more awareness to the importance of protecting artistic integrity," Criscuolo said. "We have found a beautiful cause that has become a second heart or bloodline of our movement—our support for the American Foundation of Suicide Prevention. The Snyder Cut movement has some of the most passionate, intelligent, talented people collectively in the world. I never thought I would be a part of something like this, but here I am. The friends we have made on here is a bond, a testament to what we can accomplish with sheer will and love."[11]

Most of these contributions wouldn't be possible without the dedication of devoted RTSC member Mick Doyle, an Ireland-based member of the tight-knit Snyder Cut community. Doyle, who also belongs to the TPZ brotherhood, prefers to quietly work behind-the-scenes on behalf of Zack Snyder. But ask any key member of the RTSC community and they will confirm that they have collaborated with Doyle on any number of successful promotional and fundraising drives on behalf of Release the Snyder Cut.

In 2019, in an article entitled "We Can Be Heroes: Superhero Fans Take Up The Fight For Suicide Prevention," posted to AFSP's website, Doyle wrote about the movement's charitable efforts. The piece beautifully summed up the unexpected charitable arm that has grown out of the global RTSC movement, inspired by the difficult loss felt by the Snyder family.

Doyle writes, "Superheroes and suicide awareness are not concepts people typically associate with one another, but in the case of one community of fans, the two have become inextricably linked. Moved to help and make a positive difference, the Snyder Cut community has created a series of fundraising campaigns and awareness initiatives which have since helped to raise over $200,000 for The American Foundation for Suicide Prevention. Along with these efforts, people within the fan community also began to have open and frank discussions around mental health on social media and in online chat groups. Fans shared their own experiences with depression and other mental health conditions, finding support among one another, and realizing that most people know at least one person in their lives who has experienced a mental health condition, or who has been affected by suicide. The supportive environment that has grown out of these campaigns and conversations has given people who had not previously talked about their experiences the comfort and encouragement to express themselves.

"While the #ReleaseTheSnyderCut movement may appear to be focused primarily on the goal of releasing Zack Snyder's original *Justice League* film, the day-to-day focus of the fan community has always been as much about celebrating and acknowledging the power and impact of Zack's existing filmography," Doyle continued. "Throughout this journey, each of us has encountered countless other fans who have spoken about how Zack's previous works have influenced us in positive, life-affirming ways. Folks who have felt undervalued or marginalized have found inspiration through the humanization of the larger-than-life heroes depicted on screen, while others have been empowered to appreciate their own sense of self-worth. Many who struggle with depression have found coping each day that much easier as they recognize the same emotional challenges that they face being experienced by their favorite heroes, who rise from situations of darkness to discover hope and inspire heroism in others. I have personally spoken to several people who have confided that Zack's art has literally helped save their lives. Powerful storytelling truly has the ability to heal, bring awareness and create change. This is why we fight."[12]

It's also, in large part, why this book exists.

9

JOSS-TICE LEAGUE

Hiring Joss Whedon to complete Zack Snyder's *Justice League* made all the sense in the world . . . and absolutely no sense at all.

As I've established, Warner Bros. and the DC Films label were chasing after Marvel Studios' formula for success. And why wouldn't they? Following the underwhelming financial returns of *Man of Steel* and *Batman v Superman: Dawn of Justice,* DC was ready to throw its counterpart to the Avengers onto the silver screen. So why not hire the guy who'd already delivered two Avengers movies for Marvel in 2012's *The Avengers* and its 2015 sequel, *Avengers: Age of Ultron?*

Whedon's accomplishments at Marvel were unprecedented. Not only did he deliver a historic team up of Marvel Comics icons, he also tied together numerous individual film franchises into one all-star package. *The Avengers* worked on its own as a superhero fantasy, but it also honored the character-based storylines established in Marvel movies like *Iron Man 2, Thor,* and *Captain America: The First Avenger.* Naturally, Warner Bros. executives believed that Whedon would understand exactly how to juggle multiple superhero personalities for a large-scale, planet-threatening mission.

On paper, Whedon personified everything that Warner Bros. executives thought they wanted from the DC Films. Even before he started working for Marvel, Whedon had established his quirky, sarcastic, pop culture-saturated yet adorably self-deprecating voice in the two beloved television series *Buffy the Vampire Slayer* and *Firefly.* The storyteller was already on DC's radar, having written a Wonder Woman screenplay in the mid-aughts that never got off the ground. Finally, DC Films' deliberate transition from mature and broody to humorous, upbeat, and audience-friendly was going to start with *Justice League* . . . no matter what Warner Bros. Pictures president Toby Emmerich might have told fans about Whedon's "minimal" direction, or the studio's alleged intention to maintain the course that had been set by Snyder in *Man of Steel* and *Batman v Superman: Dawn of Justice.*

That's where the Whedon hire stops making sense, however. Because Joss Whedon's voice sounds nothing like Zack Snyder's, and no amount of rewrites or reshoots would ever get these two distinctive creative forces to sing the same tune.

If Warner Bros. truly wanted a *Justice League* movie that felt like the existing *Avengers* films, then hiring Whedon to perform rewrites and oversee reshoots wouldn't be enough. The studio, in hindsight, probably needed to allow Whedon to wipe the slate clean, start over from square one, and construct a Justice League story told from his unique point of view. But there wasn't time. *Justice League* had a November 17, 2017, release date, and Warner Bros. had no intention of postponing it. Also, too much money already had been spent by Snyder and his team on the developing production. The studio merely hired Whedon to fix *Justice League*. He failed.

OPPOSING PHILOSOPHIES

Joss Whedon actually joined *Justice League* while Zack Snyder was still at the helm. This was first reported by *The Hollywood Reporter* in its May 22, 2017, story about Snyder stepping down following the death of his daughter, Autumn.[1] It was later confirmed by the AP in November 2017, when it noted that Whedon "had already been helping to punch up the script."[2]

Entertainment industry website Vulture additionally reported that it was Geoff Johns and Jon Berg who brought Whedon into the *Justice League* fold as they wrestled with the backlash to *Batman v Superman* and figured out how to instill hope and optimism to their revamped DC cinematic universe.[3] *The New York Times* later confirmed that a *Justice League* footage summit was held in 2017, where Zack Snyder's version of the film was screened for respected screenwriters Andrea Berloff (Oliver Stone's *World Trade Center*, the N.W.A. biopic *Straight Outta Compton*), Allan Heinberg (Patty Jenkins'

Wonder Woman), and Whedon. Shortly after, Whedon was hired by the studio to oversee *Justice League* reshoots and complete rewrites to better bridge existing scenes that Snyder had already shot.[4]

"Everyone was excited about Joss being a part of DC, and we thought he'd be great to write the [*Justice League*] scenes, the additional photography scenes that we wanted to get," Johns recalled in that September 2017 article for Vulture.[5]

That included the fans—or, a good portion of them—at first.

"When Joss Whedon was hired, I honestly wasn't worried," said Lindsey Staton, a twenty-one-year-old author from West Virginia. "All the producers were saying that the reshoots were given the green light by Zack, and that Whedon was following his direction."[6]

That sentiment was echoed by David McEachrane, a thirty-one-year-old Zack Snyder supporter who lives in Trinidad and Tobago. McEachrane owns and operates his own business and assists the RTSC movement at every possible turn. He remembers being "cautiously optimistic" about Whedon's *Justice League* hire.

"I mean the guy did *Avengers* 1 and 2," McEachrane said, "and according to Toby Emmerich, he was being brought in to do pickups and finish the movie whose template was already set by Zack. Only later, we found out that was a blatant lie."[7]

Count Kansas-based RTSC family member Brandon Valenza as another fan who bought into the studio's reasoning that Whedon was merely carrying out Snyder's vision.

"I believed the original story that [Whedon] was already working on a few new scenes to help lighten the movie a touch," Valenza said. "It had already been stated that the movie would be lighter in tone than *Batman v Superman,* so it made sense. Plus, Joss was already accomplished in big superhero movies. Not that it mattered, since we were promised [by Warner Bros.] in the official statement that the new scenes were approved by Zack, would be minimal, and would adhere to the already established vision set forth by Zack. So nothing to worry about right?"[8]

Well, not exactly.

There are fans who claim, years later, to have seen through the smokescreen established by Warner Bros. as they changed horses midstream and saddled up to Joss Whedon.

"I saw this hire as a clear attempt by WB to pander to Marvel movie audiences," said Ben Wellington, a twenty-six-year-old software engineer from Oklahoma.[9]

Meanwhile, Staton admits that as she learned more about both Snyder and Whedon and their creative approaches, she gradually became more concerned.

"Back then I had no idea what the process of filmmaking was, and they are two very different filmmakers," she said. "So if I had known what I know now, mostly about Zack's process, I would have been terrified. Because there was no way Whedon could emulate Zack's artistic vision."

The fundamental difference between Zack Snyder and Joss Whedon and their approach to superhero storytelling also stood out to Release the Snyder Cut founder Fiona Zheng, and not in a positive way. "We love how Snyder communicates a lot of themes through visual iconography of the religious or philosophical," Zheng said, adding that in her opinion, Whedon "does not possess that kind of layered, nuanced eye."[10]

"Snyder's philosophy, when it comes to superheroes, is that he respects them so much, that he takes them seriously. As opposed to Whedon, who portrays them with a sense of self-parody or self-deprecation," Zheng said. "Snyder's female characters are always strong and powerful. Even if they aren't wearing obvious costumes, they are heroines without capes. That's exactly the opposite of Whedon's filmmaking style."

These diametrically opposed philosophies stood out to Justin Lesniewski, a thirty-seven-year-old high school English teacher who has spent years analyzing the thematic layers and visual imagery in Zack Snyder's filmography. "Snyder's movies celebrate individualism and the wonders of life," Lesniewski said. "And do you know what doesn't get supported by the cultural elites, especially those people in Hollywood? Romanticism, and the celebration of the individual."[11]

Lesniewski admits to enjoying Joss Whedon's pre-*Justice League* work. "His writing in *Avengers* at least understood the characters to the point that the [Tony] Stark-[Steve] Rogers conflict was at its most interesting in the MCU," the teacher comments. But there's a flaw to Whedon that, in Lesniewski's eye, sets him apart from Snyder.

"For me," he said, "Whedon is an infuriatingly frustrating artist. He is an extremely talented artist who flirts with being a Romantic. However, the ultimate resolutions of his narratives are usually clichéd Hollywood tropes."

Let's use, as an example, an addition to *Justice League* that was all Whedon—the Russian family we meet at different intervals of the film who exist only to be in danger throughout the story. Snyder has confirmed on Vero that he has no clue who or what the "Russian family" is, so the characters had to have been added as part of Whedon's reshoots. Every scene they appear in contains a forced joke or painful punchline. The family's young daughter pulls out a can of bug spray, hoping it will fend off the Parademons that are swirling outside their home. When The Flash (Ezra Miller) rescues them in the film's finale, he responds with the only Russian word he knows: "*Dostoevsky!*" It's amateur-hour humor. But the Russian family also acts as a surrogate for the misguided belief that comic book audiences better invest in suspense when there's a recognizable victim in peril. And while it's true that audiences do tend to root for the dramatic rescue of characters they've grown to love, it's simple-minded to assume that *Justice League* needed these Russian family scenes to force us to connect to the story.

The difference between Whedon and Snyder can be boiled down to lighthearted quips versus somber personal dramas. Whedon hasn't met a snarky comeback he didn't immediately want to work into his dialogue, while Snyder's generally happier letting conflict breathe and evolve through discourse. Whedon's approach to genre tends to be easily digestible and highly enjoyable. You tend to forget it as you are leaving the theater. Snyder, on the flip side, usually invites analysis and challenges the viewer. It's that deeper approach that fans are expecting to see in Zack Snyder's *Justice League* when it arrives on HBO Max.

So, how would these polar opposite filmmakers find a common ground on *Justice League*? The short answer is that they wouldn't, but the studio reportedly would spend a whole lot of money in a short amount of time to learn that painful truth.

BARRY'S BAD BRUNCH

We know Joss Whedon conducted reshoots on *Justice League*. The extent of these reshoots remain a mystery to this day and may never get revealed now that Snyder has his own *Justice League* on HBO Max. But fans went to great effort to scour early trailers for *Justice League* that included Snyder's footage, comparing it to what was included in the theatrical version and lamenting what could have been. Whedon has not spoken on record about his time spent working on *Justice League* (and requests for an interview for this book went unanswered).

But reports that have surfaced regarding Whedon's time on production documented complicated scheduling conflicts with the A-list members of the League, ballooning budgets, hurried rewrites to punch up dialogue, and one hilarious obstacle involving Henry Cavill's facial hair that gets its own chapter in this book. In July 2020, Ray Fisher reported allegations of abusive on-set behavior by Whedon during the *Justice League* reshoots, which led to Warner Bros.' launch of an internal investigation. Whedon has denied these allegations. The investigation's findings had not been released at the time of this book's publication.

On July 24, 2017, seasoned *Variety* film reporters Justin Kroll and Brent Lang cited the two-month-long *Justice League* reshoots as costing Warner Bros. approximately $25 million.

"Reshoots, or additional photography, to use the preferred studio nomenclature, traditionally cost between $6 million and $10 million, and rarely have to juggle so many competing schedules. They typically last a week or two," the duo wrote. "*Justice League* is spending the kind of time and money on reshoots that mid-budget films would have to shoot an entire movie."[12]

Watch the theatrical cut of *Justice League,* though, and you can easily spot the places where Whedon fit new material into existing Snyder footage . . . but didn't try very hard to match it up. You can basically judge how a scene is lit to tell the two apart. Snyder's footage tends to have proper shading and a blue-grey tint to it, while Whedon's reshoots are bright, shiny, and have a technicolor tone that almost resembles a three-camera television sitcom. There are countless, egregious examples in *Justice League* of conflicting footage that is mashed together in the very same scene, with jarring effect.

One such disjointed pairing takes place in the specific scene that Zack Snyder chose to show the film journalists who had traveled to London in 2016 to witness the *Justice League* production in action. As you recall, Snyder showed us the scene where Ezra Miller's Barry Allen returns home, unlocks his front door, steps inside and finds Bruce Wayne (Ben Affleck) seated in a large chair in the speedster's living room. Bruce hands Barry a

CinemaBlend Managing Director Sean O'Connell on the London set of Zack Snyder's *Justice League*, June 2016. (Photo by Clay Enos)

The Times Square billboard rented by the Snyder Cut community in 2019 to advertise the mythical film. (Photo by Giovanni Torres)

The Snyder Cut community launched "Project Comic-Con" in July 2019, flooding downtown San Diego with marketing. (Photo by Nicole Ruiz / Cole of the Nerd Queens)

Posing with costumed DC fans to raise awareness for the Snyder Cut of *Justice League*. (Photo by Ben Wellington)

Zack Snyder poses with long-time fan Austin Vives at the 2019 Pasadena event that has come to be known as SnyderCon, the birthplace of the truth about the Snyder Cut. (Photo by Austin Vives)

In addition to meeting Snyder, Vives and a friend made *Release the Snyder Cut* signs and stood outside of Warner Bros. studios to spread the word and get executives' attentions. (Photo by Austin Vives)

Deadpool creator Rob Liefeld, a long-time Snyder Cut supporter, poses with shirts and a sign at New York Comic-Con in October 2019. (Photo by Giovanni Torres)

The Snyder Cut community made a marketing splash at the 2019 New York Comic-Con, getting photos with fans shared on social media. (Photo by Giovanni Torres)

This post, shared by Zack Snyder on Vero, was the nail in the coffin of the argument against the existence of the Snyder Cut of *Justice League*. (Photo by Zack Snyder)

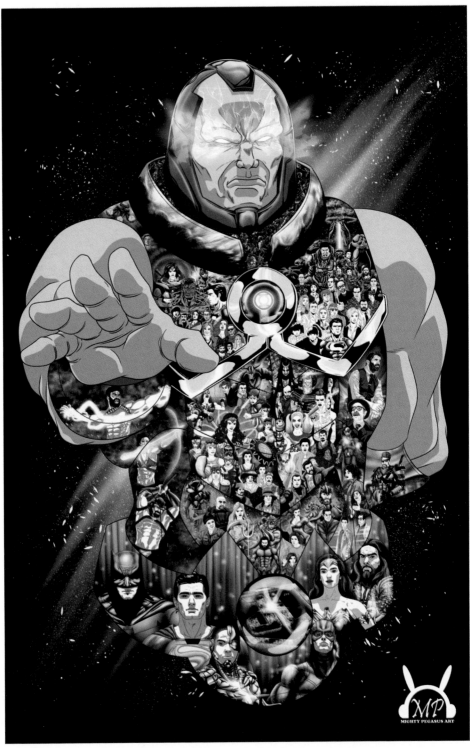

Victor Ku's original *Justice League* poster, which won Zack Snyder's official contest. Ku's prize? A trip to the set of the *Justice League* reshoots. (Photo by Victor Ku)

printout of a young man who had been captured on video thwarting a convenience store robbery. Barry tries to deflect, but Bruce throws a Batarang at Allen's head. The hero uses his Speed Force to catch the pointy weapon in midair, giving his secret identity away.

Almost everything that's included in the theatrical cut mirrors exactly what we saw in the footage shown to us by Zack Snyder on the set of *Justice League* back when it was still Zack Snyder's *Justice League*. Until Ezra Miller's Barry Allen breaks into a comedy routine about brunch.

"People are difficult," the character says in footage that clearly has been reshot. "They require a lot of focus. They have like a rhythm that I haven't quite been able to . . . like brunch. What is brunch? You wait in line for an hour for, essentially, lunch. I mean, I don't know. People are a little . . . slow."[13]

It's meant to be a laugh line, a joke added way after the fact to punch up a serious scene that originally ended on Barry Allen admitting to Bruce Wayne that he needs friends. But the blatant addition stands out like a hastily tacked-on blemish and distracts from the scene instead of enhancing anything. Even Miller's haircut is different from the existing Snyder footage, where he has longer bangs that fall near his eyes. In Whedon's reshot footage, the hair falls shorter (because the actor was filming *Fantastic Beasts and Where to Find Them* simultaneously and was sporting a remarkably unique hairstyle for the character of Credence Barebone). Miller's face also is lit differently in the Whedon footage, looking smooth because the director bathed him in light. Little to no effort was made to match the reshot Whedon footage to Snyder's original footage, and the end result is embarrassingly amateurish.

"TO BATTLES LOST"

Warner Bros. and the *Justice League* executive team tried to maintain its spin about a happy marriage between Snyder and Whedon's styles until the very last minute.

In an AP interview posted on November 13, 2017—days before the world would get its first look at the finished product—Oscar-nominated producer Charles Roven (*American Hustle, Man of Steel,* and the Nolan Batman trilogy) tried to ease the fanbase's collective mind by declaring that the studio's goal always was to make sure *Justice League* felt "cohesive" with the vision started by Snyder and continued by Whedon. Roven claimed that the actors "already [were] pretty much down the road on their arcs," and gave a rough estimate that 85 percent of what would be shown on screen in *Justice League* would be material that was originally shot by Snyder. In Roven's own estimates, Whedon would only oversee and control 15–20 percent of the overall movie.[14]

"Cohesive" definitely isn't a word that's used to describe the theatrical cut of *Justice League*. And Snyder supporters will happily tell Roven that if cohesion was the goal, they missed the target by a country mile.

"We know now, Whedon was not brought in to finish the film, he was brought in to reverse engineer it and 'de-Snyder' it to the best of his ability," concludes hardcore Snyder fan Matthew Criscuolo of Rockland County, New York, who makes it clear he's not trying to knock Whedon as a film-maker. "Anyone brought into a film of that magnitude, with five months to do a total overhaul, would have failed miserably at it. This is a knock on WB for totally destroying *JL* and the future films by making that decision to reshoot the entire film, knowing there was not enough time to deliver a quality product."[15]

So, how much of *Justice League* did Whedon actually reshoot? Fabian Wagner thinks he knows.

Wagner served as director of photography on Snyder's film, but did not return for the reshoots (which goes a long way toward explaining why Whedon's added footage looks nothing like Snyder's original scenes). Wagner is also one of the few crew members to go on record about the version of the film that Zack made and the version that was released into theaters on November 17, 2017.

ComicBookDebate's podcast interviewed Wagner in August 2019, where the hosts asked him how much footage he estimates was reshot for the theatrical cut. Wagner admitted, "It's really hard to say because I was watching it and I think I was crying all the way through. So it's hard for me to say exactly how much was changed, but a lot was changed. It looked very different, and it's sad for me because I loved working with Zack."[16]

A few months later, Wagner addressed the same topic during a Q-and-A session about his career that was captured by Twitter user Leonardo Oliveira.[17] In a detailed and devastating answer, Wagner explained, "I did

principal photography for Zack. We finished shooting, and he started editing. We went to L.A. to do the color grading for the trailers. So the first three
trailers, they were all things we shot. Then they started the reshoots several
months later. I wasn't there. It was a completely different team. They actually reshot 55 days. The movie that was in cinemas was maybe 10 percent of
the stuff that we shot. Everything else is a reshoot."

Let that sink in. Zack Snyder's cinematographer, Fabian Wagner, estimated that the theatrical version of *Justice League* contained nearly 10
percent of what Snyder shot. That claim alone gave sufficient evidence to the
armies of fans who believed that Snyder had all the material he needed (and
then some) to deliver his own cut of the movie. And it likely confirms that
the version coming to HBO Max will look nothing at all like the theatrical
cut. They're basically different projects.

Joss Whedon, meanwhile, was asked to reshoot roughly 90 percent of the
movie in under sixty days, add humor to an already lighter endeavor, juggle
the production schedules of a league of A-list talents . . . oh, and satisfy a new
mandate allegedly issued by former Warner Bros. CEO Kevin Tsujihara that
Justice League come in under two hours.

The Justice League themselves couldn't complete that mission.

That type of studio interference could be blamed, ultimately, for *Justice
League*'s failures. Zack Snyder's blockbuster definitely got caught in the
crosshairs of a major movie studio trying to shift gears midrace. Reacting to
the success of Patty Jenkins's solo Wonder Woman movie, and perpetually
chasing the highs that were being enjoyed by Marvel Studios, WB put *Justice League* under the knife, and then braced for the inevitable consequences.

Watch the theatrical cut of *Justice League,* however, and you'll see what
I am choosing to interpret as a blatant explanation, and apology, from
Whedon to the audience. The opening-credits montage for *Justice League*
is set to a somber and reflective cover of Leonard Cohen's song "Everybody
Knows," sung by Norwegian singer-songwriter Sigrid. The haunting tune is
characterized by its dark humor. In context, the use of the melancholic song
could refer to the end of the Snyderverse, as fans knew it.

A deeper dive into the lyrics for "Everybody Knows" suggest that
Whedon chose it as his movie's opening song because it potentially sug-
gested the uphill battle he was facing by accepting the ill-fated mission to fix
Justice League and meet the studio's requirements.[18]

The song's lyrics talk about dice being loaded, or the war being "over," with the good guys already lost. The lyrics acknowledge that "the fight was fixed," that "the boat is leaking," and "the captain lied." It's about as confessional as one gets.

Now, couple that song choice with the bizarre shot in the movie of a homeless man sitting curbside next to his dog as the opening credits conclude. The man has a cardboard sign resting by his feet. The camera zooms in on it. It reads, "I tried." Tried what? What could the homeless man possibly have tried that he needs to make a sign explaining his failure? There's no reason for the sign's inclusion, unless it's interpreted as a message from Joss Whedon to his detractors. Don't blame him too much. The dice were loaded. The war was over. The captain of the leaking boat had lied. The good guys lost.

Very few people tied to the *Justice League* production speak on the record about what happened when Whedon took over for Snyder. There's no director's commentary track on the *Justice League* DVD (though I'd pay top dollar to hear one), and Whedon never participated in the press events for *Justice League* when the movie came out. For what it's worth, the movie is still credited to Zack Snyder, a fact that likely infuriates the most ardent Snyder supporters.

But every once in a while, a bit player in the *JL* soap opera will weigh in, giving us a little more insight into the chaos that took place behind the scenes. It's like tearing off a chunk of stale bread and tossing it to a starving prisoner. We devour it instantly and immediately crave more crumbs of gossip to help us see the whole picture.

This morsel came from Holt McCallany, who conducted a 2017 interview with *Men's Journal* on behalf of his brilliant Netflix drama, *Mindhunters*, where he plays a criminal psychologist. But McCallany also shows up briefly in Joss Whedon's *Justice League* in an opening fight scene. He plays a thief who confronts Ben Affleck's Batman on a Gotham rooftop. Eventually, his character is detained and used by Batman as bait to lure out a menacing Parademon creature.

The way that McCallany recalls it, he had a blast shooting the scene with Affleck, whom he described as "easygoing."[19] McCallany claims that he was once considered for a significant role in the MCU, but since it went to another actor, he was thrilled to finally get a chance to be in a big-ticket superhero film like *Justice League*.

As he went on about his fight choreography, and losing a battle to Batman, McCallany also remembered a battle Whedon lost while arguing with the studio.

"My scene with Batman was originally conceived as a comedic scene," he said. "That's how Joss wrote it, and that's how we shot it. I thought it came out great, but the studio felt it would be a mistake to open the film with a completely comedic scene, so it was re-edited a little bit. I was disappointed, but when I got home to New York I found a bottle of my favorite Champagne and a note from Joss that said 'To Battles Lost. Gratefully, Joss.'"

McCallany would be neither the first nor the last person disappointed by *Justice League* because of compromises pushed on the movie's two directors by the powers-that-be. As it stands, the theatrical cut of *Justice League* is an abominable amalgamation of conflicting creative decisions made by executives trying to figure out a path forward long after the journey had begun. You've no doubt heard the analogy about how difficult it is to turn an unwieldy cruise ship? That's what happened with *Justice League*. They tried to make a sharp left, and the massive boat capsized.

Affleck actually has a better analogy. While promoting his 2020 basketball drama *The Way Back,* the former Batman spoke with CinemaBlend and addressed the confusion on the *Justice League* set after Whedon took over. The way that Affleck described it, "Having two directors is a very weird thing. And for *Justice League*, the director had a family tragedy. . . . And so you have a kind of cow's body with a horse's head a little bit, with two directors a lot of times, for better or for worse."[20]

It's worth noting that in that same conversation, which took place months before the HBO Max reveal, Affleck concluded with, "I do think Zack's cut should be available."

There are many small examples of terrible decisions made in support of completing *Justice League* in time for its announced release date, come hell or high water. But there's one huge example of a Band-Aid applied to the theatrical cut that shouldn't exist in any version of the superhero blockbuster, under any circumstances. Your mission, should you choose to accept it, is to read on and learn how Henry Cavill's *Mission: Impossible—Fallout* mustache proved to be the hairy straw that broke the *Justice League*'s back.

🔟

MUSTACHEGATE

Fifty-five seconds.

That's how long you need to watch the theatrical cut of *Justice League* before you realize something has gone horribly wrong.

Less than one minute goes by and you're already questioning the film's reason for being, because that's the moment when a specific visual effect punches you square in the face. Survival instincts implore you to look away, but you can't tear your eyes off the shoddy effect, wondering how something so slapdash, substandard, and unacceptable could have been left in the finished cut of a wildly anticipated blockbuster superhero movie.

Of course I'm talking about Superman's CGI'd face.

At the fifty-five-second mark of *Justice League,* a bulbous blur first appears on Henry Cavill's lip and cheek, once Superman shakes hands with a firefighter and turns to face two boys asking to interview Kal-El for their podcast. Would kids this young even *have* a podcast? And why is one of them recording sketchy iPhone video for this endeavor? None of this makes any sense. The clumsy interaction between the boys and their hero is so painfully awkward, I've no clue why Joss Whedon chose it as his opening moment for *Justice League.* You can almost surmise, in hindsight, that Whedon knew everyone would be transfixed by the hatchet job performed on Cavill's face, so the dialogue being spoken in the scene would largely be ignored.

Back to the blur. By the 1:05 minute mark, Superman has turned to fully face the camera and answer the boys' questions, but the right side of his face can only be described as swollen, as if the icon was in the midst of painful oral surgery and had to unexpectedly leap from the dentist's chair to save a kitten from the top branch of a tall tree. When Cavill, in the scene, looks down at the red "S" emblazoned on his chest to tell the kids that the letter represents hope and is meant to "wind like a river," the blur on his lip almost subsides. But anytime the actor looks up and stares directly into the camera, the distracting eyesore returns.

Brandon Valenza, a Kansas-based marketer for a financial education company, distinctly remembers the painful shock that overwhelmed him when he first saw this scene on screen.

"The curtain opened, the lights went down, and the movie started," he recalls. "The opening scene was a cell phone camera shot of children interviewing Superman! At this exact moment, I knew this movie was going to be a disaster. Not only was the Superman suit brightly colored with awful chrome plates visible underneath, [but] they chose to OPEN the film with the absolutely horrendous CGI mouth on Henry Cavill! How was this even possible? This was a $300 million movie!"[1]

Terrific question. How is this possible? DC superfan Will Rowlands actually thought it was a creative choice. The thirty-nine-year-old actor from Portsmouth, England, calls Superman his all-time favorite character. Rowlands has been enamored with Snyder's approach to the classic DC hero over the years. He remembers seeing this opening footage for *Justice League* and assuming it was some sort of mistake.

"The opening cell phone scene of Superman was confusing," he said. "My first thought was, 'Umm, he's dead.' Which immediately [was] followed by observing the awful quality of the image. This was completely unexpected, as it fell far below the Zack Snyder standard, not to mention what you would expect from a Hollywood production. Superman's weird face . . . I put down that the footage must be deliberately poor and old, hence a visual style to depict a child's attempt at filming a hero that they have met."[2]

In a way, that could make sense, but that's not the reality. Similar thoughts ran through the head of RTSC community member Ben Wellington, a twenty-six-year-old software engineer from Oklahoma who described his reaction to the *Justice League* theatrical cut in far more harsh terms.

"Through a strange number of circumstances," Wellington explained, "the IMAX theater I watched *Justice League* in on opening night was almost completely empty. But several times throughout the viewing, while I was sitting in my chair, I was so outraged by what I saw, that I actually yelled, out loud, 'What the fuck is this *shit*?' while pointing at the screen."[3]

In hindsight, that's a totally valid response to the theatrical cut of *Justice League,* and specifically to the CGI, ahem, "enhancement" to Henry Cavill's chiseled jaw and upper lip. What is this thing and how did it end up in *Justice League*? The story behind the CGI butchery is almost too strange to believe.

THE *FALLOUT* OVER A MUSTACHE

By most accounts, Zack Snyder wrapped filming on *Justice League* in October 2016, leaving himself several months for the movie's postproduction needs. Jason Momoa shared the most "Jason Momoa" Instagram message around October 1, thanking the cast and crew for their hard work and stating how much he was looking forward to the wrap party.[4] On October 6, 2016, Snyder himself tweeted a one-minute, twenty-two-second video filled with behind-the-scenes footage from his shoot at Warner Bros.' Leavesden studios in southeast England. "Last day filming in the UK," he wrote. "It has been an amazing shoot. Big thanks to everyone involved. #JusticeLeague."[5]

That video contains some fascinating Easter eggs, now that we know what has made it into the theatrical cut, and what remains to be seen in the Snyder Cut of *Justice League*. For instance, we see finished footage from a bomb explosion that reportedly goes off while Wonder Woman is attempting to save children from a London terrorist attack at the beginning of the story. The explosion is absent from the theatrical cut, confirming that Snyder shot scenes that fans now will see on HBO Max. Additionally, Snyder's production video ends with a bulk of the crew sitting on bleachers that were used for Victor Stone's football game at Gotham City University. Stone goes on to become the Justice League member Cyborg, and footage of the young man playing football in the snow is one of many examples of a scene included in Snyder's version of the film that fans knew existed and clung to when they didn't see it in the theatrical cut.

Once filming wrapped in October 2016, the main *Justice League* cast members were free to move on to their next projects. For Ezra Miller, this meant trading in his Flash suit for the wizarding robes of *Fantastic Beasts and Where to Find Them,* where he was set to reprise the role of Credence Barebone in Warner Bros.' planned sequel, *Fantastic Beasts: The Crimes of Grindelwald.*

Jason Momoa, meanwhile, kept it in the DC universe. Casting for his *Justice League* follow-up, *Aquaman,* was in full swing in 2016, as director James Wan surrounded Momoa with the likes of Amber Heard (Mera), Nicole Kidman (Queen Atlanna), Patrick Wilson (Aquaman's half-brother, Orm), and Yahya Abdul-Mateen II (Black Manta). After months of preparation, principal photography began on the movie on May 2, 2017, in Australia (according to a tweet on Wan's now-defunct Twitter page).

As for Henry Cavill, he was moving from one high-powered film franchise to another, and the shift was about to cause massive, hairy headaches for the eventual *Justice League* reshoots.

SHAVING MONEY

On March 16, 2017, director Christopher McQuarrie confirmed via Instagram that Cavill was being offered a significant role in the sixth *Mission: Impossible* film, which eventually would be titled *Mission: Impossible—Fallout.*[6] Cavill would play August Walker, a barrel-chested CIA assassin who's ordered to shadow IMF agent Ethan Hunt (Tom Cruise) on a planet-saving mission to retrieve stolen plutonium. Walker is meant to be the counterbalance to Hunt. He's described in McQuarrie's *Fallout* script as a "hammer" to Hunt's "scalpel." Walker skydives, pilots helicopters, and even cocks his arms before entering a fistfight as if they are pump-action shotguns.

And he sports a luxurious mustache, one that suggested August Walker was the love child Burt Reynolds and Tom Selleck never had.

Putting a mustache on Henry Cavill's character wasn't an issue until the *Justice League* team realized they needed the actor back for reshoots, which proved to be far more extensive than anyone could have predicted. Remember, initially, Joss Whedon only was going to oversee a handful of pickups meant to add levity to Zack Snyder's original footage, and possibly bridge a few scenes that now needed to be better connected. Except, current calculations suggest Whedon instead reshot anywhere from 80 to 90 percent of what audiences see in the theatrical cut of *Justice League,* and that included most, if not all, of Cavill's Superman sequences.

What would Warner Bros. do about Cavill's problematic crumb catcher?

Variety first reported the mustache conflict on July 24, 2017, when the trade noted that Paramount officially "would not allow Cavill to shave the facial hair" while production on *Mission: Impossible—Fallout* was taking place.[7]

Naturally, the true story came out a year later when the parties involved could look back on the insanity and chuckle through their own tears.

In an August 2018 interview for *Empire* magazine's podcast, *Mission: Impossible—Fallout* director Christopher McQuarrie made it clear that he was willing, at the time, to shut down production on his own film to allow Henry Cavill to shave the mustache, film his *Justice League* scenes as Superman, then grow the facial hair back before returning to the role of August Walker.

As McQuarrie remembers it, *Justice League* producer Charles Roven called asking for help because the superhero film needed Cavill to shave to complete the reshoots. And to his credit, McQuarrie claims he worked with his team to figure out how to pull this impossible mission off. McQuarrie tells *Empire* that he and *Mission: Impossible—Fallout* producer Jake Myers cooked up a solution that would allow Cavill to shave, then start growing back the facial hair, prompting the *Fallout* team to digitally fill in whatever was missing.

"Because like it or not, a fake mustache in close-up on a 75mm lens is never going to look like anything but a fake mustache," McQuarrie said.[8]

The cost of said compromise? McQuarrie estimated it at $3 million worth of visual effects.

An additional $3 million for a *Justice League* movie that reportedly would go on to cost somewhere in the vicinity of $300 million? That's less than pocket change. But Paramount balked, unwilling to budge an inch to help a rival studio. Per McQuarrie, in the same *Empire* podcast interview:

> We said, here's what we'll do: give us the $3 million and we'll shut down, and that will give Henry Cavill the time to grow his mustache back. . . . At which point, somebody from Paramount Pictures said, "What is going on? What are you people even talking about?" They're like, "There's no way we're going to do that." We were just like, "Okay." That was the best plan that we could come up with.

It was a better plan than what was actually executed.

CG AYE YAI YAI

Justice League, instead, digitally removed Henry Cavill's facial hair in his reshot Superman scenes. Well, they attempted to, at least. Budget and time constraints meant that the VFX teams responsible for the work weren't able to complete the task properly, and so the petty studio dispute over a possible mustache shave leads to facial devastation in the *Justice League* theatrical cut.

It's slightly beneficial that Superman isn't in the bulk of *Justice League,* having sacrificed himself to stop the monstrosity Doomsday at the end of *Batman v Superman: Dawn of Justice.* The Man of Steel remains dead throughout this sequel, while Batman (Ben Affleck) and Wonder Woman (Gal Gadot) debate the morality of reversing his mortality.

But the movie needs Superman eventually, and that meant digital alterations to Henry Cavill's face. The actor rarely speaks of the CGI mustache removal, or the *Justice League* reshoots, in interviews. The studio never comments on it. And while I did manage to connect with a visual effects artist who confirmed that they worked on the *Justice League* reshoots, they were unable to speak on the record about the work that was attempted because of nondisclosure agreements they had signed.

What curious fans get, instead, are brief moments of insight, mixed with heavy doses of levity, where the actor will make self-deprecating asides in movie junket interviews regarding the mustache and its impact on the DC cinematic universe. Something deeply unusual happened during the press junket activities surrounding the release of *Justice League.* Cavill participated in interviews, but he couldn't ever confirm—or even acknowledge the possibility—that Superman was back from the dead. He couldn't even admit in the interviews that his character would show up in the theatrical version of the film. Instead, he danced around probing questions from journalists and played coy about his actual involvement in the film, even if he did a poor job of hiding how silly he seemed to find the whole publicity charade.

Cavill did address the mustache directly when speaking with noted celebrity interviewer Kevin McCarthy of FOX 5 Washington D.C., a cohost on the *ReelBlend* podcast. McCarthy, who specializes in asking technical production questions of filmmakers and actors, wondered what the mustache looked like on set during the *Justice League* reshoots.

"What we do is, we try and pull it back from the top lip as much as possible. So they kind of wax it up, and then I have dots all over my face," Cavill explained. "And they try and put dots, which are barely visible, in the various points on the face which you would see them during normal . . . not facial placement, but whatever CGI element they may be applying to a face. And yeah, I was covered in dots and had a big mustache! It was definitely a new look for Superman."[9]

That's an understatement.

The mustache controversy, as you would imagine, instantly became a running joke on social media. Twitter had a field day, with hashtags such as #HenryCavillsMustache trending worldwide, and multiple users creating fake accounts honoring the actor's facial hair. The controversy took on a life of its own, and memes poking fun at Superman's mustache still continue to pop up on social media years after the fact. My personal favorite was a re-creation of the *Justice League* poster, where bushy mustaches are added to every member of the rest of the team, including Gal Gadot's Wonder Woman. It's a masterpiece.

Cavill himself played along on social media, posting an image of himself in the Superman suit while still sporting his fantastic, face-hugging *Mission: Impossible—Fallout* facial hair. It was April 28, 2017—National Superhero Day—and Cavill used the post as an excuse to thank and celebrate all his fellow actors who play comic book legends on the big screen, from his DC colleagues (like Jason Momoa, Ben Affleck, Margot Robbie, Ezra Miller, and Gadot) to numerous Marvel stars, including Chris Pratt, Ryan Reynolds, Hugh Jackman, and Scarlett Johansson.[10]

Months later, Cavill kept the joke going. On July 26, 2017, he shared a behind-the-scenes photo of a massive glowing stage that would become part of a set piece for *Mission: Impossible—Fallout*. Only Cavill used it to lampoon what he referred to as "this moustache fiasco."[11]

"It is time to finally set the record straight in this moustache fiasco," he wrote, with tongue planted firmly in that chiseled cheek. "Pictured above is not a set on *MI6* but is in fact the latest in a series of weapons being designed by Warner Bros and Paramount Studios to combat the entity know as 'Henry Cavill's Moustache.' There has been no discussion over whether to shave or not to shave for the *JL* reshoots, simply a relentless campaign to put an end to the seemingly inexorable conquest of this despotic 'stache.

It is not a question of IF I should shave—it is a question of how can we possibly be victorious against such a beast without bringing our own doom raining down upon us."

NO LAUGHING MATTER

The above quote is a textbook example of Henry Cavill's dry, intelligent wit (a skill the actor possesses that hasn't yet been utilized properly on screen). Yet in poking fun of the "beast" that his *Mission: Impossible—Fallout* mustache had become at the time, Cavill truly underestimated the "doom" that it brought down onto the *Justice League* legacy, as the punchline of Superman's CGI lip still punctures holes in the movie's credibility to this day.

The opening cell phone scene isn't the only place where Cavill's handsome face has been visibly altered. Later in *Justice League,* the team confronts a resurrected Superman at the monument erected in his honor. It should be a legendary fight sequence—the members of the Justice League using their combined forces to try and take down the team's most powerful member. Only you can't enjoy the moment because of the hackneyed CGI that consumes Superman's visage.

One shot in that sequence should have been a deal breaker for any discerning studio executive. It's an up-close shot of Cavill's face and mouth, when the Kryptonian snarls at a bested Batman, "You won't let me live. You won't let me die. . . . Tell me, do you bleed?"[12] That unmistakable blur returns, signifying hasty digital correction that likely was made during reshoots to change that scene from Zack Snyder's original intent to Joss Whedon's reworked approach. Superman doesn't quite have five o'clock shadow (a side effect of being dead and buried for months) so much as he has a grey swirl that makes his cheeks, lips, and chin appear larger than the rest of his facial features. It's beyond disturbing.

Watching it, even now, has us asking the same question Brandon Valenza of Kansas demanded. How is this possible? How did anyone associated with *Justice League* look at these scenes and decide, "Yep, that looks good enough to release into theaters." This isn't a student film. It's not an independent feature from a first-time filmmaker who is forced to cut corners because of budget constraints. It is the industry's first *Justice League* movie, a historic on-screen team up of iconic DC superheroes who have been worshipped by fans for entire lifetimes. And this is what you are giving them? A blatantly unfinished work?

It's a reality of *Justice League* that still boggles my mind. Even understanding, in hindsight, that the powers-that-be had decided to switch DC's gears away from Snyder's vision, you still have to wonder what compelled the studio to keep the film's announced opening release date and not give Whedon and his team the time needed to perfect the effects and complete the work.

As is usually the case in Hollywood, the reason probably boils down to money. Not the money it would have taken to satisfactorily finish the reshoots. Rather, the money that Warner Bros. executives stood to claim in the form of bonuses if *Justice League* ended up being a hit.

Right around the time that Zack Snyder was wrapping *Justice League* filming in October 2016, AT&T announced plans to acquire Time Warner in a blockbuster deal reported to be worth $108.7 billion.[13]

What does this have to do with *Justice League* and Henry Cavill's CGI shave? Reports at that time claimed that Warner Bros., at the time of the merger, needed to project strength. Delaying the anticipated *Justice League* beyond its November 17, 2017, release date could have signified weakness. Especially when the studio still believed that the first-time teaming of these beloved DC characters would produce a box office hit, no matter the quality of the film.

Additionally, pushing *Justice League* into 2018 potentially would have delayed bonuses that key studio executives stood to claim. Speaking to trade industry website The Wrap for a November 29, 2017, article, one Hollywood executive, commenting anonymously, surmised that the president of Warner Bros. Pictures, Toby Emmerich, as well as Warner Bros. CEO Kevin Tsujihara, "wanted to preserve their bonuses they would be paid before the merger," and further explained that the duo was concerned that "if they pushed the movie, then their bonuses would have been pushed to the following year and they might not still be at the studio."[14]

And so, *Justice League* maintained its release date. Creatives raced the clock behind the scenes, corners were cut, and a less-than-acceptable version of *Justice League* was given to fans. Viewed in that light, Superman's blurry face represents so much more than just a crude and sloppy CGI effect. It's a jarring, perpetual reminder that the studio executives in charge at the time didn't care enough about *Justice League* or its passionate fanbase to give them the best possible version of their highly anticipated story. It screams a message that it was more important for executives to receive bonuses from a monumental merger than it was for DC fans to have a memorable on-screen team up of their beloved heroes.

And if that's the case, it's an unsalvageable mistake, one that forever will be as clear as the CGI blemish on Henry Cavill's lip.

11

IT'S A BIRD!
IT'S A PLANE!
IT'S . . . A DISASTER

Richard Bullivant wasn't able to see his beloved DC Comics superheroes on screen when *Justice League* finally opened on November 17, 2017. He was too busy being an actual superhero in real life.

Bullivant, forty-one years old, serves as a hydrographic surveyor for the Royal Navy, a position he's held for more than a decade. His job often whisks him to the farthest corners of the globe where he aids in scientific research by collecting oceanographic data and delivering supplies and personnel to bases. As fans curiously, perhaps begrudgingly, shuffled into theaters on November 17 to see how much (if any) of Zack Snyder's vision had been preserved in *Justice League,* Bullivant found himself in the middle of the South Atlantic Ocean, miles from the coast of Antarctica.

"An Argentinian submarine had 'gone dark,'" Bullivant remembers, referring to the ARA *San Juan*, which had stopped radio contact on November 15. "No communications were had between the [Argentine] Navy and the boat. As a hydrographic vessel, we were called in to assist the search."[1]

The Royal Navy deployed its own elite submarine rescue team to help scour the South Atlantic, so Bullivant ended up glued to a computer screen instead of a movie screen. His orders? Scroll through a sea of data points looking for anything that could potentially signify a manmade object.

The mission was arduous, but Bullivant didn't complain. "The search went on and we could not abandon it," he said. "Many lives were on board that boat, and mariners won't abandon fellow mariners lives, for any reason. . . . Our search area stretched hundreds of miles at the request of the

Argentinian government. More ships joined the search. Americans, Russians, Norwegians, and others. Days, then weeks, went by.

"In the end, the Argentinians themselves thanked us and told us to get back to the Falklands to conduct the watch handover," Bullivant continued. "The oxygen on board the boat would have run out days ago, and now it was a search for a hull, not lives."

The search-and-rescue operation for the ARA *San Juan* officially was abandoned on November 30. The remains of the sub wouldn't be located until a full calendar year later, when the Argentine Navy discovered the wreck on November 16, 2018. But Bullivant explains that throughout this tense, emotional time at sea, he used the DCEU—specifically Zack Snyder's *Batman v Superman: Dawn of Justice Ultimate Edition*—to distract himself and relieve stress during pockets of downtime that occurred in between searching.

"I watched [that movie] in my cabin, with my headphones on, whilst at sea, and had fallen in love with that film," Bullivant said. "It takes a lot for me to like a film, and it takes a hell of a lot for me to watch a film more than once. *BvS* had done it. Completely unaware of Zack Snyder, or his DCEU or his potential movie plans, all I knew is that I had enjoyed *Man of Steel* and truly loved *BvS*. I was becoming excited for a movie universe and I felt like, finally, a movie studio had allowed something special to be created that would appeal to someone like me."

When he finally returned from service at sea, Bullivant spent his first night back in the UK at the cinemas. Having fallen head-over-utility-belt for *Batman v Superman: Dawn of Justice,* Bullivant psyched himself up to learn where the story went. He remembers paying a little extra for a VIP recliner seat at his local theater. He purchased a beer and settled in for what he presumed would be an engaging, thought-provoking, comic book movie experience.

Asked to sum up his reaction to *Justice League* in one word, Bullivant offers, "Horrified."

"As soon as that film began, I knew something was wrong," he said. "The music was off. The visuals were awful. The color scheme was garish and the story literally made no sense. There were no stakes. . . . Batman was now camp. Superman was somehow ugly. Wonder Woman was simultaneously a mother figure and a sex object. There was bug spray.

Aliens had stolen husbands. . . . There were some truly cringeworthy jokes, and I felt uncomfortable."

Bullivant's experience wasn't unique. When *Justice League* opened on November 17, the film was met with a stifling wave of negative critical reactions. With more than 380 reviews filed, the movie struggled with a 40 percent Fresh grade on the review aggregate Rotten Tomatoes, where the consensus nitpicked the "murky aesthetic, thin characters and chaotic action" offered up in the theatrical cut.[2]

Aware of the rocky road *Justice League* endured through its production, professional critics seemed to approach the movie with a razor-sharp dagger in one hand and the proverbial poison pen in the other.

"A pointless flail of expensive (yet somehow, cheap-looking) CGI that no amount of tacked-on quips, or even [Gal] Gadot's luminescent star power, can rescue," wrote *New York Post* film critic Sara Stewart in her 1.5-star review.[3]

Toronto Star film critic Peter Howell tried to put *Justice League* into context with the rest of the DCEU movies, summarizing, "The film is marginally better than last year's sour and dispiriting *Batman v Superman: Dawn of Justice,* but that's like saying that dental surgery is preferable to passing a kidney stone."[4]

Damning the movie with the faintest of praise, *Us Weekly*'s Mara Reinstein wrote, "*Justice League* is just fine. But considering that the would-be blockbuster features a collection of A-list superheroes, the word 'fine' is like kryptonite."[5]

But it was long-time film critic Todd McCarthy, writing for *The Hollywood Reporter,* who delivered the death blow for *Justice League* and its potential as a catalyst for positive change at Warner Bros. for the DCEU. "This hodgepodge throws a bunch of superheroes into a mix that neither congeals nor particularly makes you want to see more of them in [the] future," McCarthy dismisses. "Plainly put, it's simply not fun."[6]

Justice League couldn't possibly have received a more devastating assessment, especially after months of behind-the-scenes studio tinkering and highly scrutinized creative decisions. Wasn't "fun" the whole reason for bringing Joss Whedon into the *Justice League* fold in the first place? Wasn't "fun" the justification used by Warner Bros. to wrestle *Justice League* and the future of the DCEU away from Zack Snyder, whose attempts at building a more mature superhero universe through *Man of Steel* and *Batman v Superman: Dawn of Justice* had been rejected by mainstream audiences and skittish studio executives? If, at the end of the day, Whedon's significant alterations couldn't even make *Justice League* fun, what was the point of these deeply disruptive changes?

"But," you can argue, "these movies aren't made for the critics! They are made for the fans." True. And *Justice League* does enjoy a 72 percent Fresh audience score on Rotten Tomatoes, which is higher than its DC predecessors, David Ayer's *Suicide Squad* (59 percent) and Snyder's *Batman v Superman: Dawn of Justice* (63 percent Fresh). So that means fans embraced the theatrical cut of *Justice League* and all was right with the world, right?

Not exactly. In fact, if you thought critics calling *Justice League* "clunky," "empty," "mediocre," and "forgettable" was unpleasant, just wait until you absorb all the disgusted terms unleashed by the Release the Snyder Cut family as they recall the heartache that accompanied *Justice League*'s butchered theatrical cut.

"IT FELT LIKE TORTURE."

The theatrical cut of *Justice League* is a Frankenstein monster made up of chintzy special effects, truncated character development, hurried plotting, and hollow fan service. None of its heroic moments are genuinely earned. It plays like the CliffsNotes version of a much more detailed superhero epic, and almost everyone involved appears discouraged that they are throwing away their shot at delivering a worthy *Justice League* for the fans.

The way that Matthew Criscuolo describes it, seeing the theatrical cut of *Justice League* totally broke him. His inner geek pendulum swung from craving the *Justice League* movie and being excited about the future of the DCEU to never wanting to see another DC movie again.

"There were scenes in that movie that disturbed me so profoundly, I feel the sudden rush of anger all over again when I think about them," Criscuolo said.[7]

The ardent DC fan remains dumbfounded over how Warner Bros. and the creative team working on *Justice League* could release the film with Superman's face looking so discombobulated (as discussed in chapter 10).

"It's simply unacceptable," Criscuolo states. "They humiliated Henry Cavill, [and] desecrated the iconic stature of Superman. They had another opportunity [to make good] in *Shazam*, and displayed Superman with his head chopped off. In no way, shape, or form did they show Superman more respect than Snyder showed him. I knew, after walking out of that theater, they totally butchered Snyder's movie and took out all the deep complex character development, and world-building blocks. Most importantly, I knew, beyond a shadow of a doubt, that was not Zack Snyder's film."

That was a common refrain echoed by members of the Release the Snyder Cut community and speaks to why they fought so hard to restore Snyder's vision for *Justice League*. Try as they might, they just couldn't find a trace of their esteemed director's fingerprints on the debacle that played on screen.

"I dislike the theatrical version of *Justice League*," says Fiona Zheng, who would go on to organize disgruntled fans, establish the RTSC movement, and keep early pressure on the studio to relent and show Zack Snyder's true vision for the superhero story. "To be honest, I find it to be an affront to core DCEU fans."[8]

A brutal assessment. But one that's totally fair. It echoes the sentiments expressed by John Aaron Garza of Austin, Texas.

"I saw *Justice League* on opening day and, for the first time, truly felt betrayed. From the opening moments of seeing Superman, I was embarrassed, as a DC fan and as a lover of cinema, to watch a film. Not only was this 'thing' a total abomination to the work Zack did, it completely evaporated any ties to *Batman v Superman*. The entire marketing had Zack Snyder's footage and yet, none of it was in the theatrical cut. . . . That night, after watching it, I couldn't sleep. I kept thinking about *everything* we were told leading up to the release. I thought about all the trailers we had seen and how none of that footage was in the movie."[9]

Rabid Snyder supporter Geraldo Cortes from Rio de Janeiro also claims that he didn't sleep right for two whole weeks following the release of *Justice League* because he was so upset by what happened to Zack Snyder's vision. "I felt like I was watching my wife going out with another guy," Cortes claimed. "I felt betrayed, cheated, [and] insulted."[10]

Unlike Zheng and Cortes, some of Snyder's faithful viewers really did try to find a silver lining in what they were being offered. Cole, of the Nerd Queens, tells me she "was still excited because I absolutely love the cast and

I enjoyed most of the cast in their portrayal. You can tell they gave it their all, even in scenes where they did not want to be there." But as the end credits rolled, Cole says the movie "just sat with me wrong, and in the days to come, with further discussion and reflection, it just sat with me even worse."[11]

Joseph Todd of Homewood, Illinois, went through a similar cycle of begrudging acceptance, which led to stinging betrayal. "I was attempting to convince myself that the film I watched wasn't a complete and utter abomination. [But] it felt nothing like previous Zack Snyder movies. It was immediately clear that as a fan base, we were robbed."[12]

The theatrical cut of *Justice League* also robbed DC fanatic Benjamin Hunt of any authentic emotion.

"My theatrical experience of *Justice League* was very . . . weird," Hunt recalls. "It was opening night, and the theater was practically empty, with this superloud obnoxious guy sitting to my left. My feelings can be described as confusion and embarrassment within the first ten or so minutes. After that? Nothing. The movie didn't stir any kind of emotion or reaction within me. Everything felt wrong. It felt like the film was just going through the motions but with no heart, soul, or style. It looked like it was filmed on a television budget, and it definitely didn't feel like a 'Zack Snyder' film."[13]

At the very least, Hunt remembered getting excited for the movie's post-credit scene, which was going to feature Joe Manganiello as the infamous DC assassin Deathstroke on screen for the very first time. In the sequence, Deathstroke boards a yacht to take a meeting with the conniving Lex Luthor (Jesse Eisenberg). The bald supervillain suggests that the two men team up and form a league of their own. However, Hunt says his excitement for this scene faded almost immediately as he walked out of the theater. As he and his girlfriend headed to their car, they were greeted by theater employees who were dressed in Justice League costumes.

"I could barely look any of them in the eye," Hunt admits. "They were handing out posters, I regrettably took one, and we headed out. Honestly, the movie was so bad that it shook me."

Not nearly as hard as it did Andrea Abbatista. The Snyder fan saw *Justice League* in Italy with a friend. The moment he saw Zack Snyder's name in the opening credits, he held out hope that the filmmaker's vision had been maintained.

"But at the end of the movie I was disgusted, embittered, and deeply sad for Zack Snyder, for me, for my friend, and for all DC and Zack Snyder fans," Abbatista proclaims. "It's not a movie. It's a farce, a soulless Frankenstein monster, an abomination. It's not a Joss Whedon movie, and it's certainly not Zack Snyder's movie! It's nothing! Every frame has an obvious scar of a cut-and-sew desired by the production. There is no gravity, no epicness, no special effects [delivered] at acceptable professional levels."[14]

Abbatista still doesn't understand why Warner Bros. wouldn't postpone the movie's release date following Autumn Snyder's death, giving Zack time to grieve but return and finish the movie he had started. In fact, I asked Snyder during our exclusive interview if anyone from Warner Bros. offered to delay the *Justice League* release date so he could complete the work after a needed hiatus. But he replied, "I don't remember, to be honest. Certainly if they did, it wasn't. . . yeah, I don't think so."[15]

"The fans would have appreciated it much more," Abbatista said. "Nobody would have complained, given the tragedy that Snyder and his family was living. They deliberately took advantage of the moment to get rid of an artist who, in addition to the tragedy, had to see his slaughtered movie, still carrying his signature. A true and deep disfigurement by the [studio]."

That betrayal is echoed by Brandon Valenza of Kansas. Like so many DC fans, he woke up on November 17 finally ready to see his favorite superhero team together on the big screen. Wearing his Flash T-shirt and an official *Justice League* movie Black Suit Superman New Era hat, he started conversations with those around him about how the behind-the-scenes drama might have helped the film.

We know how that turned out.

"It was obvious something major had happened, and that this was no longer the movie Zack envisioned," he said. "So much of what was shown in the trailers was nowhere to be found in the final film. The powerful female characters were reduced to sex jokes and humiliating moments, all for a good laugh. The powerful score was replaced by whimsical melodies and terribly placed uses of the original John Williams *Superman* theme, as well as [Danny] Elfman's own *Batman* theme. There were still a few Snyder moments to keep the movie entertaining enough. But this was definitely not his film."[16]

Valenza touches on an important element of these opening weekend screenings of *Justice League*. All weekend long, in theaters around the globe, fans were clinging to their memories of *Justice League* trailer scenes that weren't showing up in the theatrical cut. These amateur detectives would begin, almost immediately, to investigate what had happened to these scenes, planting the seeds of the Snyder Cut movement.

Sheraz Farooqi, the editor-in-chief for the website Comic Book Debate as well as a reporter for *Newsweek,* would be one of the earliest and most ardent supporters of the RTSC movement. He admits to being in what he calls "rose-colored glasses mode" when he first watched the *Justice League* theatrical cut, ignoring all the red flags that were popping up and powering through, virtually forcing himself to like it.

"It was not until my second watch where I felt the truth come down," Farooqi said. "That is when I knew something was not right and started the first process to learn more."[17]

We'll pull harder on that thread in the next chapter. For now, Snyder's fans were too busy dealing with the overwhelming and painful disappointment that accompanied the release of the theatrical cut of *Justice League*.

"Walking out of the movie was the most disappointed I have ever been after seeing a film," Valenza said. "I really could not believe what I just witnessed. I literally said, 'Goddammit Warner Brothers' out loud, shaking my head and trying to hold back the tears of my emotional pain. It was now entirely obvious that WB had lied in an effort to get me, and other Snyder fans, to show up to this film so they could make as much money as possible. Was it actually possible that they used the death of Zack's daughter to remove [him] and cover up their intentions? Do people like that actually exist? And as news trickled out that they could have delayed the film but chose not to in order to secure multimillion dollar bonuses for their highest level employees, [that] told me what I already knew. Yes, there are actually people capable of such terrible acts to a grieving family."

Believe it or not, that didn't stop Valenza from going back to the theater.

"At the time, I had MoviePass [from AMC Theatres], and chose to go see the movie again. Four more times actually. Every time I went, I hoped that I had just had a terrible dream and that the real movie would start. But every time the movie began, the same scene opened with a Superman with a terrible CGI mouth."

Giovanni Torres has that story beat. His suffering over *Justice League* followed him, like a nagging Parademon, to multiple parts of the globe thanks to dashes of hope and some unfortunate travel plans.

"The film came out the day before I flew to Singapore for a little vacation, with a stopover in Tokyo," Torres remembers. "I had booked movie tickets in both cities. Telling myself, 'This is gonna be great! I get to see this amazing flick in three different cities!' I had to sit through that shit three times. It felt like torture."[18]

SNYDER'S JL REVIEW?

Did everyone hate *Justice League*? Not right away. As mentioned, the film does have a 72 percent Fresh audience score on Rotten Tomatoes, proving a majority of ticket-buying patrons liked what they saw. And the movie did sell tickets. Just not enough for Warner Bros. to claim any real profit.

Justice League earned $657 million in worldwide box office grosses. That total makes it the sixth-highest grossing film in the DC Extended Universe, meaning it earned less than the two movies that directly built up to it: *Man of Steel* ($667 million) and *Batman v Superman: Dawn of Justice* ($873 million). That's certainly not the trajectory Warner Bros. envisioned when it embarked on this mission to build a cinematic universe from the treasure trove of DC characters. *Forbes* even reported, at the time of release, that based on their educated guess (since studio math isn't the most transparent subject), WB was looking at a loss in the $50–$100 million range on *Justice League* alone.[19]

Still, select members of the RTSC family found some positives in the theatrical cut, and aren't afraid to admit it. Chris Wong-Swenson of the You-Tube channel Ping Pong Flix talked about his opening weekend experience with *Justice League* saying, "Despite the blatant cursed lip on Superman, I actually enjoyed it overall coming out of it, as some of my local friends seemed to have had a good time. My local friends don't like the 'Snyderverse,' so it was refreshing to see them kind of liking it. I even did a good review of it, despite feeling slightly underwhelmed. It was very clear to me that it did not feel like a Zack Snyder movie. Then, as the weeks went on, it started dropping down in the ranks of DCEU movies as I continued to learn more of what happened to it."[20]

David McEachrane, a small business owner from the Caribbean nation of Trinidad and Tobago also fell into the camp of those who didn't hate *Justice League* until they processed how much of Snyder's vision had been gutted. "When I saw *Justice League* initially, I chalked it up to it being little more than a live-action version of a WB animated movie," he said. "It was . . . fine. It was only when more info came out that I started to hate the film. They completely gutted the film and tarnished it."[21]

That's nothing compared to West Virginia-based author Lindsey Staton, who actively tried to convince herself that she had to embrace this *Justice League,* no matter how unsatisfactory, for fear that Warner Bros. might not make more DC movies if fans rejected this offering.

"I tried to like the movie," Staton confessed, mainly because the Justice League ranks as her favorite superhero team, and she wanted to appreciate seeing them on the big screen for the very first time. "I tried to put all the reshoot buzz and two-hour mandate behind me. A part of me kept saying, 'You HAVE to like this movie. It has to be good. If it's not, they won't make another one.' But deep down, the movie didn't make me feel anything like I felt when I watched *Batman v Superman.* And soon, I grew to hate it. I started wondering where all the scenes that were missing went, and why on earth they CGIed Superman's upper lip. It was official. I hated this movie."[22]

Do you know who still hasn't seen the theatrical cut of *Justice League?* Zack Snyder. Well, if he is to be believed.

Snyder first admitted to avoiding *Justice League*'s theatrical cut in a text message sent to Fiona Zheng in November 2017. In the text, which Zheng shared on Vero, Snyder wrote, "I will be honest. I have not seen the film since I stepped away. You know I love these characters. I only wish I could only have finished it for you and the others who love MOS BvS."[23]

"This interaction was very important, because up until that point, we hadn't really heard Zack Snyder's verdict on the film," said Lupe, one of the cohosts of *The Film Exiles* podcast.[24] On November 16, 2019, Lupe and his cohost, Chris Vinaldo, recorded three consecutive podcasts celebrating the two-year anniversary of the theatrical release of *Justice League.* In the process, they documented how far the movement had come to that point. Lupe singled out Snyder's text to Zheng as a watershed moment in the formation of the RTSC movement.

"That lit a fire under a lot of people," he said.

Even after that text, Snyder kept the lines of communication with his fanbase open. The director frequently answered questions directed at him in the comments section of his preferred social media tool, Vero. Fans would reference specific scenes from the theatrical cut, asking if they belonged to Snyder's original version or were added in later by Joss Whedon. For example, there's a moment in the film, prior to the team's first engagement with the villain Steppenwolf, where Ezra Miller's Flash admits to Ben Affleck's Batman that he's afraid to fight because he's never really been in a superpowered battle before. "I've just pushed some people and run away," Flash confesses.[25] It's an out-of-character reaction for a hero to fear confrontation, and it didn't sit well with most DC audiences. Asked point-blank by a fan if that scene exists in the Snyder Cut of *Justice League,* Zack Snyder responded on Vero with an incredulous, "What the fuck?"[26] It implied that Snyder was both unfamiliar with the scene and offended by what they'd made Flash say.

On Vero, Snyder finally explained to fans why he has avoided sitting down with the theatrical cut of the movie that was ripped from his grip. And it makes all the sense in the world. Underneath a series of posts shared on Christmas Day 2019, Snyder said, "People who I trust and who have seen the theatrical cut and the true cut have told me never to watch it."[27]

Sitting down for an exclusive interview for this book, Snyder took the argument of avoiding the theatrical cut of *Justice League* one step further. In his opinion, that version of the film is tied directly to the DCEU's broken narrative. Snyder explains that the *Justice League* that's going to HBO Max holds so much potential because it's no longer attached to any larger picture, the way his initial *Justice League* would have been.

"The movie that was released—whatever's in that movie, I still have not seen it—is in a lot of ways, for the DCEU, that's canon," Snyder said. "And what I'm doing [now] is its own thing. Which for me, as a filmmaker and as a storyteller, I'm very happy about. Because I don't have to serve all these other gods. All that's required is for me to just make it as cool and as fun and as immersive and complete as possible. The movie can be true to itself.

"When I'm looking at the cut now, I feel just that everything is . . . when I was doing it before, it was under such duress," he continued. "Anything I wanted to do was a struggle. Where the nice thing is that now, that's just not the case. Everything I want to do is just, it is what it is. And so in that way, it's just much better. . . . Anytime you put '*Zack Snyder's Justice*

League' on it, the rules have changed. I don't have any responsibility to this giant billion-dollar franchise insanity. The movie doesn't have to exist in that way. That part has passed. Whether it's successful or not, that moment has passed."

The whole scenario remains so very bizarre. And in hindsight, with the proverbial "Big Picture" laid out before us (including the released Snyder Cut), it continues to make zero sense. Warner Bros. spent years, and millions of dollars, trying to establish a DC superhero universe that rivalled the one built by Marvel Studios, but then the powers-that-be allowed a handful of rash decisions to detonate the entire structure and wipe out any possibility of a grand, connected universe. The studio's executives decimated Snyder's choreographed arc, and even snared Ben Affleck and his planned Batman solo film in that destructive wake only to have to admit defeat and pour millions more into allowing Snyder to finish the version he wanted to deliver in 2017.

Somewhere in the rubble left by Joss Whedon's *Justice League,* these fans discovered something else: hope. Hope that the foundation of an alternate cut of *Justice League* existed. Hope that the damage inflicted on Snyder's vision could be undone. Hope that, if they presented a unified front as a fandom, they'd somehow convince Warner Bros. to release the Snyder Cut of *Justice League*. And it worked.

Let's dig deeper into how that journey officially began.

12

#RELEASETHESNYDERCUT

Passionate fanbases are nothing new to the entertainment industry. Both the *Star Trek* and *Star Wars* franchises, as an example, have successfully cultivated generations of dedicated followers over the years, while more recent series such as *Doctor Who, Supernatural,* and *Harry Potter* have grown similar-sized armies of loyal supporters. They write fan fiction, binge watch films and TV seasons, and attend conventions all around the globe. But there's a unique, possessive, and protective dedication found in the Release the Snyder Cut community that sets them apart from these other groups. There's a reason why, when writing about the RTSC movement in 2019, Rob Harvilla of The Ringer called it "the most bizarre sustained fan campaign in modern superhero-movie history, arbitrary and fearsomely dedicated, fascinating and bewildering, possibly hopeless and legitimately inspiring."[1]

And they've been that way from the moment they formed, which essentially happened minutes after the first worldwide screenings of *Justice League* concluded on November 17, 2017. The credits hadn't even finished rolling when distraught fans began clamoring for the release of Zack Snyder's intended version of the film. These passionate DC and Snyder enthusiasts felt confused. They felt betrayed. They wanted answers. Most complained to friends and family who had tagged along to the theater on opening night. Many vented their frustrations on social media. But one fan decided to take significant action.

The RTSC movement's "birth" wasn't flashy or explosive, stylish or cinematic. No, the movement's "big bang" moment can be traced back to the creation of a petition on Change.org, an open, online platform that encourages people to start campaigns and mobilize supporters to accomplish goals in virtually any field.

Sexy origin story, right?

The week that Warner Bros. opened *Justice League* in theaters, Roberto Mata of Puerto Rico launched a petition titled, "Zack Snyder's Director's Cut and Tom Holkenborg's (Junkie XL) Score for Home Release."[2] The petition, now closed, was a massive success, receiving 179,322 supportive signatures. In the plea, Mata appealed to Warner Bros. to allow Snyder to finish his version of the story, which obviously would have been drastically different from what was being shown in theaters around the globe. He explained that the director's work in *Man of Steel* and *Batman v Superman: Dawn of Justice* had cultivated a large enough following to justify Snyder's completion of his movie. Mata seemed to want closure for Snyder and for the fans who had followed him on this creative path.

The website KnowYourMeme dates the creation of Mata's petition as November 11, 2017, meaning it launched before the movie had even opened (though that date has not been confirmed anywhere else of note). Major entertainment news sites like Mashable and The Wrap didn't start covering the petition until November 19 and 20, respectively, but by then the site had collected more than thirty thousand supporters, proving it had been online for a number of days. And many of those supporters were already gathering in chat rooms, having just seen the atrocity that is *Justice League*'s theatrical cut, to speculate about what had gone wrong.

When these fans arrived online, they found Fiona Zheng, which is ironic because Zheng wouldn't have even *been* online if not for her passion for and fascination with Zack Snyder.

Zheng owns and operates a small medical clinic in the city of Harbin, China. She says she became obsessed with Snyder and his filmmaking style after watching *Batman v Superman: Dawn of Justice* for the first time. "His films have been criticized as 'too dark,' 'serious,' and 'ponderous,'" Zheng told me. "But in fact, he is using these pop culture myths of superheroes to examine ourselves in a nonironic or self-parodying way. This makes his films more powerful, relevant, and meaningful than any other film in the subgenre."[3]

Zheng says that her passion for Snyder's work drove her to social media in search of like-minded movie fans who also wanted to more deeply explore the themes and imagery the director was layering into his films. After watching *Batman v Superman: Dawn of Justice* and falling in love with Snyder's style, Zheng chose to use her social media presence on Twitter, Vero, and YouTube to amplify the filmmaker's accomplishments. "[He is] the reason I became vocal online," she says.

Roberto Mata may deserve credit for properly launching the idea of a Snyder Cut request from fans, but it's Zheng who put fuel in that engine and kept the campaign racing forward. Speak with anyone who was involved with the Snyder Cut family in those earliest days and they'll tell you Zheng rallied the troops, started organizing campaigns, and gave the fans purpose.

"She was a beacon to all those wanting to see Zack Snyder's original *Justice League*," says Alessandro Maniscalco, a thirty-eight-year-old long-shoreman from New Jersey who would eventually become very active in the Release the Snyder Cut community.[4]

"I count Fiona as a friend," said Darren Benson of Norman, Oklahoma. "She had a ferocious intensity in rallying support early on in the movement. She also had a friendship with Zack and she really wanted to do right for him and Deb, the cast, and crew."[5]

Following the release of *Justice League,* Adrienne Marie, a Colorado teacher, admits that she reactivated her defunct Twitter account so that she could interact with other DC fans who were trying to piece together what had gone wrong.

"It wasn't long before I found Fiona and several others who were disturbed and puzzled by what we saw and several of the scenes that were in the trailer but weren't in the theatrical [cut]," Marie said. "I was especially perplexed about the removal of the 'I'll take that as a yes' scene with Lois and Clark on the Kent farm. There's absolutely no reason to cut that beautiful scene. It was gorgeous with the sunset, and the actors looked their absolute best. After that, it was analyzing everything piece by piece. Scene by scene. Word by word."[6]

Will Rowlands of Portsmouth, England, says he also scoured the early *Justice League* trailers, noticing all of the footage that didn't make it into the theatrical cut. "I even went to see the movie again, but noticed the issues even more," Rowlands said. "Within weeks, online chat confirmed my feelings and I guess you can say the seeds of the movement began to sprout."[7]

Matthew Criscuolo of Rockland County, New York, confirms that sentiment. He started tweeting with DC fans as soon as he got back from *Justice League* on opening night. He says the hardcore fans were already hard at work dissecting the theatrical film, picking it apart, and looking for evidence of Snyder's work. As Rob Harvilla notes in that profile for The Ringer, "The #ReleaseTheSnyderCut movement thrives on this sort of detective work and informed but necessarily incomplete speculation."

Criscuolo chatted with Zheng online in those early days. "She had some pretty bold claims from an insider that Warner Bros. had an alternate version, the real *Justice League* movie by Snyder," he said. "That was the birth of the Snyder Cut movement. She was so sure of her statements, so urgent about telling us, it really convinced me to take this seriously."[8]

Around this time, Scott McClellan and Tim Yoko also sat up and took notice. The duo has been podcasting about the DCEU since August 2015. They started with *The Suicide Squadcast*, which in time evolved into the *DC Films Squadcast,* part of a larger Squadcast Media Network, with multiple shows dedicated to comic books and comic-themed entertainment. McClellan, thirty-eight years old, lives and works in the suburbs of Birmingham, Alabama. And because he was so active in spreading the gospel of the DCEU, he says that Zheng reached out to him on November 22, 2017, with a request to join the fight for Zack Snyder's cut of *Justice League*.

"She was a listener of our show, and we were mutuals on Twitter," McClellan said. "The discussion with Fiona, along with additional information we received, is what proved to us that there was a Snyder Cut. We never shared that information publicly at the time, and still haven't until now, for reasons of confidentiality."[9]

Zheng's online influence was global. Jonathan Nordia is a thirty-three-year-old electrical engineer from Eilat, Israel. A husband and father of two, Nordia's a lifelong Superman fan who was attracted to the Snyder Cut movement from day one.

"Because Zack matters to me," Nordia explained. "Because I think we deserve better films. We deserve art that challenges us, that helps us grow and learn."

He remembers seeing messages at the time that Zheng shared with the community between herself and Snyder, which confirmed that the director had not seen the theatrical cut of *Justice League* and never intended to. Nordia calls Zheng the movement's "captain" and commented that because of a connection she forged with Snyder, Zheng "found herself in an interesting position, between an army of brokenhearted fans and a director who genuinely likes to communicate with real life, genuine, and passionate people. That is how I'd describe Fiona. She went above and beyond, trying to give us an orderly direction, to gather our strength in unison, to raise awareness and evolve the #ReleaseTheSnyderCut cry to a legitimate call for arms."[10]

Ah, yes. The hashtag. We may not know the exact day that the Snyder Cut movement was born thanks to the lack of specific detail on Roberto Mata's Change.org petition, but we *can* pinpoint the precise moment that the effort received its nickname, as well as its pithy, vital battle cry.

A CATCHPHRASE, A CALLING

Sean Maher will forever hold a special place in the fascinating and colorful history of the RTSC movement. Maher first tweeted the phrase "#ReleaseTheSnyderCut" at 5:24 am on November 21, 2017. That act basically has become a turning point for the RTSC family, the equivalent of Gerard Butler screaming, "This is Sparta!" before kicking that poor Persian messenger into a bottomless well in Snyder's movie *300*.

"I remember thinking, after I saw *Justice League,* of all the scenes that didn't make it into the film from the trailers," said Maher, a twenty-two-year-old student from Ireland who tweets under the Username @MovieBuff100. "I couldn't understand why they didn't make the cut of the film. There were a few people discussing the possibilities of a Snyder cut on Twitter, and I engaged with those people.

"I was convinced that a cut existed because of the trailer [shots] and stills we didn't see," Maher continued. "Also, I talked to a few extras from the film who said a lot of their scenes didn't make it into the film. [So] I tweeted #ReleaseTheSnyderCut, and I was the first to do that, I've been told."[11]

Without realizing it, Maher gave the movement its rallying cry. He couldn't possibly understand the sheer value of that tweet though. Writing for *Forbes* about the importance of a tagline for any coordinated campaign, Vladimir Gendelman said, "Taglines . . . have the potential to build value over time. When you use a tagline for long enough, it can become one of the most memorable parts of your identity. . . . Overall, taglines help to fill in the information gaps that the rest of your marketing doesn't cover as effectively—be it what your product or service actually is, or why a customer should choose you over someone else. Think of a tagline as the glue that holds your brand together."[12]

Over the years, the phrase "Release the Snyder Cut" has become shorthand code in pop culture for the global fight to get Warner Bros. to restore Zack Snyder's ultimate vision for his *Justice League* movie. But it also has been used as a substitute to mean any push by eager fans who'd want to see a preferred version of a bad movie over the one they have been given. Disappointed by the slapdash version of the *Suicide Squad* movie that landed in theaters in 2017? Then get behind the "Release the Ayer Cut" campaign, which continues to lobby for David Ayer's extended cut of the film. *Star Wars* fans in 2019 tried these tactics following the resolution provided by J. J. Abrams's *Star Wars: The Rise of Skywalker*. They took to Twitter and attempted to get #ReleaseTheJJCut trending on social media (even though no evidence of an alternate cut of *The Rise of Skywalker* existed).

Oftentimes, the hashtag is used for comical effect. Remember Tom Hooper's failed on-screen adaptation of the Broadway musical *Cats*? We've tried to forget it as well. But on March 18, 2020, when information was revealed that a visual effects producer was hired on *Cats* "to remove CGI buttholes that had been inserted a few months before," you better believe that #ReleaseTheButtholeCut started trending on Twitter in the United States.[13] Ultimately, because these fan bases lack the passion, scope, and drive of the Snyder Cut family, those hashtag campaigns tend to die out almost instantly. Yes, even the CGI butthole one.

NOT ALWAYS UNITED

That's not to say every member of the RTSC movement is a pious saint blessed with the best intentions. For all of the unity expressed by the community, the RTSC family isn't immune to infighting and schisms—as can be expected when passions for a particular subject run hot.

Stephen Colbert, an editor for ScreenRant who also cohosts the *Batman v Superman: By the Minute* podcast, notes, "The idea of the movement, and many people in it, is inspiring. However, for much of the past three years, I've had a handful of dedicated trolls attacking me for the way I cover it and I've had numerous cases of slander or character assassinations or threats made against me, sometimes by prominent individuals in the movement. I know it's only a few bad apples, and I also know I've done my legwork and gotten proper sourcing for everything I've written, so I'm able to brush it off. But it's hard for me to even think of the organized movement without thinking of all that."[14]

Some members of the movement hold a serious grudge against Warner Bros. and refuse to support anything in the DCEU that followed Zack Snyder's removal from the series. This has also led to a handful of members of the RTSC movement attacking people like *Birds of Prey* director Cathy Yan or *Shazam!* star Zachary Levi on social media, usually with paper-thin justification. There's an anger and frustration that still exists in the movement, and it bubbles up and tarnishes the good deeds that many in the RTSC family seek to achieve. It even continued after the Snyder Cut of *Justice League* was obtained, as different factions in the movement argued over who deserved more credit, or clout, for the work that was done on Snyder's behalf.

Still, Colbert is able to look past most of these online disagreements in the very small percentage of RTSC members and conclude, "I have made many friends from the movement, and it's inspiring to see how motivated they all are in one way or another by Zack Snyder. Zack says, 'Powerful art can heal, bring awareness, and create change,' and I see that every day. The fact that the movement is still going strong proves that quote true."

Further demonstrating that not every member of the movement is infallible, even Roberto Mata fell out of favor with key members of the RTSC family after triggering the petition that started this all. In the weeks following the launch of the campaign, significant RTSC members like Zheng, Chris Vinaldo, Justin Lesniewski, and ComicBookDebate's Sheraz Farooqi revealed that they helped Mata polish the language in the Change.org statement, while also giving it a signal boost via their social media platforms.

"After he created it, and it started to get traction, Roberto Mata reached out to me to help him write a better draft," Lesniewski said. "I did. It was up for a while. Myself and my friends were excited because I was on the forefront of this cultural battle where I belonged."[15]

But Mata started to negatively interact with fans and post "petition updates" that many in the RTSC community deemed racist, sexist, and Islamophobic. "Mata started going off on Twitter at journalists, media, and fans," Lesniewski continued. "I was trying to help him run a media campaign. I wrote a few updates that got media coverage. But he eventually turned on me, attacking me personally in DMs. I tried to get Change.org to hand over petition ownership to me, but they wouldn't do it without his consent. I threw in the towel on the petition. He eventually went off the rails completely."

As Mata's hurtful language ballooned, Zheng, Farooqi, and the DC Films *Squadcast* cohosts Yoko and McClellan drafted their own statement distancing the RTSC movement from him, completely.

"As DC fans, none of us condone this behavior and, in fact, see it as a direct insult to many of the fans," they wrote. "The DCEU fandom is universal, and many are in the direct line of fire of Mata's words. Adding to this, Zack Snyder and his films, something Mata is fond of, don't ever condone this hatefulness. On the contrary, they speak on the need for inclusion. Zack Snyder's Superman is the ultimate immigrant. . . . Islamophobia is something no Snyder film, especially his Superman films, condone. Snyder's films also treat women by the highest standard. The treatment of Lois Lane, Martha Kent, Wonder Woman and more show that these characters have their own agency and are just as impactful, if not more, than the male characters. No bigotry, sexism, or racism is tolerated by myself, the co-signers of this statement, Zack Snyder, or the DCEU Fandom."[16]

Swift and decisive action like that demonstrates exactly how Fiona Zheng and a handful of dedicated Snyder fans held the RTSC family together and kept it productive in those early days when the movement easily could have splintered into selfish infighting and unfocused squabbling. When discussing Zheng's impact on the Snyder Cut effort during their two-year-anniversary podcast episode, *The Film Exiles* cohost Lupe simply states, "Fiona is about the most powerful force that started this movement."[17]

Fellow *Film Exiles* cohost Chris Vinaldo proudly adds, "Fiona is the one we all looked up to at that time, especially after her interactions with Zack [on social media]. We trusted Fiona implicitly. And hearing [updates] from her, again, reenergized us. Reenergized the movement. She had to bear so much responsibility in those early days. Honestly, it's incredible what she did for us."

SUSTAINING THE MOVEMENT

Giving birth to a movement is one thing. You are passionate about a cause. You find others who agree with you. You decide, perhaps hastily, to do *something* about it. You even have a belief system, a wrong that you feel deserves to be righted. "The fundamental reason we started the movement is that we want [the] future films of the DCEU franchise to keep the same artistic integrity as previous works like *Man of Steel, Batman v Superman,* or *Wonder Woman*," Zheng tells me. "Not like the theatrical *Justice League,* which was downgraded to a mediocre action-comedy."

Organizing, sustaining, and leading a movement forward in a productive fashion, though, is another challenge altogether. Not content to simply engage in conversations on social media, Zheng took the next massive step for the RTSC community, establishing a website that would act as a hub for any and all new information pertaining to the fight for the Snyder Cut.

ForSnyderCut.com contains articles written by fans about the DCEU, the SnyderVerse, the #ReleaseTheSnyderCut accomplishments, and more. The site collects storyboards from Zack Snyder's *Justice League* that have been shared by the director, showing off characters like Darkseid and Deathstroke. Behind-the-scenes photography documenting the *Justice League* production can be found there. Most important, the site boasts a comprehensive timeline that documents virtually every step on this lengthy process, from a 2014 *Variety* article first reporting that Snyder had been hired to direct a *Justice League* movie, to the latest updates on progress the RTSC family has made in terms of raising awareness for the existence of Snyder's preferred cut. For some odd reason, the site doesn't have information regarding HBO Max's agreement to release *Zack Snyder's Justice League.*

With these actions, the movement was off and running. And it's still running to this day, even after they have achieved their single-most important goal of securing Snyder's abandoned film. But why? Why did these supporters pour their own heart, soul, time, money, sweat, and tears into the #ReleaseTheSnyderCut movement, year after year?

When you ask them, their answers vary.

"I wanted to be a part of the movement because I wanted justice for Zack and everyone involved with *Justice League,*" said Devin Fuerte, a nineteen-year-old film student from Orange County, California. Fuerte gets credit for recording Zack Snyder confirming the existence of his Snyder Cut of *Justice League* at the 2019 fan event "SnyderCon" in Pasadena. That was a seminal moment. As part of a three-day screening event at the ArtCenter College of Design, Snyder showed off his extended director's cut (or, Ultimate Edition) of *Batman v Superman: Dawn of Justice,* then participated in a staged, postscreening Q-and-A. Fuerte asked the director about the existence of the cut—still a mystery at that moment—and Snyder confirmed for him, "I mean, all I'll tell you is that, you know, sure there's a cut. It's done. I have a bunch of them. So, it's not like . . . that's up to them."[18]

Looking back on his participation in the movement, Fuerte reflects, "I felt like it was the least I could for Zack, because his DCEU introduced me to one of my biggest passions now [DC as a whole], and has helped me through a lot during the tough times in my life. The Snyder Cut movement means so much to me. It lets me know that I'm not alone, and that there are thousands on thousands of people who share the same love for Zack and his vision for the DCEU as I do. It really does feel like a big family to me."[19]

That passion for Snyder and the desire to vindicate the filmmaker after the way he was treated by his studio collaborators is echoed by so many who spoke up for this book. Scott McClellan of the *DC Films Squadcast* tells me, "I wanted to be part of the movement because I wanted to see the Snyder Cut of *Justice League,* and I had a platform from which to make my voice heard. So instead of just moaning and groaning and complaining about it, I decided to put 'my money where my mouth is' per se and actively do something about achieving what I wanted and believed in."

While Adrienne Marie adds, "Hearing what happened to Zack both personally and professionally, how could I not give back and fight for him when he and his creative team had given me so much? I just couldn't *not* give back. No matter what. It was the right thing to do, and my hype and love for what he had brought with these films had never waned despite all the onslaught of negativity. It only emboldened me and solidified my commitment."

And for others, it's the charitable aspect of what the RTSC movement accomplishes that keeps them dedicated on a nearly daily basis. Nana and Cole, aka the Nerd Queens, gravitated to the movement because of its stated emphasis on raising funds and awareness for mental health.

"The topic of suicide and mental health is very close to our hearts," said Nana. "And Zack Snyder's movies helped me personally through the darkest time of my life. This is my chance to give back to the community. I've met friends for life thanks to this cause. If we don't stand for something, we'll fall for anything. The Snyder Cut movement is what I choose to stand for."[20]

Cole adds, "Personally, as someone who has struggled with mental illness for a very long time, the charity aspect has just made the movement so much more unique and amazing. Being fans of Zack and wanting to advocate for suicide prevention just made this the perfect marriage of passions.

"This movement is a beautiful mixed bag of unique faces from around the world," Cole continued. "From so many different abilities and talents to different walks of life. [We] all come together under one banner and one love of Zack and his work, and our desire to fight for this film, but also while doing good. It's a beautiful thing, unlike any other, and this movement means the absolute world to me."

That passion, shared by many, helped form a community that has forged miraculous bonds as they rally behind their common goals. As DC enthusiast Ben Wellington from Oklahoma states, "We are fighting for each other."[21]

"This is a global movement [that was] willing to fight for what we believe in," he says. "The Snyder Cut movement has become my family, as we've all lost loved ones and had to deal with the heartbreak. I, too, lost my best friend and father in early 2018. The Snyder Cut movement was there for me in my time of need, and I for them. This movement means so much more to me now than just a movie. It's my life. Day in and day out, we all do our best, to fight the hate and show WB our support for this film."

Do you know what helped to keep the Snyder Cut movement afloat, while also lending it a crucial air of legitimacy? The fact that the RTSC family's most famous and influential supporter happened to be Zack Snyder himself. It can be argued that Snyder did as much to fan the flames of support for the movement as the most active members of the community.

"Literally, every single thing they've done, any outward-pointing activation that they've triggered and accomplished, I'd been astounded by," Snyder told me about the movement. "We all have. Debbie and I both are always like, 'Oh, have you seen this? Look what they're doing?' And it's always, 'Those guys are awesome. They're unbelievable. This is unbelievable.'"[22]

That continuous boost from their beloved filmmaker kept this community engaged in the battle, even when the relentless resistance to their efforts threatened to wear down their enthusiasm and desire to fight. Combat analogies? Make no mistake. The RTSC movement was, in every sense, a battle. And Snyder, like a seasoned general, figured out how to gain the upper hand in the effort to educate his fan base on his cut, and subvert misinformation about its existence. Snyder introduced his followers to a "secret" weapon that he strategically unleashed whenever it was time to rally his troops. Let's shift our conversation and learn all about Vero.

13

SNYDER, VERO, AND THE EVERBURNING TORCH

Here's what fascinated me the most about the hysteria associated with the Snyder Cut—from its rumored existence (something that was actually *debated* for years) to the possibility of its release. Zack Snyder encouraged it. Hell, he virtually triggered it any time momentum seemed to lull in the ongoing quest to get his *Justice League* in front of fans. Whenever I was asked by skeptics of the movement why I'd give credence to a campaign that, in their eyes, fell somewhere between "hopeless" and "useless," my answer revolved around the fact that Snyder himself wouldn't let the story die. Why, then, would his fans?

This entire time, Snyder had the ability to stop the RTSC movement dead in its tracks. All he had to do was record a short video on social media and say something to the tune of, "Guys. I love you. You are the best, most passionate, and dedicated fans in the universe. I don't deserve you. But it's time to stop. This 'Snyder Cut' you seek . . . it doesn't exist. I don't have it. I didn't shoot enough footage. We'd need way too much expensive CGI to complete it, and it'd cost more than I care to invest. I couldn't show you my rough assemblage even if Warner Bros. granted me permission. And by the way, they'll *never* do that! So, while Debbie and I admire your commitment, and deeply appreciate the amount of money and attention you have generated for the American Foundation for Suicide Prevention, I feel like I finally must tell you to move on. I have. You should too. The Snyder Cut of *Justice League* will never, ever happen."

Only Snyder never said that. He said the exact opposite every chance he got, keeping the dream alive. He continuously shared behind-the-scenes photos or black-and-white screen grabs from his cut of *Justice League* on his preferred social media tool, Vero (more on that in a second). He'd even interact with fans in the comments of these posts, answering their questions or clarifying bad information they may have been receiving elsewhere. When a fan reached out to Snyder with a dire, "Say something. I am losing hope," he'd quickly reply, "Don't." Snyder even posted the ultimate mic drop photograph on December 4, 2019, when he showed off four film cannisters that were labeled "Z.S. JL Director's Cut. Running Time: 214." Accompanying the image was the text, "Is it real? Does it exist? Of course it does." And in the comments beneath the photo, Snyder confirmed that he posted this on Vero because he's "just tired of people saying it's not real."[1]

By encouraging the RTSC movement and egging it on by sharing material from the movement's metaphorical "grail," Snyder essentially was confirming the cut's existence and teasing its probable release. And while I wasn't able to say anything with certainty until Snyder finally confirmed the film's release plans on May 20, 2020, these sentiments were shared by the director back when I visited the set of his Netflix film *Army of the Dead* on October 2, 2019. That's how far back I'd assumed the Snyder Cut quest had entered its endgame. Questions about the Snyder Cut movement were asked that day and Snyder delivered incredible answers.

HONORING THE FANBASE

In October 2019, Netflix traveled a small band of media outlets (CinemaBlend, included) to Atlantic City, New Jersey, where Snyder and his crew had taken over the Showboat Hotel and Casino. The hotel allowed the *Army of the Dead* production to convert its gambling floors into the harrowing aftereffects of a zombie apocalypse, meaning skeletal remains hunched over slot machines and blackjack tables while action star Dave Bautista (*Guardians of the Galaxy*) attempted to retrieve a large sum of money from a casino vault. This shouldn't even have to be stated, but yeah, the whole thing looked amazing.

Snyder, who was overwhelmed with the day-to-day tasks of managing a bustling film set, took a break during lunch to sit with us and discuss his latest project. Eventually, though, talk gravitated to Snyder's ongoing situation with *Justice League*. It had to. *Army of the Dead* was the first film Snyder was mounting after having *Justice League* ripped from his grip. He hadn't done much press since that uncomfortable circumstance, and this was our first real opportunity to gauge his reaction to what had happened, as well as address the work being done on his behalf by the RTSC family.

Snyder was asked, point blank, if there would come a time where he'd want his fans to stop clamoring for a project he once worked on—*Justice League*—and focus instead on his upcoming features. He replied, "Of course I want everyone to be like, 'Look, I made this movie! Let's talk about it.' That's what I want, you know? 'Here's this new thing I made.' One hundred percent, I feel that way. But, I will say that I don't really separate . . . the work to me is sort of a singular thing. And the process is a singular thing. And is there a relationship between this movie and my other films? Of course there is. And is there, like, in the filmography, is there a hole? Yeah, there is. I mean that's just a fact."[2]

The impact of that statement carried more power than a punch thrown by General Zod in the culminating battle of *Man of Steel*. This was, for the first time on record, Zack Snyder confirming that he didn't consider the existing *Justice League* to be an entry in his filmography (regardless of the fact that the theatrical cut comically credits him as the director). Taking it one step further, Snyder admitted that he actually felt that a "hole" now existed on the timeline of his professional career. But he also believed that the fans interested in *Justice League* would accept the work that he was doing on *Army of the Dead* as well.

"I kind of feel like anyone who's interested in that [*Justice League*] movie, whatever that movie was supposed to be, and then what I'm doing now, those things aren't mutually exclusive," he said. "I'm pretty sure that someone who's interested in [my *Justice League*] will go see this movie. I don't think there's a lot of people who are, like, 'No, no, I just want to know about *Justice League,* and that's it. And I don't care about what else he does.' I don't think that that's a thing."

Snyder was correct to assume that he has a dedicated fan base that will follow him from project to project. We've discussed, in this book alone, the sheer number of fans who came to the DCEU because of their fascination with Snyder's filmmaking, and countless others who were DC fans to begin with but got swept up in the director's distinct style and agreed to support him, whether in the DCEU or outside of it.

Then the conversation took a really interesting turn. Because, in connecting the potential audience for *Army of the Dead* with the fans who have been vocally lobbying for the release of Snyder's cut of *Justice League*, the director finally opened up about the efforts of the movement and the sacrifices that they have made on his behalf. And in doing so Snyder shed light on his personal motivations for encouraging the RTSC movement instead of lowering their expectations.

"I think a lot of people in fandom have sacrificed a lot as far as to maintain their interest in that movie," Snyder said about the relentless fight that kept momentum rolling on his version of *Justice League.* "I don't want to *not* honor the commitment that people have to that, and the interest they have in that. Because I find it, personally, as a filmmaker and as an artist, incredibly cool. And it makes me happy that there's that much caring about a thing that they don't even know what it is, you know? To me, I find that really awesome.

"Do I want to drag those people forward with me into the future? Of course!" Snyder continued. "But I definitely don't want anyone to get this impression that I'm saying, 'Move on! It's fine! Forget about it.' Because I think that dishonors the work that so many people have done in the fandom. There's a lot of money that has been raised, and a lot of strong relationships have been forged out of this struggle. And I don't want to dishonor it."

It was at this point that Snyder's wife Debbie, who had been sitting near Zack at the same long table, chimed in about the efforts of the RTSC family and the charitable work they have done for the American Foundation for Suicide Prevention in honor of Autumn Snyder.

"It's superamazing to me how a movement which *could* be seen as, 'Oh, we want this thing,' could bring so much awareness for suicide prevention, and so much money," she said. "It's supermoving, and has been so touching to us, that aspect of it. Because I think its the fans, not only showing support for Zack's art, but [also] something very personal to us. It means a lot to us."[3]

As much, I'd imagine, as these words of support and encouragement will mean to Snyder's fans—the ones who spent years in the online "trenches," enduring cyberattacks from vocal, mean-spirited critics who called them crazy for even suggesting the possibility that Zack Snyder's *Justice League* exists. As in any sustained war, there were peaks and valleys, wins and losses. But it undoubtedly meant a lot to the members doing the fighting every time they saw Snyder joining them on the front lines online, sharing a vital piece of information or confirming that the cut they argued for existed, and that their energies weren't being spent in vain.

So, we've answered *why* Zack Snyder encouraged the movement to continue. To ignore or possibly downplay their collective efforts would have been, in his own words, a dishonor to their work. But it's equally important to explain *how* Snyder engaged his fans during this time, because his exclusive use of the social media tool Vero opened a direct and valuable line of communication and gave his fans unprecedented access to the man responsible for the unreleased movie they'll finally get to see on HBO Max.

A BREADCRUMB TRAIL

Back when CinemaBlend was reporting on the *Justice League* production—from Zack Snyder's departure to Joss Whedon's hiring and the fallout that spewed from that debacle—only one writer on staff had access to Vero. So the running joke became that anytime Snyder posted something salacious on the social media tool, that reporter either had to cover the story themselves or go to Vero and screengrab whatever Snyder had shared so that someone else would be able to write an update.

None of us wanted to bother signing up for Vero because, at the time, it felt like Snyder was the only person of note using it—while the rest of the world wasted its time on Twitter, Facebook, Pinterest, Snapchat, and Instagram. So, what is Vero? It's a streamlined, cleaner-than-normal social media experience that was launched in 2015. "Vero" borrows the Esperanto word for "truth," and the company's slogan advertises it as the "Authentic Social Network." There are no ads on the tool, hence no need to mine user data. Vero claims to avoid the algorithms employed by Twitter and Instagram, giving users direct access to recommendations from their friends and followers. But even though it placed its focus on popular genres such as music, movies, books, and travel, Vero never caught on with mainstream users.

Snyder fans didn't care about all of that though. They only knew that their beloved director used Vero, and shared content on it religiously. And he used it exclusively because he's friends with Vero cofounder Ayman Hariri, the son of the assassinated former Lebanese prime minister Rafic Hariri. The two met after Hariri, an avid collector of rare comic books, won a charity auction for a walk-on role in Snyder's *Batman v Superman: Dawn of Justice,* as reported by CNBC.[4]

Snyder's first Vero post has nothing to do with DC or any of his films. It's a twenty-five-second video of himself diving in slow motion off a yacht in Monaco, posted on September 16, 2016.[5] But since that date to present, Snyder's Vero account has been the one-stop shop for exclusive *Man of Steel, Batman v Superman,* and *Justice League* content, including numerous Snyder Cut posts that kept the RTSC family engaged in the battle.

"The content Zack has shared on Vero has always felt like a nod to the #ReleaseTheSnyderCut movement to keep up the fight," said Giovanni Torres, a dedicated Snyder fan from New York City. "Personally, and I know a lot in the movement share this sentiment, but the subtlety of his posts and comments are really fun and engaging."[6]

The director's Vero page provides a virtual timeline of his involvement in and contribution to the DCEU. Jason Momoa, in one example, posed against what looks to be the rural backdrop of Djupavik, located in Iceland's most remote region. Snyder captioned the image, "One king" on October 10, 2016, signifying that the duo and their production team were filming scenes of billionaire Bruce Wayne (Ben Affleck) attempting to recruit the reclusive Arthur Curry, aka Aquaman, in an isolated fishing village.[7] You know the scene. "There is a stranger who comes to this village from the sea," Wayne growls to a gnarly gathering of protective townsfolk. "He comes in the winter when people are hungry and brings fish. He comes on the King Tide. That was last night."[8]

Snyder continued to make waves when he posted "Working on my birthday" on March 1, 2017, accompanying video of Aquaman swimming up to meet an Atlantean leader who was sitting on an underwater throne.[9] While only a nine-second clip, this was the first known demonstration of how the DC hero and his unique aquatic environment would look on screen, answering a major question many had in the run-up to the release of *Justice League.*

A week later, on March 7, Snyder followed up with a photo of Momoa in a technical harness against a massive green-screen backdrop, explaining, "People are wondering if he was CGI or not. He's not . . . hair and environment CG, otherwise all Jason."[10]

These types of updates trained Snyder and DC enthusiasts to keep their eagle eyes locked on the director's Vero page for news regarding their anticipated blockbuster. "Vero allowed for a controlled environment in which Zack could share content about his work for his fans without all the negative or toxic 'noise' other social media platforms usually bring," said Carlos Orbegozo of Toronto, Canada. "It is a great meeting point for creator and fans. In my opinion, Vero played a large role in moving the discussion forward in regards to the cut. Because of it, Zack was able to share his work and progress directly with the fans in a very positive manner."[11]

As it turns out, that's *exactly* why Snyder says he remained so active on Vero. "I just felt like the community there was superpositive," Snyder told me. "I felt like the community there was open to what I was trying to lay out. And I just felt like, in that way, the posts kind of grew on each other. I'd put something up, and there was a lot of—in those early days, especially—I would chat with the responses. I would go back and forth with everybody, a little bit. It was like a mini Q and A."[12]

Snyder admits that he found these interactions with the fans to be cathartic. "I would always say, 'Well, there is a small group that thinks this is cool,'" he said.

During those difficult years, when the future of his cut seemed uncertain, Vero also offered Snyder a platform on which to vent after *Justice League* was taken away from him. A cryptic photo showing a silhouetted figure staring at a body of water at sunrise was posted on May 23, 2017, which would be the day after *The Hollywood Reporter* broke the news that Snyder was stepping away from *Justice League* to be closer to his family.[13] The picture had no caption associated with it. Some of Snyder's Vero posts in the weeks and months following would have DC connections. He'd show support for Patty Jenkins, Gal Gadot, and their *Wonder Woman* movie, which opened on June 2, 2017 (and which Snyder helped produce). He even posted "I (Heart) RF" on August 6, 2017, replying to his Cyborg star Ray Fisher wearing an "I (Heart) ZS" shirt on the Hall H stage during San Diego Comic-Con in July.[14]

Snyder used the tool to communicate with followers, and even showed moderate levels of support for the *Justice League* movie he'd toiled on for years. On September 28, 2017, however, the tone of these posts majorly shifted.

On that day, Snyder first shared what would become a steady stream of looks at *Justice League* material. The hand-drawn sketches shared that day showed a scene that was present in the 2016 San Diego Comic-Con trailer, but was edited en route to Whedon's theatrical cut.[15] In the scene, medieval knights hover over a deep hole, burying one of three Motherboxes, which eventually would be sought by the villain Steppenwolf. Snyder called the sketches "JL storyboards," and having visited the set of *Justice League* in June 2016, I can confirm that the director planned to open his version of the movie with this history lesson of the Motherboxes on Earth. One would be hidden by the Amazonians. One would be protected by the Atlanteans. The last would be buried by what appears to be King Arthur and the Knights of the Round Table. (Given Snyder's professed fascination with John Boorman's 1981 film *Excalibur,* this should come as no surprise.)

Snyder still might open *Justice League* with these scenes, or he might evolve to a new idea as he brings the story to HBO Max. But this sketch became one of the first clues unearthed by RTSC supporters that Snyder shot a lot more for *Justice League* than was offered in the theatrical cut. It was all the proof they needed, though Snyder happily fed the fan base's insatiable hunger for Snyder Cut evidence every chance he could get.

More hand-drawn sketches posted on October 8, 2017, showed a different version of Clark Kent (Henry Cavill) and Lois Lane's (Amy Adams) cornfield reunion than the one fans eventually would see.[16] Shortly after that, Snyder ramped up the number of behind-the-scenes images he'd share from his *Justice League* shoot. But now, in hindsight, it's vital to realize what type of content the director decided to show fans in the weeks leading up to the film's theatrical release. Almost everything chosen by Snyder to be shared on Vero in October 2017 (one month before the film's release) reflected scenes he shot that would not be in the theatrical cut. Fans didn't know it yet. Did he? These behind-the-scenes images included a "City Limit" sign for The Flash's hometown of Central City, and Victor Stone (Ray Fisher) in his football uniform for Gotham City University.

None of this would appear in the theatrical cut of the film.

"It was important to me that Zack was continuing to share content on Vero," said Scott McClellan, cohost of the DC Films *Squadcast*. "One, it continued to reinforce how different his cut of the film was from the theatrical version. Two, it also reinforced how much of his cut had been completed before he left the film, which only continued to help provide evidence against the naysayers who kept arguing the 'does not exist' or 'it's only an assembly cut' arguments.

"Third, it personally motivated me, and obviously motivated the movement, because it was concrete proof that Zack hadn't moved on or wanted the movement to forget about his cut," McClellan continued. "He obviously cared about his cut and the movement because he kept sharing this content for his fans. Even his comments where he said, 'I'm doing this for you,' were encouraging."[17]

Was that the point? Did Snyder deliberately lay down a breadcrumb trail for fans to pick up and follow after they had seen the theatrical cut of *Justice League*? Did he want to document, on his Vero page, the proof they'd need to one day begin lobbying for the release of the material he was showing them? Giovanni Torres certainly believes so.

"If you think about it, in a few frames and comments here and there, Zack completely dismantled the thought that *JOSStice League* kept what Zack was trying to do in the true *Justice League*," Torres said. "He never just gave us stuff. The posts were clues, and he challenged us to figure it out."

While Orbegozo adds, "Of course, the stuff Zack Snyder shares keeps everyone [in the movement] positive and motivated. It keeps the curiosity and the possibilities in the fans' consciousness. It's a great marketing tool, and one where there's nothing but positivity and demand."

Snyder's Vero account now serves as the official time capsule for his experiences in the DCEU and points to where he's likely going with *Justice League*. It holds a treasure trove of Easter eggs that enticed amateur sleuths to join in the quest for the elusive Snyder Cut. The director posted photos of Deathstroke on a yacht in Monte Carlo and a cave drawing of Darkseid alongside the caption, "A bell can't be unrung."[18] It's no coincidence that the Darkseid scene became the basis for Snyder's first *Justice League* teaser trailer on HBO Max, which he released on June 18, 2020.[19]

Over time, Snyder increased his support for the RTSC movement on Vero too. Snyder first shared his connection to the RTSC family's unofficial founder, Fiona Zheng, on February 25, 2018, practically endorsing the work being done online and in the field by the movement.[20] And his supportive comments, posted in response to some of the movement's most significant accomplishments, demonstrated how in awe this celebrated filmmaker was of his own fan base—even though the feeling was mutual.

"Many people in the fandom used [that] exclusive content not just for the fight for the cut, but as healing tools for their daily struggles," said Hamad Al-Mansouri of Qatar. "It made this fight a lot easier."[21]

"There were definitely times in this movement where those posts were all we had," Torres added, "and I'm truly grateful to Zack for sharing them."

14

THEIR BIGGEST ACCOMPLISHMENTS

The RTSC movement's most important goal undoubtedly was the release of Zack Snyder's *Justice League,* a mission they accomplished on May 20, 2020. The release on HBO Max will allow fans the chance to see the proper version of the film, after a three-year, uphill battle.

"The moment Zack showed the HBO Max promotional image, I was grinning from ear to ear," said Jon Aaron Garza of Austin, Texas. "I knew that Zack and everyone that worked on the original *Justice League* was vindicated. All of the fans that helped get this through were vindicated. And that is something that will never be forgotten."[1]

While they waited for that historic announcement, the movement worked overtime to maintain high levels of awareness for the Snyder Cut, leading to some truly remarkable wins. Several of them were publicity-driven victories—organized campaigns that helped spread the latest news about the cut to the skeptical or uninitiated. However, the group's most commendable achievements, in my opinion, come from its staggering charitable contributions, which have been mentioned over and over in this book as I attempt to share this movement's story.

To be perfectly honest, the Release the Snyder Cut campaign probably wouldn't be as captivating of a subject if not for the group's decision in its earliest days to link its campaigns to the American Foundation for Suicide Prevention (AFSP). Motivated by the tragic loss of Autumn Snyder, Release the Snyder Cut leaders woke up to the fact that they could use their spotlight to increase awareness and funds for a very important organization in the AFSP.

Mick Doyle, forty-one years old, of Dublin, Ireland, often spearheaded these campaigns. Doyle, a father himself, confesses that his heart aches every time he thinks of Autumn Snyder and the pain Zack and Debbie must endure. Motivated by his strong desire to contribute, Doyle researched the AFSP and the services it offered. It opened his eyes, wide.

"Their entire reason for existing is to save lives. They are real-life superheroes," Doyle said. "As such, organizations such as the AFSP and their volunteers are, in some ways, an embodiment and manifestation of the ideals of these mythic heroes which we are all inspired by. Life savers. We are fortunate enough to have both the opportunity, and the power, to do something to help make a difference. Inspired by heroes of our own, many of us [in the movement] collectively felt that same wrenching call to service and action."[2]

Doyle, along with his compatriots in TPZ and several other members in the RTSC family, helped ensure that the marketing campaigns done on behalf of Release the Snyder Cut would also benefit the AFSP.

"If I am most proud of any one thing in relation to my time in the #Release TheSnyderCut movement, it is the extent to which I was able to work with other compassionate people in raising awareness and funds for suicide prevention through a series of #ReleaseTheSnyderCut awareness campaigns supporting The American Foundation for Suicide Prevention," Doyle said. "Many of the good people from all over the world who I've gotten to know and work with on this journey have become not just friends, but family. Brothers- and sisters-in-arms in a fight for the artistic and personal integrity of a man whose life, family, and work inspire us to do better, and to be better—for ourselves, and for each other."

The small team driving the RTSC bus in those early days first got their awareness campaigns going in 2018. One, held in March, raised eight hundred dollars for AFSP by getting the hashtag #JusticePledge trending on Twitter. During that campaign, members took the money they would have spent on a *Justice League* DVD and donated to the AFSP instead. Doyle says the movement considered that a trial balloon for what was to come.

"The #JusticePledge had proven that we could raise significant awareness and funds for AFSP with ideas and campaigns that resonate with people in Zack's and DC Films' fan communities," he said. "Other hashtag-themed campaigns sprung up in the wake of #JusticePledge, asking folks to give what they could to AFSP as a component of participating in the campaign, with each subsequent campaign growing in terms of the scope, breath of awareness, as well as fundraising totals."

Those included a social media push on May 17, 2018, in honor of the six-month anniversary of the theatrical release of *Justice League*, followed by the #5for5 Twitter campaign on July 13. In celebration of Wonder Woman, RTSC organizers asked followers to donate five dollars to AFSP, then post five photographs of the famed DC warrior on social media.

"It was a bit slow to begin with," admitted *Film Exiles* podcast cohost Chris Vinaldo when recalling that early #5for5 campaign on their November 16, 2019, episode. "But at the end of the day, this drive was really worth it because we raised over $1,600 for the AFSP in one day."[3]

The group successfully managed to double its initial contribution from the #JusticePledge drive, which helped them discover their true purpose— giving the fight for the Snyder Cut a deeper, more emotional aspiration.

These efforts, as you might imagine, are also incredibly important to the American Foundation for Suicide Prevention. The New York City-based voluntary health organization has been around since 1987, fulfilling its stated mission to "save lives and bring hope to those affected by suicide." The AFSP workers are superheroes without capes, which is why the RTSC family does all it can to donate to AFSP's herculean efforts.

American Foundation for Suicide Prevention CEO Robert Gebbia weighed in on the value and importance of the Release the Snyder Cut community, stating, "For more than two years, the American Foundation for Suicide Prevention has been fortunate to receive the support of Zack Snyder's fans through the #ReleasetheSnyderCut movement. We are grateful for this partnership, which is promoting the importance of mental health and suicide prevention. This dedication to AFSP's mission, and the willingness of Zack Snyder's fans to build a community that is supportive of one another, has been truly remarkable. Every step of the way, suicide prevention messaging has been incorporated into their outreach, and they have been invaluable in reducing the stigma surrounding seeking help when someone is struggling with their mental health.

"We are honored to partner with #ReleasetheSnyderCut and to be a part of this amazing community," Gebbia concluded.[4]

The fundraising campaigns came in all shapes and sizes during this three-year span. The RTSC members would hold a "Birthday Fundraiser," asking friends or family members to make AFSP donations as a personal gift. A charity screening of *Batman v Superman: Dawn of Justice* that was held on March 28, 2020, raised $1,440 in donations for the AFSP.

Then there was the "Snyder Dollar" marketing campaign, conceived of and launched by Brandon Valenza of Kansas. He had participated in some of the earliest RTSC initiatives, including a letter-writing campaign that sent "Release the Snyder Cut" requests to Warner Bros. executives. Through this involvement, Valenza realized how much he enjoyed serving as a self-proclaimed "hype man" for new campaigns so much so that he came up with one himself.

"My event was to write to Warner Bros. and 'show them the money,'" Valenza recalls as he described the creation of the "Snyder Dollar," a replica of a one hundred dollar bill with Zack Snyder's face on the front and the Justice League team members on the back.[5]

"I worked with our groups' amazing graphic designer to bring my idea to life, and we even packed as many Easter eggs into the design as possible," Valenza continued. "We had great success with it between two Comic-Con events, and even comic book artist Brett Booth wrote a letter and hand drew a picture of Superman. I couldn't have been happier with how it turned out!"

These fan-driven initiatives kept the members engaged while they waited for news on the possible release of Zack Snyder's *Justice League*. And every once in a while Snyder put his weight behind an idea, which led to significant fan contributions.

The website Ink to the People helps people design custom apparel then promote it for charitable causes. Snyder uses the site to offer exclusive shirts, sweatshirts, and beanie caps, with remarkable results. In January 2019, for example, Snyder presented the "All the Gods" charity T-shirt. It sported an intricate logo, which fans believe maps out the story of his five-film DC story arc. The RTSC members continue to debate and translate the meaning of the design. Meanwhile, sales of the "All the Gods" merchandise led to an $85,866 donation to AFSP.

Brent M. Coffee says he jumped at the chance to support the clothing drives that are run on Ink to the People. Coffee is a San Antonio, Texas-based lawyer and a lifelong DC fan. He's been supportive of Zack Snyder since seeing *300* in theaters, and now uses these Snyder-themed T-shirts and sweatshirts to educate people on the existence of the Snyder Cut of *Justice League*.

"Because the campaigns are for limited periods of time and future campaign dates [are] uncertain, I took a leap of faith and purchased a personal stock of them that I carry with me wherever I go," Coffee said. "I have met a number of people who want to purchase one on the spot once I share the movement, and I will have one immediately on hand for them. . . . Having the hoodies and shirts with me has done wonders in sharing the movement with others in all its aspects.

"I also made a 2020 New Year's resolution to share the movement with every person I see wearing a DC hero shirt and show them the hoodie and T," Coffee continued. "The conversations I've had have been nothing short of amazing."[6]

And for a few in the movement, these financial contributions to the AFSP equal (or maybe even outweigh) the desire to see Snyder's *Justice League*. "If we can save one life by all our charity efforts, then that's my biggest hope accomplished," said Nana of the Nerd Queens. "I know we will get the movie one day. But that doesn't stop the fight. Suicide prevention and mental health is a vital part of who we are. And if we can save a life, that's the biggest accomplishment of all."[7]

IT'S A BIRD! NO. . . . IT'S A PLANE

But the AFSP donations were not the only achievements the RTSC movement put in the "win" column as they fought to keep the movie on the radars of the decision makers at Warner Bros. Usually, the campaigns launched by organizers were modest. Every once in a while they got extreme.

"That plane over Burbank was pretty cool," reminisced Charlie Buda, a twentysomething New Yorker who studies computer science while working part-time as a produce associate.[8] He's also known in the RTSC community as the guy who organized to have a plane fly over Warner Bros.' studio lot in Burbank, California, with the message "#ReleaseTheSnyderCut" attached to its tail.

"I don't remember exactly when or how I got the initial idea, but I know that at some point I had this urge to do something more than just tweet about the Snyder Cut," Buda recalls. "I'm not saying tweeting is useless. I guess I just wanted to do something more tangible than words or pictures on a screen."

Buda grew up on DC comics and came to appreciate Snyder's interpretation of Superman after seeing *Man of Steel*. He admits to initially liking *Justice League* when it opened in 2017 ("Superman's fight against the JL was awesome," he states), but turned against the theatrical cut the more he learned how much Snyder's vision had been altered. He started following RTSC pioneers like Fiona Zheng and Dave Pena online, learning all the stories about the postproduction edits and drastic reshoots. By then he was fully aboard the movement's train.

"After realizing that what we got was just a shell of what Zack Snyder's real *Justice League* would've been, I started following Fiona on my personal twitter account. I kept up with everything she said about the Snyder Cut but didn't really tweet anything out. It was May of 2018 when I decided to make an account dedicated to trying to spread the news about the Snyder Cut," Buda said. "As we kept getting new bits of information throughout the weeks and months, I began to think that there might really be a shot at the Snyder Cut getting released someday. I guess I figured that maybe adding my voice (and some bad-to-sometimes-good Photoshops) could help bring that to pass."

On November 19, 2018, Buda traded words for actions. After researching the costs, and polling the RTSC membership to see who'd participate in a fundraiser, Buda went through the process of renting an airplane to transmit a "Release the Snyder Cut" message to Warner Bros. He coordinated his efforts with Doyle and scheduled the flyover for lunchtime on a Monday, hoping employees would see the plane in the sky as they took their afternoon break.

"The banner flew right over WB headquarters," Buda said. "I still remember the day the banner flew very well. I was in a geology lab, checking my phone every few minutes to see if anyone on the ground had gotten pictures of the banner. Eventually, Mick sent me a photo someone had taken, but the plane was far away, and it was kind of hard to see what the banner said. I was crestfallen! Half of the fundraiser money was wasted, [because] barely anyone could see the banner."

At least one significant person saw the banner, though. As Doyle recalls, "Zack Snyder had seen talk of the campaign circulating online in the days ahead of the flight and made sure to be on the WB lot during the flyover. He captured some spectacular footage—it's Zack Snyder, of course it was spectacular—of the plane and the #ReleaseTheSnyderCut banner flying overhead."

The airplane stunt additionally was covered by most of the entertainment trades and movie news websites promoting the #ReleaseTheSnyderCut hashtag and raising awareness around the movement. An $891 donation was sent to AFSP in conjunction with the plane promotion. And Charlie Buda made an online friend.

"I think it was a few days before the banner flew that Zack followed me on Vero," he recalls. "That was definitely the highlight of my year (until the day the banner flew, that is). I hadn't set out to do this with the hope or expectation that Zack would recognize me for starting it, but I'd be lying if I said I wasn't absolutely thrilled to have one of my favorite directors following me on social media.

"Never in a million years would I have thought [that] Zack Snyder is going to record and post a video of the #ReleaseTheSnyderCut banner flying over the WB lot with the caption 'That is caring,'" Buda continued. "But he did. And it was amazing."

THE SNYDER CUT IN SAN DIEGO

The plane stunt over Burbank was such a needle-mover that the RTSC movement tried it at least two more times: once more over the Warner Bros. studio lot in an attempt to snag the attention of newly-hired chairperson of Warner Bros. Entertainment Ann Sarnoff, and once over San Diego during the city's annual Comic-Con event.

San Diego Comic-Con (SDCC) is a massive gathering of comic, movie, and television fans, a mecca to which thousands annually pilgrimage to get updates on hotly anticipated projects. The Snyder Cut family often looked to the regular Warner Bros. panel in SDCC's renowned Hall H (the largest exhibition hall in use during the event) in hopes of hearing possible release plans for their cut. But they also used their time in San Diego to drum up support and spread awareness of their ongoing fight.

"I think that a major event like SDCC is THE place where you want to be the loudest," explained Kerry Vanderberg, a thirty-nine-year-old middle-school teacher from Los Altos, California, and a loyal RTSC member. "That's where you have as much of the fan base there gathered together in solidarity, and almost like this mass crowd, so that it is impossible for conventiongoers and WB to ignore us."[9]

The RTSC family made its presence known at the two San Diego Comic-Con events that were held after *Justice League* was released theatrically (the 2020 gathering was moved online due to public health and safety concerns during the COVID-19 global pandemic). Nana and Cole of the Nerd Queens deserve the lion's share of the credit for kicking off activities in 2018 with an event they called "Operation I <3 ZS." The ladies were given two hundred T-shirts with the words "I (Heart) ZS" on the front and challenged by RTSC organizers to hand them out during the convention. That design was inspired by the shirt Cyborg actor Ray Fisher wore on the Hall H stage in 2017, months after it was revealed that Snyder was stepping down from *Justice League*. At the time, many saw that fashion statement as one actor supporting his former director, though in hindsight some Snyder fans now consider Fisher's action as a subtle protest waged against replacement director Joss Whedon.

"Little did Ray know, or could predict at the time, that his gesture of love and support for Zack would inspire fan campaigns which would become a powerful theme and recurring symbol within the #ReleaseTheSnyderCut movement," Doyle said.

The Nerd Queens succeeded in handing out all two hundred shirts and even posted to YouTube a grainy video of them distributing the merchandise to Snyder fans who were camping out overnight in the Hall H line. It's incredibly touching and inspiring to see the SDCC attendees who were willing to support Snyder while they waited to go into the hall.

"The idea was a great success. The T-shirts were snapped up quickly and got attention at Hall H," Doyle said. "Zack did not attend, but he saw online photos and was moved by the incredible level of fan support on display. Ultimately, interest grew beyond the convention as fans wanted to know where they could buy such a cool shirt to proudly support Zack. It was at this point that the idea of marrying fan T-shirts and support for AFSP came together."

The movement made plans to return to San Diego the following year, 2019, with the hope of building on the foundation laid by the Nerd Queens. They called the effort "Project Comic-Con," which became a massive marketing endeavor that recruited several loyal RTSC members for an all-out blitz on downtown San Diego.

"After the SnyderCon [event] in Pasadena, the chat rooms were buzzing," explained Will Rowlands of Portsmouth, England. "Many of us discussed how we could capitalize [on] the new confirmed info. The next big event coming was San Diego Comic-Con, possibly the biggest and most well-known of all cons. So, as a group, we decided we should target the event with advertisements and a ground team to raise awareness outside of the SnyderCut bubble. . . . The ideas were growing and growing. However, I felt that a lot of talking was happening and not enough action. We were limited on time for such a big idea. So, I offered to get the ball rolling and create the GoFundMe campaign and make the idea public."[10]

This initiative ended up generating more than $27,000 in donations, according to Rowlands, with $14,930 of it going to the AFSP in Autumn Snyder's name. The rest was spent on roadside billboards, bus stop signage, a half-page color advertisement in *The Hollywood Reporter*, the aforementioned flyover from a plane sporting a #ReleaseTheSnyderCut banner, and marketing materials that were handed out by volunteers on the ground. The team behind Project Comic-Con was large, with Alessandro Maniscalco coordinating a lot of the moving pieces, assisted by Eric Blake, Dustin Sheffield, Lindsey Staton, Jeff Purdy, Ben Wellington, Kristen Holmgren, Shawn Morgan, Kerry Vanderberg, Brad Curran, the Nerd Queens, and many more.

"There were many late nights and long hours of brainstorming and discussion, as well as dealing with the vendors and finances," said Maniscalco. "It was quite a lot of hard work. But it was all worth it because I believed in what we were fighting for, and we were helping a good cause with AFSP."[11]

"The 'Project ComicCon' campaign was probably the single most important and impactful effort in terms of breaking out #ReleaseTheSnyderCut from the confines of the Twitter and Vero echo chamber, out into mainstream popular culture," Doyle concluded. "It is also the single biggest fan-initiated fundraising campaign to date, raising approximately $15,000 for AFSP. It also drove the highest level of positive press coverage for #ReleaseTheSnyderCut with major publications from *The Washington Post, The Hollywood Reporter,* and *Business Insider* covering the story.

"But what is most impressive about 'Project ComicCon,'" Doyle continued, "is that it was a true example of fans from different parts of the DC and Snyder fandoms coming together, putting personal and preferential differences aside, and making a difference for Zack. It was a true act of unity and proved that what unites us is always more powerful than what divides us."

Personally, Project Comic-Con is when I started taking the RTSC movement seriously. CinemaBlend reported on the first banner flight over Burbank in 2018, primarily because of the eccentricity of the stunt. And anyone covering the film industry would see the #ReleaseTheSnyderCut hashtag sporadically trending on social media. Truthfully, though, I didn't pause to give the movement much thought until I walked past a San Diego bus stop in July 2019 and saw the eye-catching, floor-to-ceiling posters with the Justice League's silhouette calling for "The 3 1/2 Hour Untold Story of *Justice League.*" It piqued my curiosity, and I made a mental note to start digging into whatever it was this movement was trying to sell.

Three months after that I officially bought in, thanks to the group's next spectacular achievement.

AT THE CROSSROADS OF THE WORLD

New York City. The Big Apple! As Ol' Blue Eyes once crooned, if you can make it there, you'll make it anywhere. And from October 4–6, 2019, the Snyder Cut movement "made" it there, in massive fashion.

Following up on the success of Project Comic-Con, the RTSC team kept its momentum going by shifting coasts. In conjunction with New York Comic-Con (NYCC) 2019, which took place that weekend in Midtown Manhattan, RTSC organizers Chris Vinaldo, Will Rowlands, and Abdul Abdullah coordinated another GoFundMe campaign. This one would be used to rent out a digital billboard in Times Square, aka "The Crossroads of the World."

"Getting a billboard in Times Square was very ambitious," Rowlands told me, "but the success of our previous campaigns gave us the confidence that we had the power to achieve it."

The biggest difference between Project Comic-Con and the Times Square billboard was the amount of time (or lack thereof) the movement had to raise donations to pay for the marketing materials. Chris Vinaldo of *The Film Exiles* podcast led the charge on this campaign and confessed to being concerned about asking RTSC members to donate to yet another fundraising campaign so soon after San Diego. After researching the cost of a digital billboard, Vinaldo's team knew it had to raise $3,742 in order to book through the website BigSignMessage.com. That money would cover the quoted fee of $1,871 for a twelve-hour rental of the billboard (where the Release the Snyder Cut message would circulate every fifteen seconds). And it would allow the group to donate the same amount to AFSP. Additionally, Vinaldo and Rowlands estimated that they'd also need $800 to be spent on materials for a ground crew to canvass the actual convention, handing out signs, and helping raise awareness.

"My main concern was ensuring we met the funding target," Rowlands said. "We, as always, needed to raise twice as much to ensure we could donate 50 percent to AFSP. Initially, I wondered if we were asking too much too soon [after the San Diego campaign], but boy did the movement step up yet again."

The overall goal for NYCC was $6,000. The campaign ultimately amassed $6,311—enough to fund the Times Square billboard rental, get marketing materials in the hands of a ground team, and donate $3,355 to AFSP.

The exposure, however, ended up being priceless. There's no telling how many people walked past the Times Square billboard and noticed the affirmative messages, showcasing positive quotes from *Justice League* cast members Ray Fisher, Ciaran Hinds, and Jason Momoa. The scrolling billboard concluded with a message from Snyder that he has a cut of *Justice League*, and that, "It's done."

And film journalists dedicated valuable coverage to the billboard, writing stories about the accomplishment in the days following NYCC, which meant the group's consistent message finally was reaching more people. And it was reaching people outside of the already-passionate circle of Snyder supporters. Social media exploded that weekend with photographs of fans who stopped by a NYCC booth to hold a "Release the Snyder Cut" sign. Numerous news outlets covered the RTSC efforts, building off the momentum that began in San Diego months prior. The RTSC volunteers on the ground in Manhattan could sense the tide turning in their favor.

"That entire weekend was absolutely insane," said New Yorker Giovanni Torres, a member of the RTSC ground team who volunteered to work the group's NYCC booth. "After almost two years of receiving nothing but hate or, at a minimum, disinterest from anyone not in the movement—after being told time after time there are ten people supporting this movement, get over it—I walked into the Javits Center thinking I was going to be Rorschach displaying my 'The End is Nigh' [sign], or in this case 'Release The Snyder Cut' sign, to deaf ears.

"But what happened was that, no joke, every two to three minutes, someone would stop me and say so many words of encouragement, [or] ask me to explain the movement," Torres continued. "Even the people who jokingly stopped me, they gave me two minutes to explain, and afterwards were like, 'Shit, man, I hope this works out! It's great you guys made this into something.'"[12]

They certainly did. The back-to-back campaigns in San Diego and New York showed that the RTSC movement was committed, capable of mobilizing, and willing to think extremely big. Flooding downtown San Diego with posters and billboards is one thing. Buying a billboard in Times Square took the campaign to the next level, and people outside of the movement—including entertainment outlets that previously had dismissed the RTSC efforts—finally viewed the fanbase with newfound appreciation.

They had each other's backs. They were picking up support from outside the movement. Now it was time to get some all-star assistance.

SUBWAY (YES, THAT SUBWAY) JOINS THE FIGHT

Numerous one-off events have been staged by the RTSC movement over the years to keep enthusiasm high among supporters. Dave Pena of California attracts hundreds of viewers to a "Vodka Stream" on his YouTube channel Film Junkee, where he discusses the most recent developments surrounding the Snyder Cut. Members participated in AFSP walks in Pasadena, California, in 2018 (which raised $2,445 for the charity) and again in 2019 (raising an additional $4,003 in donations). Once, the group paid to rent a digital advertisement with the #ReleaseTheSnyderCut hashtag during a 2020 English Premiere League FA Cup match between Middlesbrough and Tottenham. The ad was seen on television sets around the globe.

And in one of the strangest interactions I've witnessed since covering the accomplishments of this movement, the Twitter account @RTSnyderCut asked the sandwich chain Subway how many retweets it would take to get the company to donate ten thousand sandwiches on behalf of Feeding America. Subway's social media team actually responded, giving the RTSC family five hours to get five thousand RTs.[13]

They accomplished the goal in minutes.

Subway immediately upped its donation to fifteen thousand sandwiches. And they used the hashtag #ReleaseTheSnyderCut in their reply. But more than that, Subway essentially joined the fight for the Snyder Cut from that point forward. The company frequently tweeted support for the hashtag. They helped lure fellow fast-food franchises like Wendy's into the marketing battle. And they even got Zack Snyder to explain what ingredients would go into a Release the Snyder Cut sandwich. On February 14, 2020, Snyder clarified, "Obviously, it's ALL meat. . . . NO cheese. . . . NO Baloney."[14]

Whenever Snyder got involved with these initiatives it ignited a special spark in the movement. His fingers were locked onto the pulse of the RTSC campaign, and he'd orchestrate momentum to keep support for his cut running high. But Snyder injected real hope into the movement when he concluded a fan-driven poster competition on February 29, 2020, that solicited original artwork for *Zack Snyder's Justice League*.

Victor Ku of St. Paul, Minneapolis—who goes by the artist name of The Mighty Pegasus—ended up winning the poster contest. He designed a gorgeous mural around the shape of the DC villain Darkseid. Within the silhouette could be found references to all the characters in the DCEU, from the Justice League to the Suicide Squad and beyond.

"Since the *Justice League* animated series was a big part of my childhood, and Zack Snyder is my favorite movie director, I wanted to show how much I loved the universe he created," Ku said. "So in July 2019, I started my Darkseid Justice League project, which took me seven months to complete. And it felt as if it was destiny that the poster contest announcement happened two days after I had completed my project! Of course I had to submit my art, but I had never imagined that I would make it to the top nor even win it."[15]

Ku's own creative journey is remarkable. Born in a little suburb in France called Corbeil-Essonnes, Ku cultivated a love for drawing by studying Anime and Manga series such as Dragon Ball Z and Saint Seiya. By the time he'd moved to the United States in 2003, Ku says he had given up on his aspirations to be a professional artist, and instead joined the US Navy in 2011.

"During my time in the Navy, I felt like I was still missing something in me, as if I had unfinished business with something else in my life," Ku told me. "I separated from the US Navy in February 2016 and I took a break for a few months to figure what I wanted to become and who I was inside. In 2017, I got back in touch with an old friend from France who has been doing comic conventions as an artist, where he showcased his art and traveled. He had motivated me to start drawing again."

Once back in the comic-artistry game, Ku says he started following Christopher Cayco, another convention artist known for his detailed projects involving pop culture universes such as *Rick and Morty,* Pokemon, and the video game series Marvel vs. Capcom.

"There were many other artists and influencers also such as Ross Draws, James Raiz, and Tyrone Magnus who inspired me. But Christopher was one of the main influences who really pushed me to start my journey."

Ironically, it was a DC-themed competition that really catapulted Ku down this path in the summer of 2017. He entered a *Justice League* fan art contest where the prize would be a premiere ticket to see the movie in Los Angeles.

"I took that chance to prove to myself that I could be a serious artist and that I could handle the pressure of drawing and expose my art to my social media," Ku said. "I created a *Justice League* piece to submit, started my journey, and never looked back."

He didn't win that contest, but he did win Zack Snyder's *Justice League* poster competition in 2019. His prize? A film slate that Snyder had used every day on the set of his *Justice League.* That souvenir, alone, would be an amazing keepsake. And Ku admits to being properly blown away by the victory.

"I remember looking at so many amazing submitted arts, and it must have been hard for Zack to pick four finalists. I also believed that the #3 poster by artist Nimo5877 would take the win, since it was my favorite from the finalists," Ku said. "So when I was announced the winner, I was so overjoyed that I didn't know what to say! For the first three days, I still felt like maybe someone was trolling me, and that I was dreaming. But I finally absorbed everything in, and I was so grateful."

It got better. On the back of the slate was a special message from Zack Snyder. It read, "Please extend to the bearer of this slate the right to pass all security protocols and the permission to operate this motion picture scene and sync marker on the set of any additional photography for the motion picture known as Zack Snyder's *Justice League* in the unlikely and purely speculative event that such photography is needed."[16]

A golden ticket—like something pulled straight out of *Charlie and the Chocolate Factory*. An invitation to operate the sync marker "on the set of any additional photography" of Snyder's *Justice League*. At the time, Snyder coyly included the caveat about it being "unlikely and purely speculative." But now that the Snyder Cut has been confirmed for HBO Max, a set visit for Ku seems inevitable.

For now, he patiently waits for the call. "I hope to meet everyone on the set of the additional scenes," Ku said. "Will it happen? I have no doubt about it."

BEN AND GAL ANSWER THE CALL

More often than not, the movement took matters into its own hands and decided when, and how, to make its biggest splashes. Few episodes in the movement's history created as much noise, and therefore awareness, as the trending event held on November 17, 2019, in "celebration" of the two-year anniversary of *Justice League*'s theatrical release. How important was it? Warner Bros. chairman Toby Emmerich singled it out in May 2020 as the catalyst for the studio finally coming to the negotiation table with the Snyders to figure out how to resurrect Zack Snyder's *Justice League* from the studio's vault, according to *The Hollywood Reporter*.[17] So yeah, it was a massive deal.

The week leading up to that trending event produced a flurry of activity in the movement. Snyder spent the week posting photos of his *Justice*

League cast on Vero, most of which showed them in scenes that were not part of the theatrical cut of the film. Ray Fisher's Cyborg stared down Steppenwolf in S.T.A.R. Labs in a photo Snyder shared on November 13, for example, or Henry Cavill is shown in his Superman suit with the added caption, "He Has Yet To Rise." Snyder was priming the pump. The movement was set to explode.

On Sunday, November 17, the fan base stormed social media with the resolve of the Spartan army defending their homeland against the marauding Persians. They set a goal: 214,000 tweets, in honor of the reported 214-minute run time of Zack Snyder's *Justice League*. They used "#ReleaseTheSnyderCut" as a battle cry to rally the troops, and they posted on social media all day long.

By the end of the day they'd nearly quadrupled their goal.

"In the early days #ReleaseTheSnyderCut was trending with a couple thousand tweets. That number grew to tens of thousands and exploded on the two-year anniversary of the theatrical release of *Justice League* to nearly 800,000 in a single day," said Maniscalco.[18]

"The November 2019 '214' event on Twitter was a fantastic day of trending the hashtag and showing WB there is a market and a fandom for Zack Snyder's *Justice League*," added Darren Benson.[19]

That wasn't all, though. November 17 further marks the day that *Justice League* stars Gal Gadot and Ben Affleck finally broke their silence and used the Release the Snyder Cut hashtag on social media. My outlet, CinemaBlend, interviewed Affleck in March 2020 while he was doing press for Gavin O'Connor's basketball drama, *The Way Back*. Instead of asking him a pointed question about his collaborations with Snyder, or even his experiences under replacement director Joss Whedon, we opted to thank the actor for voicing his support of the RTSC movement with that unexpected November 17 tweet. The actor admitted that he was unaware of the trending event but that Snyder was the one who reached out and asked Affleck to chime in.

"I didn't know about it," Affleck said. "Zack was like, 'Hey, they are doing this thing.' And I said, 'Zack, I love you, and I support you. However I can help you.'"[20]

It was interesting to hear Affleck confirm that it was Snyder who reached out to ask his Batman to tweet in support of the RTSC movement during the trending event. It shows that the director tracked the progress of these events and wasn't opposed to recruiting celebrity talent if it meant a high-powered jolt of exposure.

Affleck and Gadot's tweets were game changers. They officially confirmed the A-listers' support for Zack Snyder's cut of the movie, joining Ray Fisher, Ezra Miller, and Jason Momoa in publicly calling for the Snyder Cut to be released. And now, thanks in part to them, it has been.

There are turning points in every sustained war, battles fought and won, that can be pointed at, in hindsight, where the victor says, "Here's where things shifted. Here's where we finally broke through and started winning. Here's where the momentum swung in our favor." The Twitter campaign of November 17, 2019, now stands as the watershed moment in the fight to get *Zack Snyder's Justice League* released on HBO Max. The occasionally fractured army of Snyder supporters put all their differences aside and united in support of one shared goal. They got the hashtag trending on social media, which led to days of coverage on important websites and news outlets. They got two all-star holdouts—Ben Affleck and Gal Gadot—to join the effort, virtually speaking. And they finally turned Emmerich's head long enough for him to concede that the Snyder Cut of *Justice League* needed to be released.

"The November 17 trend was the game-changing turning point that brought WB to the table of *Zack Snyder's Justice League*," Doyle said. "If there is one other thing, apart from working closely with passionate people to be a force for good for AFSP, that I am most proud of, it is having the honor to be a part of a massive global voice that day, and to have been a contributing part of the organization of events and giveaways surrounding it. It will be a day long remembered."

By Zack Snyder as well. "Humbled by the outpouring and support," the director wrote on Vero in the hours following the event.[21] It wasn't exactly a victory speech, but it can, in hindsight, be read as a heartfelt acknowledgment for all the spectacular achievements that the RTSC family will continue to accomplish.

15

THE LEAGUE CELEBRATES

Naysayers spent years arguing with Release the Snyder Cut supporters about Zack Snyder's *Justice League*. They claimed the cut didn't exist. Even if it did, they argued that the special effects and postproduction work would be too expensive to properly finish and that Warner Bros. had no interest in investing more money into a movie it had abandoned years before.

Even after Snyder announced that his cut of *Justice League* would in fact screen on HBO Max, ardent anti-Snyderists continued to engage in tepid online takedowns. They claimed the version coming to HBO Max wasn't really the "Snyder Cut" anymore because of the director's intended reshoots and additional photography. They argued that AT & T's decision to collaborate with Snyder was a victory for toxic fandom (though people pushing that claim ignore any and all goodwill achieved by the RTSC community because it doesn't fit their narrative). Honestly, the resurrected Jesus Christ had an easier time convincing the apostle Thomas, dubbed "Doubting Thomas." Some people simply don't want to accept the reality that the Snyder Cut exists and finally is going to screen for fans.

Snyder, for one, isn't buying the argument that a victory for the RTSC movement is a win for toxic fandom. Following the May 20 announcement, writers at select media outlets typed their concerns over vocal fan bases who were able to convince studio heads to reverse course and release alternate versions of handpicked films. They feared such action would create a harmful precedent in the industry, allowing any disgruntled fan community to demand an alternate cut of a bad film to be released.

"I just think that's sour grapes," Snyder told me. "There's really no other way to say it. We know the people who were the architects of that narrative, and it's pretty obvious what their agenda is. Those are people that I've been held back from confronting, by wiser people in the room. Because I'd love to get at some of these characters. Some direct conversation would be nice. Just to say, one, you don't know shit about what you're talking about. And we can break down everything they've ever [said]. I can make a list. There's a few of these guys where I could just get a list of everything they've ever said, that they thought was right, and [I could tell them] every single thing they've said is wrong.

"And so, in what world do you have any credibility anywhere, to anyone?" Snyder continued. "I would love the opportunity to just say to the world, and to fandom in general, who these fakers are and what should be done to them, or with them. It's just a bunch of BS. In regards to that toxic fandom, or it's 'a win for toxic fandom,' again, in what world does this 'toxic fandom' raise hundreds of thousands of dollars for suicide prevention? How is that toxic fandom? They've probably achieved more than any other fan base, [and done more] good than any other group. So I don't understand."[1]

These cinematic cynics that lurked on Twitter and YouTube grew quiet, however, whenever actual Justice League members spoke on the subject. And when Snyder confirmed his plans to release the cut on HBO Max, no one celebrated harder than the *Justice League* cast themselves.

"It has felt like a birthday mixed with every other gift-giving celebration you could ever, ever, ever have. All in one," Ray Fisher said when he guested on *TheNiceCast* podcast on May 24, 2020. "It's still hard for me to wrap my head around. I don't have enough distance from the actual [announcement] and from everything to get some clear perspective on it. I feel like my brain is just racing with the possibilities. . . . My thing is, I don't care *what* it is. I know whatever it is, it's going to look great. It's going to sound great. And it is going to *be* great."[2]

That's because when it drops on HBO Max in 2021, *Zack Snyder's Justice League* will be exactly that—Snyder's version of the anticipated material. Meanwhile, Ben Affleck filmed a video for Kevin Smith's *Fatman on Batman* podcast on May 21, 2020, that also celebrated Snyder's victory and the overall win for artistic integrity.

"I'm very excited Zack's getting a chance to finally see his vision realized," Affleck said. "I think it's a great thing. I'm really excited for fans to get to see it. I want to say thank you to the fans because it was their enthusiasm and their passion that made it happen. Without the fan support, I don't think it'd ever happen. I love Zack, and I love his version of the movie. I look forward to everyone getting a chance to see it."[3]

That enthusiasm was quadrupled by *Aquaman* star Jason Momoa, who screamed into his cell phone camera the day after the announcement for a video posted to his social media accounts. "You see that shit? You put it out there! You believe that? Releasing the Snyder Cut? HBO Max, man, I can't believe it," Momoa shouted. "It's happening! Finally. Release the Snyder Cut! Give it!"[4]

He ended the video by punching his phone.

One-time Lex Luthor Jesse Eisenberg was more demure when discussing the historical precedent HBO Max's decision would set. He praised the work of the RTSC movement during a *Digital Spy* interview, clarifying, "I can't think of any other precedent in history where there was something of this scope. Because it's not just about releasing the movie, but it required all of this . . . we call it post-production. So it's not just they're releasing scenes that are finished. They had to do a lot of post-production, and it's such a big process. And yeah, I'm so happy for him. He's a great guy with a very, very specific vision and so, yes, I'm happy that he gets that."[5]

The *Justice League* cast deserves an awful lot of credit for beating the Snyder Cut drum over the years, knowing full well that they were playing the media like a fiddle. Momoa nearly broke the internet in August 2019 when he shared an Instagram video of himself with Zack and Debbie Snyder accompanied by the following caption: "Mahalo for showing me the Snyder Cut. Here is a token of my appreciation. Leica Q2, for inspiring me as an artist through and through. @leicacamerausa I wish I was a better actor but I can't lie. The Snyder Cut is ssssiiiicccckkkkkk #luckymesucksforu."[6]

Those words of support from the *Justice League* leads carried weight. Almost as much weight as the celebratory screams of the Snyder Cut family. They may not be movie stars, but without their constant support for Zack Snyder's vision of *Justice League* there'd be no version of the film screening on HBO Max.

"It didn't feel real," said Megan Loucks about the HBO Max announcement on May 20. "It felt as if I was in this crazy, amazing dream. I was sitting next to my boyfriend, and I just burst into tears. We have been fighting for this moment for so long, and to finally see it happen was very surreal. Seeing Zack, Debbie, Henry, and many of my friends there to help usher this announcement was beautiful."[7]

Loucks' post-announcement celebration ended up being an all-star affair, made up of RTSC community founders and members of Snyder's *Justice League* cast.

"I had a few beers and got on a Zoom call with my friends the Nerd Queens and TPZ," she said. "We were also joined by Ray Porter, Darkseid himself, and the legendary Jay Oliva. We drank, laughed, and cried. It was an amazing time, and one I will remember for a long time."

"The moment that Zack Snyder finally revealed that his *Justice League* was coming to HBO was one of jubilation for myself. Happiness for Zack and his family, happiness for the fans, and for myself as well," said *Newsweek* columnist Sheraz Farooqi. "Henry Cavill was the final *Justice League* cast member to speak on the Snyder Cut, and much like Superman, he arrived exactly when we needed him. Having Cavill be the one to take it to the finish line was awesome."[8]

Carlos Orbegozo added, "It was special to see Henry on board. It was very appropriate for the original trinity to reintroduce the world of these DC films to all the fans. They give birth to a world of possibilities, once again. [Afterward], I just smiled by myself for a few minutes, remembering how far we got. How it all started with a depressed confusion, and it ends with the thrill of victory. I communicated with a few brothers and sisters in the movement and then went on to tell my wife, 'It happened. It finally happened!'"[9]

"THIS IS GOING DOWN IN CINEMATIC HISTORY."

Snyder may not have been able to deliver on his dream scenario of announcing the Snyder Cut at San Diego Comic-Con, but he did get to stage a celebratory victory lap at his very own fan event, Justice Con, which was held on YouTube on July 25–26, 2020.

Organized and hosted by Loucks and the Nerd Queens, Justice Con featured an array of informative panels conducted by many who were part of Snyder's process while filming *Justice League*. Ray Fisher, Darkseid voice actor Ray Porter, and photographer Clay Enos participated in Justice Con panels that celebrated the joys of collaborating with Snyder on a project of this size. Debbie Snyder joined the hosts of the Snyder's Amazons podcast for an in-depth discussion of female representation in Hollywood, and the DC movies. And dedicated Release the Snyder Cut team members Jonita Davis, Sheraz Farooqi, and Chris Wong-Swenson staged a Justice Con panel discussing diversity in the DCEU, and Snyder's complete filmography.

Snyder even held his own Saturday evening presentation during Justice Con—which was, in a word, eventful. The director used his time to discuss the lengthy restoration process conducted on his existing *Justice League* footage in order to get it ready for its HBO Max distribution. He praised the executives at HBO Max for their support of the Snyder Cut, and dodged spoiler questions about Green Lantern and Martian Manhunter, DC heroes who are expected to show up in Snyder's cut of the film. And in the most colorful conversation of the panel, Snyder definitively cleared up the misconception that his cut of *Justice League* might include any footage that Joss Whedon shot during his controversial reshoots.

"I would destroy the movie. I would set it on fire before I use a single frame that I did not photograph," Snyder said. "That is a fucking hard fact. . . . I would literally blow that fucking thing up."[10]

Those passionate sentiments reinforced the concept of artistic integrity, a flag waved by the RTSC movement as they fought to restore the director's vision for this eventual blockbuster. As if to reward their effort, Snyder shocked the Justice Con panel crowd by presenting the first official video clip of the resurrected Superman (Henry Cavill), wearing his signature black-and-silver suit, in a scene that only can be seen in *Zack Snyder's Justice League*.

Justice Con was an opportunity to tease the work that would show up on HBO Max. It also was a chance for Snyder and his crew to thank the members of the movement for making their dream come true.

"More than anything, I'm in shock and awe, and proud especially, of the people who contributed to getting the Snyder Cut released," Fisher said during his panel. "There's no way that any of this would have happened without the support of the fans, without the support of the individuals involved. There's just no way. I mean, this is history. It's monumental. There's nothing that's ever been done like this before. So for me, it's like . . . this is something I've said over the years. If this is the only experience I'm blessed to have in this business, I'm fine with that. This is going down in cinematic history, for a lot of different reasons."[11]

Justice League cinematographer Fabian Wagner added during his Justice Con panel, "I'm just superhappy for Zack, you know? It's just nice for any creative to be able to finish something that they've done the way it was created by them. That's the main thing. I'm really happy for Zack. I'm happy for Debbie, his wife and producer. And I'm happy for everyone else who worked on it. And obviously I'm happy to see the film that, when I was there, we were making."[12]

Whether intentional or not, Wagner's Justice Con comments sum up the mission statement of the RTSC movement, in a nutshell. The work they did was all for Zack. The battles they fought were on behalf of the crew who worked hard on a movie that was discarded. And the victory they achieved was celebrated intensely by basically everyone involved in the *Justice League* production process.

When members of the movement step back now, they hopefully will be able to recognize just how far the Release the Snyder Cut campaign came in three short years. And they should realize how proudly they stand, shoulder to shoulder at the finish line, with their favorite director, who told me during our interview, "It's the difference between a ten-year journey of my life that ends with nothing, that ends with literally the thing in ruins and destroyed, or it ends with the fulfilling of a vision that I had in my childhood. . . . And I'm sure that, with monies raised, these guys have literally saved lives with their movement. It's undeniable that these hundreds of thousands of dollars hasn't gone to suicide hotlines and help calls. And literally, there is no doubt in my mind that lives have been saved by these people.

"I can only say thank you to the movement," Snyder concluded. "And to the fandom for the incredible hard work of all these individuals who have come together to create a singular voice that would not be silenced and could not be silenced."

Not until the Snyder Cut had been released.

EPILOGUE

THEIR MESSAGE TO ZACK

When Zack Snyder revealed HBO Max's plan to release the Snyder Cut of *Justice League,* he gave this book its best possible ending. The announcement provided closure to the three-year-long fight to convince Warner Bros. to collaborate with Snyder once again. And it personally gave me a celebratory punctuation mark to place at the end of this narrative. The victory lap has been run. The story of the RTSC movement has now been told.

That wasn't always going to be the case. Prior to Snyder's historic May 20, 2020, event, I wrote this book with an open-ended but optimistic finale. And at the time, I came up with an idea that I'm choosing to retain, even though the story has a concrete ending. Back before the Snyder Cut announcement, I turned the book's conclusion over to the people whose emotional, mental, and physical contributions made this journey possible: Zack Snyder's passionate fans. The perpetual uncertainty swirling around the status of Snyder's cut forced me to pivot, midproject, and make *Release the Snyder Cut* less about the actual movie (which we feared we might never see) and more about the people fighting for it. Why do they do it? What keeps them engaged? What have they accomplished so far? I hope the book answered those questions and raised a few more.

The last word, however, should still belong to the RTSC community. That feels right. So I asked the Release the Snyder Cut family members to send me messages they'd want Zack Snyder to read. I wanted them to have an opportunity to tell him what his films mean, what the movement means, and how both have affected them in their daily lives. They spoke from the heart. I've amplified their voices. This is what they had to say:

Eduardo Candelaria: "Thank you, Zack, for saving my life. I wouldn't be here if it wasn't for *Batman v Superman*. You literally gave me a reason to keep going with my life, that the brighter stars shine in the darkest nights. Thank you for inspiring me to be better, to do better. You're a role model for me. I love you and your films. Thank you, Zack Snyder. #ReleaseTheSnyderCut."

Jack Farrelly: "I don't know how to put into words how much you've changed my life. . . . Everything you put into your work has inspired me to think deeper for everything I do. All forms of media must evolve to stay relevant and to do better, whether that involves modernizing mythology or holding a mirror to society and politics. It all adds so much more to a movie or book that some fail to realize. None of this even begins to tell you how much you inspire me, and I could go on forever. Thank you, Zack Snyder."

Julius Tora: "I'd like to say that *Man of Steel* and *Batman v Superman: Dawn of Justice* came at a pivotal time in my life. I was battling a mental illness diagnosed as clinical depression. And the weight of the world was crushing me beneath it. Then I saw your Superman—not lighthearted, but heavy-hearted by the world, and it clicked to me that I can be like Superman and survive the weight of the world too. . . . Thank you so very much. I believe in your art, and I believe in the Snyder Cut."

Jacob Sackleh: "Zack Snyder. Through *Batman v Superman* and *Man of Steel,* you permanently changed the way I view these characters, the comic book film genre, and comic books as a whole. *Batman v Superman* is an absolute masterpiece that will always hold a special place in my heart. Thank you for giving so much of yourself to this arc for these characters and in turn giving me such remarkable films that only become richer and deeper every time I watch them."

Daryn Kirscht: "You are the single biggest inspiration in my life and have made a significant positive impact on my life. I will be forever grateful for it. You and your films have given my life a much greater sense of meaning, understanding, and importance. Your films, particularly *Man of Steel* and *BvS,* have completely altered and enhanced the way I view films—thank heavens! . . . To you and your amazing cast and crew, I say: Thank you for giving me and the rest of your fans an ideal to strive toward and, for the record, #ReleaseTheSnyderCut."

Eric Blake: "Mr. Snyder, it's truly been an honor to take part in all these efforts to help ensure that you'll be able to see your vision through. As it stands, your *Man of Steel* and *Batman v Superman: Ultimate Edition* have both filled me with a deep passion and interest for these comic characters I didn't have before. . . . Your works have opened my mind to new horizons— and to that end, I wish to do whatever it takes to help ensure that you will reach the horizons once denied you, yourself. Thank you so much, sir, for doing what you do. Here's to the release of your *Justice League*—and God willing, your *Justice League 2,* and beyond."

Sam Martin: "Thank you for *Batman v Superman: Dawn of Justice.* When I could no longer cope in this new world, this film gave me back hope and control again. I fight for the Snyder Cut because you fought for me, and I want to feel that light again."

Richard Lynn: "I remember sitting in the movie theater watching Zack Snyder's *Watchmen* back in 2009 in Manhattan. I loved everything about it and had never seen a comic book come to life quite like this. The colors, characters, and imagery. . . . I remember walking out of the theater thinking Zack Snyder needs to do *Justice League.* Years later (especially after *MOS* and *BVS*), I still think he needs to do *Justice League.* #ReleaseTheSnyderCut."

Thomas Gemmell: "I like all superhero and comic book movies, but many of them are about the humans dealing with their skills or powers. Lacking superpowers, I can't relate, although I can enjoy the thrill ride. *Man of Steel* and *Batman v Superman* are thrill rides which are really about characters struggling with mortality, love, family, friendship, identity, regrets, loss, grief, and the battle to be better. In short, they are about what it's like to live life as a human. I can relate to that. Thanks, Zack."

Kyle Ericksen: "I knew Zack was something special and unique when I walked out of that theater the FIRST of many times seeing *Dawn* . . . then *300* came along and flipped my world upside down in the best way possible, and I never looked at movies the same after that. . . . Thank you again Zack for your out-of-this-world filmmaking style and movies."

Keith Davis: "Zack, your interpretations of my childhood-favorite DC characters have been amazing (as the theatrical release of *JL* should've been). Awaiting the release of Zack Snyder's *JL* has truly been one of my superhero-life's passions. When I'm finally able to see it, it will be one of the milestones of my superhero life. Many thanks to you for making my superhero dreams come true. Good luck to you with this and all future endeavors. Be safe and be well."

Scott McClellan: "While I talked elsewhere about how much I appreciate your movies artistically and how they've inspired me creatively in podcasting, I wanted to take this opportunity to thank you for providing me countless opportunities to spend quality father/son time with my dad. We saw *300* together for our first time. I took him to see *Watchmen* in theatres and used that as an opportunity to inspire him to read the graphic novel. But it was seeing the Thursday night previews for both *Man of Steel* and *Batman v Superman: Dawn of Justice* that have led to countless conversations between us over the years. Thank you for that. As I've gotten older, seeing movies with my dad have not been as frequent as they once were, but thanks to you and your movies, I will also have some special times with him to cherish."

Matt Morris: "Zack, no one can imagine what you and Debbie have gone through over the years, but as you already know, the community is 100% behind you guys. We love you and hope to one day see your vision for the DCEU come to light. I want the Anti-Life Equation. I want Darkseid. I want J'onn J'onnzz, the Green Lantern, and everything else you had planned that was robbed from us. All the best in your future endeavors and, as always, #ReleaseTheSnyderCut."

Pedro Giuffra: "[*BvS*] tells a story of these fantastic heroes in a real world, always maintaining the essence that has made these characters mythical throughout the ages but giving them real, political, philosophical, and moral problems. Where you can always find something new over and over. Zack made that. After this, I could not see this genre of movies in the same way as before. . . . This is why I am here fighting for the movie, Zack Snyder's *Justice League,* which closes the *Man of Steel* story arc as its director had it in mind. And fighting for Zack, the director, the man, and the father . . . who gave me the best movie of superheroes ever . . . until now (#ReleaseTheSnyderCut)."

Alessandro Maniscalco: "Your storytelling ability is like a superpower. *Batman v Superman: Dawn of Justice* has had such an enormous impact on me. It means a great deal how much respect you've given the characters. The film is sheer genius. I'm so sorry for all the hardships you and your family have had to endure. Thank you for all your hard work and care! I can't wait to see your *Justice League*! #ReleaseTheSnyderCut!"

Frank Marchant: "The catalyst for inspiring my love for film as an art form was one of your films—*Batman v Superman: Dawn of Justice.* The careful craftsmanship of interweaving references to Greek mythology, the Bible, pop-culture media and historical figures and events, all of which is used to serve the themes of the movie, made a huge impact on me. It is that type of excellent craftsmanship in art which I strive to achieve, and which you have inspired me to pursue. Thank you, Zack Snyder, for igniting a passion within me to strive for higher goals with my artistic skills, in the hopes that our art can make a positive impact to our world for the days to come."

Irving Mendieta: "It's hard for me to put into words just how much your films mean to me. How much your films have inspired me. How personal and intimate the experiences are to me. How absorbed I get into the worlds you create in every film, and how many emotions I get through with every rewatch. I wanted to say, Boss, that in your films, I have found very strong ideals of honor, kindness, and heroism. Your films have made me grow, have made me a better person, and are part of my identity. So I wanted to say, Zack, sir, THANK YOU."

James: "Zack, your passionate vision in movies and storytelling has had a profound effect on me the last six years. I am turning 30 next month, and it's only now I realize that making movies and telling stories is what I want to do in life. I've never felt happier about that, and sure of who I am, and in moments of challenge and adversity, it's still always worth the risk. So for this, I thank you, sir."

Simon Persson: "Thank you for being such an amazing guy. I'd like to say thank you for making movies that I can't even describe how much I love, such as *Batman v Superman, Man of Steel, 300,* and *Watchmen.* Your movies have inspired me, made me happy, made me cry, and so much more! I would like to extend my thanks to you for all the hard work you put down in every movie you make, and I look forward to seeing Zack Snyder's *Justice League.* You're amazing. Have a good one!"

Kevin Miller: "You're one of my favorite directors, and I knew you would craft another gorgeous and satisfying epic. It still breaks my heart how the theatrical release of *Justice League* came out. You deserve better, and the day you're able to release your true vision, I will cry with joy. That day can't come soon enough."

Jacob Guzman: "I love all your films and filmmaking style. [You are] truly one of the best directors working today. It was awful what happened to *Justice League.* I hope everyone in the world gets to see your completed vision be brought to the big screen. Take care, and I hope you and your family are doing well."

Marcus Brown: "Just want to let you know that you inspire me, and I love all of your films. Never stop making art."

Sahib Ari: "I just want to basically say that you mean the world to me, and to everyone who is a part of the fandom! And thank you for bringing my favorite characters to the big screen!"

M. Khizer Butt: "I just want you to know that you and your work changed the life and mind of this hopeless boy from Pakistan forever. You taught me the importance of 'HOPE' and optimism. Thank you for everything. I hope to see Zack Snyder's *Justice League* soon."

EPILOGUE

Kieran Fraval: "Thank you, Zack Snyder, for all the things you have done for your army of fans. Thank you for being yourself, a beautiful soul and a phenomenal director, the best of our time. You can't even imagine what your work and yourself mean to me. You gave me hope and strength when I needed it the most. I am sending all my love to the Snyder family."

Abraham Hernandez: "I'm not a man of many words. I'm usually pretty shy. I would just say, I love your movies. Been a fan since *Dawn of the Dead*. I want to thank you for bringing to life the characters I love, for bringing on iterations of Batman I've always wanted to see on the big screen. I hold *MOS* and *BvS* closely to my heart as my favorite movies ever. Thank you, much love, and many blessings to you and Debbie. Can't wait to watch your *Justice League*."

Tony Nyakundi: "Mine is a short message. I wanted to tell you thank you for being an inspiration to me, a young African kid. Your movies have been a big inspiration to me, especially *Batman v Superman*. Your work together with Chris Terrio has helped me a lot in my essay writing, speech making, and it drove me into wanting to read vastly, especially about Greek mythology. I also indulged some Norse mythology. Anyway, what I'm saying is, keep being you. I admire you as a person and movie maker."

Helder Oliveira: "I just want to say thank you for making true a 37-year dream. My whole life, I wished to see a Batman and Superman crossover in flesh and bone. Warner denied fans this crossover for years, and it wouldn't have finally happened without the amazing *Man of Steel*, directed by you. I still have hopes of seeing a larger world of DC heroes come to life, with you in command, beginning with the REAL *Justice League* movie that was denied to us."

Travis Duty: "Zack, your films have helped me process and deal with my own struggles in life. Thank you for giving hope to the hopeless."

Ahmad Kamal: "I hope by the time the book comes out, Zack Snyder's *Justice League* is already here. And boy, I can't wait for that day to happen. The ultimate prize for the fight we have fought for years. I cannot imagine something better as a prize. . . . #ReleaseTheSnyderCut for us, and justice for Zack Snyder. From Malaysia, with love."

Dallin Hancock: "You are my favorite filmmaker and one of my favorite people, and it's difficult to describe how much your movies mean to me. How do you explain a love that defies all description? . . . Your movies transcend the medium of entertainment to depict these dark, cruel, and violent worlds, and you insist that even in such worlds, goodness and beauty and sacrificial love can still exist and are even more powerful than the darkness itself. That is a message I take with me far beyond the movie medium. It is a charge I lead with every day of my life. It wouldn't be facetious of me to say these movies saved me. So thank you, Zack. Thank you for everything."

Mariano Gomez: "You did the impossible, making these characters real, and I'm very grateful I got to see it. I want you to know that I can see what you've done and I know who you are. I will not stop supporting your work, even after Zack Snyder's *Justice League* is released! You brought the heroes I love to life the way I needed them. You made them real. Thank you."

Brian Scully: "The quest for the holy grail that is Zack Snyder's *Justice League* has let me be a part of an amazing and determined worldwide fan movement, and it has been my pleasure to partake. I cannot wait for its release to vindicate everyone involved, from the cast and crew to Zack himself, and to finally have the original vision out there for the fans who, like me, have been unable to let go and get the appropriate follow up to *BvS* that we deserved. I hope it's already out, or at least announced, by the time this is published. But if not, then you'll find me online, still hyping it and asking for it. I'll never give up."

Renato Gomes: "Your films have always deeply moved me. What I appreciate more than your style is your personality. It is deep, strong, and honest. You are an example that I truly admire. When your career was attacked, you stayed human. You have admirers watching your back. Hero!"

Ollie Zenzer: "You made me fall in love with my childhood heroes all over again, and made me discover a passion in my life: movies. It's my hope (Superman's 'S') that one day I can be involved in the movie industry somehow, whether it's performing, or coming up with ideas. All the best Zack, and keep making movies you love and are passionate about."

Steve Buryk: "You've changed my life, and changed how I feel about these characters forever. I will never stop fighting and being vocal for your films, and especially getting your version of *Justice League* released. After all you've done for us, it's the least we can do for you. Thank you."

M. Haider Ali: "I hope that one day we get to see your *JL*. Zack Snyder's *Justice League*. We love you, and this movement means the world to us. Know that we won't stop. Know that we wouldn't stop. Know that we will stand united and fight until the end. We will Unite the Seven if we have to, but we will not rest until I have Zack Snyder's *Justice League* in my collection. Much love and respect to you, Boss."

The ACS Universe: "Thank you for modernizing Superman, my favorite comic book character of all time! Thank you for the constant fan interaction. Thank you for *BvS*, because it has helped so many get through tough times in their lives!"

Josh Byrdic: "Simply stated, Zack Snyder is an inspiration to many. Whether it's through creative filmmaking, or by the way he encourages others to live an active lifestyle. Many are inspired by his interest in racquetball, working out, or simply by doing what he loves, but he never holds back. His approach towards conflict is a testament of his character. Zack pursues life as we know it with a relentless passion, which is a breath of fresh air for younger generations and up-and-coming filmmakers."

Vishal K: "This movement is all about artistic integrity, and directors getting freedom from the studios to express their vision on screen, and I would love to let you know that your movie *Man of Steel* is my favorite comic book movie of all time. It has impacted me personally, when I was going through a tough phase for seven months in the last year. The dialogues in the film are simply so inspiring, and I'm in a better place now thanks to you. I will always be grateful to you for that, and will continue to watch your movies and get inspired."

Chris Hutton: "To me, the Snyder Cut of *Justice League* is a MUST SEE! . . . Us fans deserve to see it, and YOU deserve to be able to show it! I hope by the time this book written by Sean O'Connell releases, we will have seen your film the way it was meant to be seen. . . . You're an amazing director, and one of the all-time best visualizers when it comes to capturing film. I hope to see your cut of *Justice League* one day and wish you nothing but the best for your career moving forward."

Ryan Bridgewood: "Your talents as a filmmaker and director hold no bounds. Your art [is] truly stunning. Your art inspires thousands of aspiring filmmakers and writers like myself to dream big. Thank you for bringing us all together in the #ReleaseTheSnyderCut movement. Artistic integrity is key, and should be a number-one rule for filmmaking. We will join you in the sun. Thanks for helping us accomplish wonders."

Carlos Maranon Cardin: "I just wanted to say thank you from the bottom of my heart. You have been able to make the best movies in the history of the superhero genre. You have honored and glorified my favorite hero, Superman, and you have reflected on him what hope really means. . . . Your movies inspire us, and even make us better people."

Luis Mederos Jimenez: "I keep fighting every day for artistic freedom and integrity, to fix this huge injustice. And on a more personal level, I keep doing this with the hope that one day, my best friend from the beyond will watch [your *Justice League*] alongside me."

Joe Kelleher: "Zack, thanks for all the art."

Tanmay Gupta: "I'm a big and proud fan of Zack Snyder from India. I'm eagerly waiting for the Snyder Cut, because the theatrical cut was a complete mess! It was not the actual Zack Snyder movie. Cringy CGI, unnecessary jokes . . . the theatrical cut was a completely different movie. I want the Snyder Cut because I want to see Darkseid, Cyborg and The Flash's backstories, Junkie XL's background score, and many other surprises. The real, 214-minute Zack Snyder's *Justice League*."

EPILOGUE

Jeremy Vincenti: "Thank you for sharing with us your art. You are so generous with us. Passionate. I will keep fighting for #ReleaseTheSnyderCut. And you know what? I pray you can finish your story. It can become one of the most impressive and artful sagas in the history of cinema. . . . I send you all the love, strength, and thanks, from Bastia, on my little island of Corsica."

Iby Shalabi: "My name is Iby Shalabi, aka the Maldivian Superman, and officially Australia's Biggest Superman Fan. An alter ego that started shortly after filming started for your *Man of Steel* movie. . . . The #ReleaseTheSnyderCut movement has truly been a beautiful movement that has brought people together from all over the world through charity and art, and I am so proud to be a part of it. We will continue to fight for creative independence in the film industry, and will never give up hope for Zack Snyder's *Justice League* to be released. After all, it's not an 'S.' It means hope."

Mark Schultis: "As an author, I know of the anxiety associated with composing a lengthy work and hoping early seeds come to fruit. The fandom was with you through it all and still are, as well as the cast, so the insights and reveals . . . stick with it. Your heroes had specific journeys, and it's time to see their intended destinations! Richard Donner got his *Superman II* cut. No reason *Justice League* can't get yours. Every drama deserves its finale."

Nathan Damasceno Gadelha Rocha: "The way Zack Snyder crafts each of his films made me appreciate cinema as a whole, and the gateway to that was falling in true love with *BvS*. The world put Superman on trial. And even if he doubted for some moments, he still tried to do the right thing . . . that is true hope. Zack Snyder made me love Superman because of that, and also made me interested to see the whole story he had prepared for that character. That's why I say #ReleaseTheSnyderCut!"

James Harrison: "Zack, there's so much I want to say. It would fill a novel. I'll sum it down. Thank you, so much, for the best movies I've ever seen. They've changed the way I see the world. I hope and pray that one day, your vision will come in full. The bell cannot be unrung."

EPILOGUE

Pedro Calderon: "You are an inspiration to me. Seeing your movies is like entering a museum and seeing pictures of extreme beauty. Thank you for everything, and I hope you continue offering your vision for many years."

Juan Pavon: "Zack, I am a great admirer of you, both as a filmmaker and as a person. I really hope to see your Zack Snyder's *Justice League,* and enjoy it like with *Man of Steel* and *Batman v Superman: Dawn of Justice.* And of course, I really hope that you can finish the movie arc that you had in mind from the beginning. Thanks for everything, Zack. #ReleaseTheSnyderCut."

Eddie Trevizo: "Hey Zack, I just wanted to take this opportunity to thank you for entertaining me for the past 15 years or so. . . . You're the best Hollywood action director in the market, for sure. Thanks so much for making movies that give me hope and inspiration, continue to do so, and maybe one day you'll get to see mine."

Tyler Drinkard: "Thank you Zack for giving us movies that not only look incredible, but make us feel something. You are a beacon of hope in these hard times for many, and your movies will always bring light to someone's darkness."

Francisco Vivallo: "The #ReleaseTheSnyderCut movement means much more than only asking for the true cut of the film (which is obviously very exciting, as well). It means union, and caring for each other. I've been a fan of these characters for a long time, and they couldn't be in better hands. Love your work. Keep it coming, please."

Morgan Maric: "My stories are my life. That's the only way I can think of to explain just how much you and your work have meant to me for the majority of my life. Thank you, Zack. For the impact your characters have had on my life, for your movies giving me hours of entertainment and immeasurable joy, for—no exaggeration—saving my life with your work. Thank you so much."

Jeffery Warfield: "I would like to tell [Zack Snyder] thank you for inspiring me to go back to my roots for my YouTube channel, so I can use my gift of dance to try to change the world."

EPILOGUE

Zac Langridge: "Thank you for helping me see the beauty, inspiration, and appeal of superheroes. Thank you for inspiring me and bringing me films that have encouraged me to keep going and pursuing hope, even in the darkest of times. Much love and support from Zac Langridge, in Wellington, New Zealand."

Captain Ramsey: "Zack not only made me appreciate cinema and slower-formed storytelling, but he puts so much thought, love, and care [into his films]. He and Deborah deeply respect the craft. . . . This is why I fight. We need to get justice for Zack, Deborah, and David Ayer. That's not up for debate. . . . I see myself in each of these characters because they're so relatable. I truly appreciate the grounded yet fantastical approach to this tapestry, and we need more of that bold voice in comic-based movies."

Levi Heitzman: "My message for Zack is just one of immense gratitude. *Man of Steel* came out earlier the same year my grandfather committed suicide. Between that and severe depression and anxiety, I was a wreck. That movie slowly became my comfort zone. Watching multiple times a week its messages of hope, coupled with therapy, helped me overcome rock bottom and get back to a version of normal. Honestly, without that movie as an anchor point, I don't know if I could have come back. I could go on forever about this. But I just want to tell him thank you!"

Chris Bazos: "When *Man of Steel* came out, it really helped me with what was going on in my life. Especially after my father had passed away 12 years prior to the movie coming out. The way you depicted Superman, a.k.a. Clark Kent, was amazing. The bond he had with his mother was akin to the bond I had made with my mother after my father passed. And the relationship between Clark and his dad was very similar to the relationship I had with my father. I hope we some day can see your version and vision of what you had."

Siddhant Jhaveri: "Hey Zack, I wouldn't know the first thing I could say to you. Honestly, you are my hero. . . . And now I feel so special being part of this beautiful family, a family driven by something so pure and passionate as art. Your art."

Juned Shaikh: "There was a time in my life, a few years back, where I wasn't okay. My health was getting worse. Also, I started to go into depression. I was frozen in my life. I dropped out of college. Something I got to know from Zack, though, is that everything can be controlled and reimagined. So I just hit the gym for the first time in my life. And guess what? Even as a lone, sad dude, I kept going, but with hope. . . . And that is why this movement is so important, and a part of my life."

Andrew J. Silva: "Thank you so much for your adaption of DC's heroes. I cannot even begin to express the amount of love, admiration, and respect I have for your work. You truly made me believe in the age of heroes. I'd give anything in the world to see you continue to work on DC films."

James Hickey: "Zack, your films mean a lot to me. You and your films have inspired me to go and study film production here in Ireland. I hope to one day see your *Justice League*. Through this Release the Snyder Cut movement, I have wonderful people who share my love for these films. Thank you for being so good to your fans, Zack."

Teo Vucic: "I want to thank you for everything you have done for me with your films. As an immigrant myself, what you did with Superman was something special. You made me see the best parts of myself every day. You created this wonderful movement that helped me create new friendships. Your impact will never be forgotten. Keep inspiring, one day at a time. Can't wait to watch your *Justice League* film as it was intended. Thank you!"

Venkata Lokesh Duvvuri: "Mr. Snyder, thank you for making me understand the character of Superman. *Man of Steel* was the first film that I saved enough money [so I could] watch in IMAX. *BvS* was a film that spoke to me on a personal level. Hope your version of *Justice League* is released soon. May you make many more films for audiences to enjoy."

Abdulredha Gadanfar: "I'd just like to thank Zack for all the amazing films he's given us. We will always be grateful!"

Megat Danial: "Just want to let you know I've been a huge fan of your work since *Man of Steel* and it is my favorite film of all time. *BvS* also inspired me to one day be a filmmaker. I have been part of the #ReleaseTheSnyderCut movement since day one, and did my best spreading the word out at a local comic book convention here in Kuala Lumpur, Malaysia. Just want to say thank you for all your hard work, and we fans will continue to support your vision."

Victor Tolstik: "What would I say if there was a chance to send a message to one of my favorite directors of all time? To a person whose movies have reached the deepest parts of my soul and filled me with inspiration and hope? To a filmmaker whose works reveal something new and exciting even after dozens of viewings? To a man whose passion towards his craft is so prominent, that it has translated itself from cinema screens around the world into us? Every of those questions can be summed up as, 'What would I say to Zack Snyder?' My answer is simple. Thank you. Thank you for what you did, are doing right now, and hopefully will continue to do. You've already built your monument, which can be seen in a lot of passionate and faithful fans across the globe. And I am proud to be one of them."

Rui Borges (MetalCreep): "Zack Snyder proved that he loves his work, and respect and loves the fans. We are united! Thank you! #Release TheSnyderCut."

Julian Terence Seguin: "I am really excited by this movement. This is definitely a first in the history of filmmaking, and you are at the center. I've always been a fan of your movies, and that was before I knew what a cool guy you were. I'm proud to be on your team. I made some new friends, shared special experiences, and I would say I've become a better person. Helping you fulfill your vision is a great honor."

Luke McClounan: "Zack Snyder's *Justice League* has become something of a legend, but I have no doubt you can live up to that legend. Though I know we will likely never see your vision completed, the enthusiasm for us to see the *Justice League*, YOUR *Justice League*, doesn't waver. Thank you for providing us with these characters and showing us that they are inherently human. #ReleaseTheSnyderCut."

Souphian Ladjenef: "I wish we could be friends and hang out together. I didn't care about Superman before *Man of Steel*. And you changed everything.

EPILOGUE

Thank you for everything you have done, and for your passion. I won't give up on you. We do this together. #ReleaseTheSnyderCut."

Alex: "Thank you, Zack, for all your movies. Hope never dies."

Josten: "You are very creative, outstanding, and a phenomenon in directing films. I absolutely love DC movies, but I want to tell that you should publish your version of the *Justice League* that Joss Whedon shot."

Alexander Khan: "I just wanted to thank you, Zack, for giving myself and many other DC fans from Bangladesh and all over the world the perfect representation of DC on the big screen. I never thought in my lifetime that I would see a movie that would impact my life so much. . . . I came as a Batman fan to the DCEU. I am leaving DC movies as a Zack Snyder fan. #ReleaseTheSnyderCut."

Chris Yuan: "I want to take this opportunity to thank Zack Snyder for bringing me into the world of cinema. *BvS* showed me another possibility of cinema back when I was so ignorant, and watched movies just for fun. It reshaped me as a film lover. Now I'm trying to watch more movies and enjoy the beauty of powerful art. Thank you, Zack, for everything! And as always, #ReleaseTheSnyderCut."

Junior Titan: "I am so grateful for Zack Snyder, the greatest director!"

Spencer Nunn: "You have been an inspiration to me as a filmmaker. I learned from your art, but more importantly, I learned from your integrity. Thank you for everything."

Carlisle Wells: "As cheesy as it sounds, Zack Snyder made me feel like a superhero while watching his films. Never has a fandom stood so firmly behind a director and his art. Why do I fight for the #ReleaseTheSnyderCut movement? For artistic integrity, for the cast and crew, for Zack, and most importantly, for Autumn."

Brandon Hess: "I want to say directly to Zack Snyder that my thoughts and prayers have continually gone out because of the tragedy that occurred.

Autumn Snyder was such a beautiful lady, and I'm sure she lived a beautiful life. I think she would have wanted you to finish the *Justice League* movie. And do it in memory of her."

David Cookson: "I'm actually grateful for the delay (though not the circumstances) as you both have connected with the fans in a way previously not seen, at least not that I'm aware of. Thank you both for all that you do."

Sharang Mulgaonkar: "Can't wait to watch your *Justice League* movie. I look forward to watching *Army of The Dead* on Netflix with excitement, and I wish that Warner Bros. #ReleaseTheSnyderCut of *Justice League*."

Jose Eduardo Leal: "Thanks for letting us see your view of our favorite superheroes. Thanks for inspiring us to be better. With all of my geek heart, I wish this comes true. #ReleaseTheSnyderCut and #ReleaseTheSnyder Vision. Giant hug from Bogotá, Colombia."

Timothy Way: "Thank you so much, Zack, for showing such unparalleled commitment to your loyal fans, who consider your efforts to reach out and connect with us a valuable and rare experience that has opened us all up to new possibilities in the way new media is created, released, and experienced. You are a genuine and very human soul we are lucky to have."

Amanda Pereira: "I've lived with an abusive family for years, and since 2016, I dealt with constant semi-open sexual harassment by a family member. Never really built much of a circle of friends and contacts due to autism, being trans, and other things that kind of push people away. . . . After the #Release TheSnyderCut movement started, I found friends over time, people who are also different in their own ways, people who did not discriminate me, people who cared. They became my friends eventually, the Snyder's Amazons being the ones that mostly took the time to send me messages of support and listen to me when I felt full of bad thoughts due to living in that place and in that condition. . . . I can finally start living now, at 28 years of age. Thank you for Zack, Justin, the Amazons, and the movement. I don't feel alone anymore."

Corey Hobbs: "I truly can't wait to see your *Justice League* film and the many others, as I've been talking about them non-stop to my girlfriend for years now. Thank you for sharing your art with the world. It has very much changed me, and made me a better man today. #ReleaseTheSnyderCut."

Marco Muscatello: "I appreciate you as a director and visionary. But most importantly, I appreciate you as a person. I can see that you are first and foremost a family man, a great person to work with, very kind, generous, and always thoughtful towards your fans."

Andre Fernandez: "Thank you for the amazing films that you have contributed to the world. They inspire creativity and imagination, and have given me a new perspective on the world. The #ReleaseTheSnyderCut movement has served multiple purposes in the world, and would not exist without the courage you inspire. Thank you, Zack, for being you."

Michael Schinke: "I can account for my life as a serious movie fan as being clearly bisected into pre- and post-*Batman v Superman* periods. Before *BvS*, I was content to let movies simply pass before me as a way to occupy time, and I didn't engage in any conversations deeper than expressions like, 'That was cool.' But when the intellectual shit hit the critical fan following *BvS*'s release, along with the re-agitation of the vitriol against *Man of Steel*, I felt like I had to elevate my film-consciousness in an extreme way to understand why the supposedly obvious problems didn't seem to irk me as they did others. I found myself reading about film theory, researching cinematography and editing, gobbling up articles about storytelling and character arc and story craft. . . . I will never not be grateful for the opportunity those movies helped me make."

Ryan Wilson: "Thank you for everything you've done for my favorite characters through your films. It's hard to sum up what your films mean to myself and many others, but just know your work makes a lot of people happy, and that we're all behind you!"

Marko Zaklan: "Thank you for all the love and support that you have given us to continue fighting for the true Zack Snyder's *Justice League*. At this moment, we still do not know when (if) it will be released, and I can only wish that you #ReleaseTheSnyderCut one day."

EPILOGUE

Christopher Graham: "I am a lifelong Superman fan. My love of the character led me to become a teacher. I have a deep love for the original movies. I love the reinvention of the character by Zack Snyder, and hope to see it continue with his version of *Justice League*."

Mike Ward: "As a retinal surgeon, I appreciate your professionalism and dedication to your craft. As a husband and father of two daughters, I can't imagine going through what you have endured. My deepest condolences. As you are fond of saying, 'Powerful art can heal, bring awareness, and create change.' . . . Thanks again for all the time and effort you put into your art. It resonates with me and many others, as you can see."

Haruko Hitomi: "Zack Snyder, I wanted you to know how much of an inspiration you've been to me. Your movies have lifted me out of dark times, even just temporarily. Times where I felt hopeless and devoid. Your movies have inspired my own stories, those of which I hope I'll be able to show you one of these days. You're not just my favorite movie director, you're one of my favorite people, period."

Andrea Abbatista: "I want to thank you for being the way you are as an artist, with your fans and with your family. I love your art. I feel it so close to my heart, your way of telling stories, your aesthetics, and the vision you capture in each frame speaks of Modern Mythology. I hope one day, not far away, you can realize and conclude your saga in five parts, because you deserve it, and it would be an emotional satisfaction to see your fresco, finally completed. Always stay as you are. Thank you from the bottom of my heart. Un enorme abbraccio dall'Italia."

Gary Harwood: "Thank you, Zack, for giving us such a great interpretation of these characters, bringing the 'Gods Among Us' theme into the modern world. I love the level of detail and context poured into these films, which adds to each viewing, and really appreciate that you were doing something different with the genre."

Sukhjinder Matharu: "Where do I begin? So much to say but the more that is said, the less it feels. I just wanted to express my deepest gratitude and heartfelt thanks for being who you are, a role model and example at being one of the greatest visionary creatives I have had the honor of acknowledging."

Juliusz Kaźmierczak: "Thank you. For changing my life, and for delivering everything that I was dreaming for since I was six. Thank you, and stay fantastic."

Tevin Antwi: "I look forward to seeing your *Justice League* on the big screen to conclude your chapter of this series. Thank you, Zack, for bringing my childhood heroes to life and giving them that depth."

Harvey Hissey: "I wanted to say a massive thank you to Zack Snyder for helping me understand the art that goes into film making, and to allow my aspirations to grow into making a short film with an iPhone, which was inspired by *Snow Steam Iron*, proving that if you want to make a film, then just film it. . . . Thank you, Zack, for inspiring me and many, many more around the globe."

Brian Boulay: "I just want to say thank you for making *Man of Steel* and *Batman v Superman*. Those films have had a tremendous impact on me, providing countless hours of joy while invoking thought and breeding inspiration. I truly hope we get to see your cut of *Justice League*. Rooting for you in all of your endeavors. Health and happiness to you and your family."

The Witcher King: "Thank you for being one of the nicest, sweetest, and coolest people in the world. Thank you for sharing your beautiful art with us. Thank you for being so daring and uncompromising in your art and work. Thank you for bringing together a great community of people. Thank you for inspiring many like me to learn and study more about film and cinema. Thank you for being a great storyteller. I can't wait to see what you do in the future, and I wish you all the best."

Naveenshankar Parameshwar: "*Man of Steel* showed me a world full of hope and optimism. *Batman v Superman* showed me a world full of pain and tragedy. *Wonder Woman* is a step forward for feminism. Clark gave me hope, Bruce fueled my strength, and Diana gave me the courage to fight the good fight. Superman, Batman, and Wonder Woman, aka DC's Trinity. These characters were an antidote for me, and helped me in the darkest time of my life. Thank you, Zack Snyder."

Haik Diloyan: "I want to thank you from the bottom of my heart for not only providing masterful artistic movies, but for leaving such a mark on the industry. . . . We are blessed to have gotten a director with your vision, intelligence, skill, integrity, and courage. We will never see another like you. Thank you again."

James: "Zack, your films go beyond just being movies. They are pieces of artwork created, scripted, and filmed with love and passion. *MoS* and *BvS* are masterpieces, and set the standard for comic book movies. No doubt Zack Snyder's *JL* will be the perfect continuation, which will show the world that WB were fools to change your vision. Your movies have inspired me and so many others, so please keep doing what you do best."

Massimiliano Orione: "I'm an art student and movie journalist from Italy. What I'd love for you to know, Zack, is that you and your art shaped my life more than you could imagine. Your *Man of Steel* made me fall in love with cinema, and your *Batman v Superman* taught me to be brave and confident. It also inspired me to make the big step towards the woman I love, my Alessia, and to propose to her. . . . You're a master, Zack. Thank you for your art. You saved me in unexpected and incredible ways, and I'll be forever grateful for that."

Jake Gannon: "I am a huge fan of your work. In fact, I consider you one of, if not my main idol. I know you have probably heard this from your other, more vocal fans, but I just wanted you to know how much of an impact you and your work have had on my life."

Daniel Notz: "Thank you for your passion, for your heart, and for bringing my favorite heroes to life in a way I've never seen before. Your movies are filled with philosophy, Easter eggs, copious amounts of detail, and the best action I've ever seen on the big screen. You've inspired me, and so many others, to follow their hearts and chase their dreams. I can't wait to see what the future holds for you, and the films you create!"

Leon Bright: "We're told that genre work and comics are 'for kids,' but you continue to prove everyone wrong by filming the unfilmable. I respect the strength of you and your wife, Deborah. The strength that it must take in order to bring everyone in your family together, to pull each other through life's many obstacles. Thank you for being a powerhouse behind the camera, and an inspiration in life."

Eddie Hawley: "I just want to say to Zack, thank you."

Boomborks: "Hey Zack, I'm a university student from New Zealand and a huge fan of yours. I just wanted to let you know that your films have had such a positive impact on my life and the lives of countless others from around the world. Your passion and enthusiasm for the craft of filmmaking is truly inspiring. It certainly inspired me, as I am currently studying film, largely thanks to *BvS*."

Faiq Sharin: "I'm Faiq Sharin, one of your Malaysian fans. . . . Sometimes when I feel like I'm being pulled down to Earth due to uninvited circumstances, [your] inspiring films will always be my favorite so I can stand firm on my feet again especially *MoS* (2013) and *BvS: UE* (2016). We can't wait to see the sequel of your upcoming films, *Army of The Dead, Fountainhead* and, mainly, your *Justice League*."

Joseph Ramos: "Your films inspired me to pursue the idea of filmmaking, because I have some big ideas I hope to show others, and hopefully, some people can relate to them or inspire them. Thank you Zack, but to Deborah, and all of those who worked on your films. I hope one day we can see your vision for *Justice League*. God bless you and your family."

James Anthony: "Mr. Snyder you are a real-life superhero. You always stand for what's right, and no matter if life puts you down a hundred times, you are the example of a man who gets up a hundred and one times."

Karan Saggi: "When I walked out of your last movie (*BvS*), I felt that I had just experienced every single emotion humanly possible. I had experienced what it must feel like to live the full cycle of a lifetime. I laughed, cried, jumped with excitement, cheered, gasped in shock, broke down, learned to pick myself up, and hope for better. Walking out, I felt that all the color that had leaked out of my life was back. I felt wiser, grateful, and removed from anxiety. . . . Your work changed my life for the better. Thank you!"

Erik Winkler: "Just wanted to let all people know that your movies made superhero movies serious, and more than movies. Real cinema."

Robert Murphy: "Thank you! Your movies have connected with my family and I in a way that no others have. Opening night for your films is an event for us, and the anticipation leading up to that first viewing is indescribable. You bring an immense amount of joy to so many, and we are all grateful."

Austin Daniels: "I just need this moment in our lives to express my gratitude. You took such beloved icons, and brought them to us in such an organic, earthy, visceral way. You've inspired so many lives, and given outsiders like me a vial of hope in this dark, confusing world. Thank you for showcasing morals on such an epic scale, through characters who, deep down, reflect our own humanity. Thank you for being real."

Mercury: "If I could let Zack know anything, I'd want it to be that he is loved, and the hard work and dedication he puts into his movies doesn't go unnoticed by a lot of us DC fans, way more than he knows. . . . THANK YOU ZACK SNYDER for everything you've done for us. You are the greatest!"

Hamad Al-Mansouri: "Your art has been an inspiration to me to work in film. You, as a person, have been an inspiration for me to become a better and stronger person. You mean the world to a lot of people, including myself. Never compromise, even in the face of Armageddon. The world needs you."

Derek Nochefranca: "As an artist, as a comic reader, as a film lover, and as someone who hopes to work with you and The Stone Quarry film and animation studio someday, thank you for all that you have created. . . . Thank you for your art, and thank you for challenging me. It will continue to inspire me and my work forever. We're with you, Zack and Debbie. It would be a pleasure to work with you someday. You've brought me, and so many, HOPE. Thank you."

Louis Bromfield: "I will keep fighting for your vision, and so too will the whole movement. There are more out there than any of us realize, and we will never, ever stop. Thank you for reminding me that all the gods are within me. It has filled me with strength on my hardest and most difficult days. Now let's #ReleaseTheSnyderCut already."

George Weston: "Thank you for giving us *Man of Steel* and *Batman v Superman,* films which are groundbreaking in confronting what it means to be a superhero in these times. I love your interpretations of the characters and how you reinvent them for the modern era."

Mark Collinge: "Like everyone else in here, I really hope to see your *Justice League* one day. It deserves to be seen. Keep up the awesome work!"

Dantius: "*Batman v Superman* is my favorite movie. It told a story about who and what these characters are, what they mean to us, and how the problems of our world would affect them. It delivered my favorite fictional character, a Superman who embodies the common decency and volunteer virtue of the average Joe. For all these reasons and more, I am thankful to director Zack Snyder, and I hope to see the third chapter of his epic story in the near future."

Sayantan Das: "An inspiring man, a role model, a great family man, and one of the best directors working in this industry. Your visionary storytelling has inspired many, and gave them hope. Your films have taught us to be brave, hopeful, and optimistic. I hope we get to see your vision of *Justice League* someday. We will not retreat. Thank you for everything."

Aakash Sengupta: "You changed my life, my perspective, my attitude towards films and life. You made me face the uncomfortable realities so simply, yet so beautifully, through your films."

Dominic Ryland-Jones: "Your kindness, passion, and creativity have been an encouragement to me over the last two years. Seeing how you have come through so much pain and difficulty, stronger than ever and with maturity and respect at all times towards even those who wronged you, continues to inspire me."

EPILOGUE

David Musil: "Our names are David (31) and Erika (31), and we love your work, Zack. . . . We wish to thank you this way for your encouragement of DC and comic fandom. We will keep fighting for you. Sending our love to you and your family from Prague. Thank you for everything."

Victor Griggio: "I want to thank Zack Snyder for being an awesome man and human being, who cares for his fans and his fans' passion. Thank you for all you've done, Boss. #ReleaseTheSnyderCut, always."

Steven Norton: "Your stories reignited my creativity, inspired my own writings (both musical and literary), and helped heal my mental and emotional health. I can't thank you enough for showing us that a person can come back from the wrong path, and to always try being the best versions of ourselves."

Rene Valdez: "I just want to say thank you, Zack, for showcasing your style and vision and having such a passion for what you do, and how meticulous you are about details in your films. Your contributions to DC on Film won't be forgotten, and I sincerely hope your vision of *Justice League* will soon be realized."

Eric Alex Cantero: "Zack Snyder has brought to me a wider landscape of cinematography, and it continues to inspire me in my projects. I am dying to see what he has done with the *Justice League*."

James Quagliarello: "My 3-year-old son has watched Superman take flight in *Man of Steel* countless times. Yet, every time, he remains in wonder and 'flies' around our house with him. It brings me so much joy. Please know that your work continues to bring joy to generations of people who love these characters. I hope one day I get to tell you this in person, but for now this will do."

Matt Appleby: "You are a huge inspiration in filmmaking, and in life, to myself and so many people. Just know that you have helped and improved so many lives, and that you and Debbie truly make the world a better place. Thank you so much for all that you do."

EPILOGUE

Cristian Penaloza: "Thanks for giving a powerful message to the artists of the world: never compromise your work. That's the only way to keep [the] purity of an idea, and beauty in art. Art truly can heal. #ReleaseTheSnyderCut."

Dennis Jensen: "Zack inspires me to pursue greater things in life and stay true to myself while doing so. I engaged myself in the #ReleaseTheSnyder Cut movement as my way of showing gratitude, and I will stay vigilant until Zack says otherwise, or until his vision comes to fruition."

Darin Crenshaw: "With all the darkness and negativity that comes through your world, thank you for always being an amazing and positive human being through it all. . . . Thank you for everything, Zack!"

Robby Monroe: "My entire career could be traced back to your work. My whole life has been shaped and inspired by your work, and then again, by your kindness. We've met only briefly [in Pasadena], but you literally changed my life. Thank you."

Francis Zhang: "As a fan from China, I want to thank you, Zack. You made my favorite comic book movie, *Watchmen*. Your work let me fall in love with Superman and Batman. You inspired me to learn photography, to never compromise when facing obstacles. I am honored to be a fan, and when Zack Snyder's *Justice League* finally comes out, I will open a beer to celebrate the victory and the end of this incredible journey."

Justin Savage: "I distinctly remember falling in love with your work after sneaking into a Friday night showing of *300* in seventh grade. Since then, I've become such a big fan of yours, and I owe it to *Watchmen, Man of Steel, BvS,* and the true *Justice League* for reinvigorating my love of comics and comics on screen."

Kerry Vanderberg: "Thank you, Zack, for your amazing films. As a long time DC and superhero fan, you gave me the best version of Superman for the modern day that wasn't cheesy, corny, or outdated. Thanks also for a comic-book-accurate Batman, and a Wonder Woman that was perfect out the gate. Your films are so deep and enjoyable, and I can't wait to see what is next from you. The movement has given me confidence to proudly speak up and defend the films I love, regardless of how others feel."

Ethan Flegg: "You're the reason I love film. I'm in school to become a film composer because of your movies. . . . In 2017, my sister committed suicide, so when I hear your story, I feel a kinship to you. The reason I was able to come through on the other side was *Batman v Superman*. It showed me real people, struggling with real pain, and made me believe that I could struggle through it, too. Without that movie, my life would be down a completely different road. I, in part, credit you with the courage I have to shoot for my dreams, and I feel like nothing I can say would express the gratitude and appreciation I have for you and all you do for your fans."

Caleb Braley: "Your movies have truly changed my life for the better. During a very troubling time in my life, I rewatched *Man of Steel*. I had always liked the movie, but watching it this time was completely different. . . . Because of [it], I've set and reached goals I never would've thought imaginable before, and I'm finally following my passions in life. I guess it's true that powerful art really can change lives. Thank you for all you've done to bring these incredible stories to life. You really are changing lives with your work."

Jonathan Verby: "I love DC superheroes. In my opinion, you have made three of the top five comic book movies of all time. . . . *Man of Steel* showed a Superman that didn't completely trust himself. *Batman v Superman* showed a public that didn't trust Superman. My belief is that Zack Snyder's *Justice League* will examine exactly why Superman is worthy of that trust."

Ian Griffin: "This hashtag took my mind away from all of [my personal tragedy]. This community, made in honor of you and your *Justice League*, honestly has helped [my] pain. This cause has become a healing process, and it's working, and that's important. You saved MY world, and you did it without a cape. I needed an 'S' to look to. A symbol of hope. Thank you for being that. We are with you."

Pete Certo: "Your version of *Justice League* seeing the light of day is the most absolute must of all the musts in the film industry. An imperative.

A mankind requirement. I talk about it endlessly to people close to me. I read everything I can, participate in Twitter threads, and wear my #Release TheSnyderCut t-shirts to the gym, always looking for more believers. We all have your back and stand with you because the truth is, we are all still waiting to see the actual *Justice League* movie and be blown away. Massive kudos to you on your work, and I hope you and the fam are well!"

Craig Dalziel and Leh Ti Loh: "Hello Zack, my wife and I would like to thank you and Deborah for giving us the absolute best rendition of super-heroes and their films, which will be remembered for years to come."

Rajat Bagga: "I just wanted to tell you that I have prayed a lot of times in the past three years for your justice so that you'll be able to release your true vision of *Justice League*. As we are close to it becoming true, this story is be going to be an inspiration for many authentic artists (even me) around the world, for generations to come."

Kevin Johnson: "Mr. Snyder, I just want to thank you sincerely for being who you are and sharing your gift, your art with the world. I've had my share of dark times while on this earth. My wife passed away in 2008, and I soon after lost my job during the financial crisis. I became a recluse for a while, but I attempted the best I could to turn all the negatives into positives. It was a long road that I don't wish on anyone. During my reclusive state, I remember going to see *Watchmen* and then *Sucker Punch* a couple years later. The style and storytelling of these films made me see that there is hope after darkness. This really hit home after seeing *Man Of Steel*. There will always be light, but seeing it isn't always easy. I enjoy helping people as a physical therapist. To help them keep hope, and to let them know that hope never dies. Thank you, again, for making me excited about comic book movies again."

Joshua Graham: "Thank you, Zack Snyder, for bringing me two of the great-est comic book movies ever: *MoS* and *BvS*. . . . I really can't wait to see what you bring us in Zack Snyder's *Justice League*. #ReleaseTheSnyderCut."

Sforzanto Goth: "I am Sforzanto2711 from Thailand. I truly want Warner Brothers to release the *Justice League* Snyder Cut and I [want you] to complete your arcs. We missed many interesting characters. I will fight until we achieve [it]. I hope you and your family stay safe. #ReleaseTheSnyderCut."

Sam Otten: "Dear Zack and Deborah. Thank you both for all your efforts bringing to life brilliant, modern interpretations of the DC characters. *Batman v Superman,* in particular, has been so rewarding because the deeper I look, the more it reveals, and it has spurred hours of wonderful conversations with other fans. I hope to see the story continued."

Gio Torres: "Zack, thank you for all the respect you have shown us as fans. You keep pushing us to dig deeper into your films, and you have always showed the utmost respect for our passion. You've been an inspiration to me to become a better human. I will forever be grateful."

Brandon Verklas: "Zack's movies inspire me to create. And seeing his artistic vision realized with #ReleaseTheSnyderCut is why I'm in this movement. Thanks for inspiring me through films that actually have something more to say."

David Rizzuto: "Hey Zack, I appreciate your work on the DC films. All the best, and I can't wait to see *Army of the Dead* and your vision for *Justice League.*"

Miguel Coll: "I joined up with the movement because I do believe his *Justice League* is just as good as his other DC films. So thank you Zack for bringing your art to life."

David Harnois: "Zack, thank you. Thank you for a bold vision of how to present these characters. I hope that one day we get to see what would have been the next step in your plan, and, if we're lucky, somehow seeing how you planned to end it."

Hamoun Mohammadi: "Thank you for your legendary movies. The meaning and depth behind them is unbelievable."

Sean Carter: "Thank you. Thank you for being bold enough to be true to your vision, no matter what the project. Thank you for deciding to share your talents with all of us. You have made your mark on movies forever, and I hope you can recognize and find some peace in that. . . . Please know how much we support you."

Marcos Flores: "Zack, thank you brining back my love for Superman for the first time since 1993. And giving me the comic book movie I always dreamed about."

Çağlar Ali Doğan: "I'm from Turkey. I want to you know, you two give me a life purpose. You two hold my hands. Thanks to you and your powerful art, I'm still alive. *Batman v Superman: Dawn of Justice* changed my life forever. It showed me how powerful I can be; how can I beat my own demons, etc. . . . I love you two so much. Thank you."

Adam Azam: "Thank you, Zack, for completely changing my opinions on Superman. The depth and unique visual style you have in your movies puts you up as one of my favorite filmmakers of all time. Keep up the great work."

Dawson J. Wiedrich: "You introduced me into a community where people like me support and follow one common goal, in a day where finding something like that is really hard. You gave the best versions of some of the most popular superheroes of all time to fans that have been starving for that for years, and you did it in such a well-rendered storytelling way that people weren't expecting. But you look now, people all over the world love your vision and want it to be shown to the world. Just know that we support you, we love your work, we love your vision and your innovation, and your devotion to the art of storytelling. This is for Autumn."

NOTES

CHAPTER ONE

1. Author interview with Zack Snyder, June 2, 2020.
2. Author interview with Giovanni Torres, January 9, 2020.
3. Author interview with Daniella Cares, June 7, 2020.
4. HBO Max press release, May 20, 2020.

CHAPTER TWO

1. Author interview with the Nerd Queens, December 22, 2019.
2. Zack Snyder's comment under Thiago Kesseli's VERO Post, December 24, 2019.
3. Author interview with Lindsey Staton, January 13, 2020.
4. Author interview with Joseph Todd, December 23, 2019.
5. Author interview with Megan Loucks, January 16, 2020.
6. Author interview with Darren Benson, April 17, 2020.
7. Author interview with Geraldo Cortes, March 28, 2020.
8. Author interview with Chris Wong Swenson, October 23, 2019.
9. Author interview with Jeff Purdy, October 24, 2019.
10. *Batman Begins,* Warner Bros., Christopher Nolan (2005).
11. Author interview with Hamad Al-Mansouri, October 26, 2019.
12. Author interview with Fiona Zheng, January 15, 2020.

13. Tweet by Fiona Zheng (https://twitter.com/fukujang0627/status/9330873 65832118272?s=11)

14. The Film Exiles podcast, November 16, 2019 (https://www.youtube.com/ watch?v=QGrhO1YFHgs).

CHAPTER THREE

1. Author interview with Geraldo Cortes.

2. "Justice Prevails for Warner Bros.," *Variety*, February 22, 2007 https://variety .com/2007/film/markets-festivals/justice-prevails-for-warner-bros-1117960018/.

3. Author interview with Carlos Orbegozo, October 28, 2019.

4. Robert Zemeckis on 'Superman' Reboot, MTV News, November 1, 2010 (https://web.archive.org/web/20130527062010/http://splashpage.mtv.com/2010/ 11/01/robert-zemeckis-superman-reboot).

5. 'Man of Steel' will open door for more DC Comics superhero movies, Enter-tainment Weekly, April 11, 2013 (https://ew.com/article/2013/04/11/man-of-steel -dc-comics-superhero-movies/).

6. 'Batman v Superman' will be a key test for Warner's film CEO and a slate of DC Comics films, *Los Angeles Times,* March 22, 2016 (https://www.latimes .com/entertainment/envelope/cotown/la-et-ct-batman-superman-warner-bros -20160322-story.html).

7. Author in attendance at SDCC.

8. Exclusive interview with Zack Snyder, director Of 'Batman Vs. Super-man,' Forbes.com, April 17, 2014 (https://www.forbes.com/sites/markhughes/ 2014/04/17/exclusive-interview-with-zack-snyder-director-of-batman-vs -superman/#679b981b7bf4).

9. First look at 'Batman v Superman: Dawn of Justice' on EW's cover, *Entertain-ment Weekly*, July 1, 2015 (https://ew.com/article/2015/07/01/first-look-batman-v -superman-dawn-justice-ews-cover/).

CHAPTER FOUR

1. Author Reed Tucker Digs Into The Trenches To Talk About Marvel & DC Comics' 50-Year War, OkayPlayer, May 2, 2018 (https://www.okayplayer.com/ interviews/reed-tucker-slugfest-marvel-vs-dc-comics-interview.html).

2. *Iron Man,* Paramount, Jon Favreau (2008).

3. Kevin Fiege Talks Iron Man 2, The Avengers and More, MovieWeb.com, April 26, 2010 (https://movieweb.com/exclusive-kevin-fiege-talks-iron-man-2-the -avengers-and-more/).

4. Author interview with Stephen Colbert, February 18, 2020.

5. 'Man of Steel' May Give DC Comics More Superpowers, *Wall Street Journal,* June 16, 2013 (https://www.wsj.com/articles/SB10001424127887323836504578 549641408007794).

6. Henry Cavill Tells Us Why 'Dawn Of Justice' Is Not 'A Superman Sequel,' MTV News, April 22, 2015 (http://www.mtv.com/news/2140143/henry-cavill -dawn-of-justice-not-superman-film/).

7. Author interview with Matthew Criscuolo, October 20, 2019.

8. Author interview with Justin M. Lesniewski, February 22, 2020.

CHAPTER FIVE

1. Seth Rogen tweet (https://twitter.com/Sethrogen/status/5046908762000 13826).

2. Seth Rogen tweet (https://twitter.com/Sethrogen/status/5046910975669 73952).

3. Author interview with Jonita Davis, April 17, 2020.

4. How To Reboot The Superman Movie Franchise, MTV News, Aug. 11, 2008 (http://www.mtv.com/news/2592674/how-to-reboot-the-superman-movie -franchise-comic-writers-chime-in/).

5. Christopher Nolan: Villains Defined The Dark Knight Trilogy More Than Batman, *Variety,* May 12, 2018 (https://variety.com/2018/film/news/chris topher-nolan-on-how-villains-defined-the-dark-knight-trilogy-more-than-bat man-1202808441/).

6. Christopher Nolan on Batman and Superman, Empire (via SuperHero-Hype), June 4, 2010 (https://www.superherohype.com/news/102090-christopher -nolan-on-batman-and-superman).

7. Author interview with Nana of the Nerd Queens.

8. The L.A. Times' Hero Complex, November 12, 2012 (http://herocomplex .latimes.com/2012/11/12/zack-snyder-on-watchmen-legacy-as-the-anti-avengers -movie/).

9. Author interview with Chris Wong-Swenson.

10. Author interview with Matthew Criscuolo.

11. Author interview with Megan Loucks.

12. Author interview with Giovanni Torres.

13. *Man of Steel,* Warner Bros., June 2013.

14. Author interview with Carlos Orbegozo.

15. *Batman v Superman: Dawn of Justice,* Warner Bros., March 2015.

16. Zack Snyder Discusses Themes Behind Batman v Superman, *Forbes,* April 1, 2016 (https://www.forbes.com/sites/markhughes/2016/04/01/interview-zack -snyder-discusses-themes-behind-batman-v-superman/#2652d94b7104).

17. 'Justice' is served with another helping of Superman, *USA Today,* July 3, 2014 (https://www.usatoday.com/story/life/movies/2014/07/03/henry-cavill -batman-superman-movie-first-look/11310229/).

CHAPTER SIX

1. 'Batman v Superman' Won't Be Joining $1 Billion Box Office Club, The Wrap, May 4, 2016 (https://www.thewrap.com/batman-v-superman-wont-be -joining-1-billion-box-office-club/).

2. 'Batman v Superman' Won't Be Joining $1 Billion Box Office Club, The Wrap, May 4, 2016 (https://www.thewrap.com/batman-v-superman-wont-be -joining-1-billion-box-office-club/).

3. Author interview with Stephen Colbert.

4. *Suicide Squad* review, CinemaBlend (https://www.cinemablend.com/ reviews/1540929/suicide-squad).

5. David Ayer's Tweet (https://twitter.com/DavidAyerMovies/status/822948 443110842369?ref_src=twsrc%5Etfw).

6. David Ayer's Instagram post (https://www.instagram.com/p/B4adVBE gxZ_/?utm_source=ig_embed).

7. 'Batman v. Superman': Married Creative Duo on That R-Rated DVD, Plans for DC Superhero Universe, *The Hollywood Reporter,* March 17, 2016 (https://www .hollywoodreporter.com/news/batman-v-superman-married-creative-874799).

8. Author interview with Benjamin Hunt, January 4, 2020.

9. Author interview with Fiona Zheng.

10. Author interview with Hamad Al-Mansouri.

11. Author interview with Carlos Orbegozo.

12. Author interview with Zack Snyder.

13. 'Batman V. Superman' Box Office Profits—2016 Most Valuable Movie Block-buster Tournament, Deadline, March 23, 2017 (https://deadline.com/2017/03/ batman-v-superman-box-office-profit-2016-1202049201/).

CHAPTER SEVEN

1. Reading the Weather, Drew McWeeny, January 10, 2020 (https://drewmc weeny.substack.com/p/reading-the-weather).

2. 'Batman v. Superman' Fallout: Warner Bros. Shakes Up Executive Roles, *The Hollywood Reporter,* May 17, 2016 (https://www.hollywoodreporter.com/heat -vision/batman-v-superman-fallout-warner-895174).

3. Geoff Johns Confirmed As DC Entertainment President, *The Hollywood Reporter,* July 27, 2016 (https://www.hollywoodreporter.com/heat-vision/geoff -johns-confirmed-as-president-915028).

4. The New Co-Chief of DC Superhero Movies Is Big On Hope and Optimism, Vulture, May 18, 2016 (https://www.vulture.com/2016/05/geoff-johns-dc-films .html).

5. Warner Bros.'s New Strategy on DC: Lighten Up, Superheroes, *Wall Street Journal,* September 8, 2016 (https://www.wsj.com/articles/warner-bros-s-new -strategy-on-dc-lighten-up-superheroes-1473350000).

6. Warner Bros.'s New Strategy on DC: Lighten Up, Superheroes, *Wall Street Journal,* September 8, 2016 (https://www.wsj.com/articles/warner-bros-s-new -strategy-on-dc-lighten-up-superheroes-1473350000).

7. Author's set visit.

8. Author's set visit.

9. Author interview with Zack Snyder.

CHAPTER EIGHT

1. Zack Snyder Steps Down From 'Justice League' to Deal With Family Tragedy, *The Hollywood Reporter,* May 22, 2017 (https://www.hollywoodreporter.com/ heat-vision/zack-snyder-steps-down-justice-league-deal-family-tragedy-1006455).

2. Author interview with Zack Snyder.

3. Author interview with John Aaron Garza, March 27, 2020.

4. Zack Snyder Steps Down From 'Justice League' to Deal With Family Tragedy, *The Hollywood Reporter,* May 22, 2017 (https://www.hollywoodreporter.com/ heat-vision/zack-snyder-steps-down-justice-league-deal-family-tragedy-1006455).

5. Author interview with Benjamin Hunt.

6. Author interview with Giovanni Torres.

7. Author interview with Darren Benson.

8. Author interview with Hamad Al-Mansouri.

9. Zack Snyder Steps Down From 'Justice League' to Deal With Family Tragedy, *The Hollywood Reporter,* May 22, 2017 (https://www.hollywoodreporter.com/heat-vision/zack-snyder-steps-down-justice-league-deal-family-tragedy-1006455).

10. Zack Snyder's Vero Post, November 27, 2018 (https://vero.co/p/b-Ng3x WjqPqK8T6D7z1XMBcw).

11. Author interview with Matthew Criscuolo.

12. We Can Be Heroes, Mick Doyle, October 11, 2019 (https://afsp.org/story/we-can-be-heroes-superhero-fans-take-up-the-fight-for-suicide-prevention).

CHAPTER NINE

1. Zack Snyder Steps Down From 'Justice League' to Deal With Family Tragedy, *The Hollywood Reporter,* May 22, 2017 (https://www.hollywoodreporter.com/heat-vision/zack-snyder-steps-down-justice-league-deal-family-tragedy-1006455).

2. In 'Justice League,' DC looks beyond Batman and Superman, AP, November 13, 2017 (https://www.washingtontimes.com/news/2017/nov/13/in-justice -league-dc-looks-beyond-batman-and-super/).

3. DC Rethinks Its Universe, Vulture, September 2017 (https://www.vulture .com/2017/09/dc-wonder-woman-movie-strategy-universe.html).

4. Why Ben Affleck and Gal Gadot Are Tweeting #ReleaseTheSnyderCut, *New York Times,* November 19, 2019 (https://www.nytimes.com/2019/11/19/movies/snyder-cut-gadot-affleck.html).

5. DC Rethinks Its Universe, Vulture, September 2017 (https://www.vulture .com/2017/09/dc-wonder-woman-movie-strategy-universe.html).

6. Author interview with Lindsey Staton.

7. Author interview with David McEachrane.

8. Author interview with Brandon Valenza, January 12, 2020.

9. Author interview with Ben Wellington, January 12, 2020.

10. Author interview with Fiona Zheng.

11. Author interview with Justin M. Lesniewski.

12. 'Justice League' Extensive Reshoots Causing Headaches for Star Schedules, *Variety,* July 24, 2017 (https://variety.com/2017/film/news/justice-league -reshoots-1202502433/)

13. *Justice League*, Warner Bros., November 2017.

14. In 'Justice League,' DC looks beyond Batman and Superman, AP, November 13, 2017 (https://www.washingtontimes.com/news/2017/nov/13/in-justice -league-dc-looks-beyond-batman-and-super/).

15. Author interview with Matthew Criscuolo.

16. *ComicBookDebate* podcast, https://www.youtube.com/watch?v=nBh-Z_c61k4.

17. Leonardo Oliviera's Twitter, https://twitter.com/Leo_Rafael99/status/1202021154917158912.

18. Leonard Cohen, "Everybody Knows," 1988.

19. Actor Holt McCallany on Getting Beat up by Batman in 'Justice League,' and Season 2 of 'Mindhunter,' *Men's Journal,* https://www.mensjournal.com/health-fitness/interview-actor-holt-mccallany-getting-beat-batman-justice-league-and-season-2/.

20. Ben Affleck Says Zack Snyder's Justice League Cut 'Should Be Available,' CinemaBlend, February 21, 2020 (https://www.cinemablend.com/news/2490644/ben-affleck-says-zack-snyders-justice-league-cut-should-be-available).

CHAPTER TEN

1. Author interview with Brandon Valenza.

2. Author interview with Will Rowlands, January 28, 2020.

3. Author interview with Ben Wellington.

4. Jason Momoa Thanks 'Justice League' Crew With Shirtless Photo as Filming Wraps, The Wrap, October 1, 2016 (https://www.thewrap.com/jason-momoa-thanks-justice-league-crew-with-shirtless-photo-as-filming-wraps-photo/).

5. Zack Snyder's tweet, https://twitter.com/ZackSnyder/status/784425976117747712?p=p.

6. Christopher McQuarrie's Instagram, https://www.instagram.com/p/BRuN63FgRr5/?hl=en.

7. 'Justice League' Extensive Reshoots Causing Headaches for Star Schedules, *Variety,* July 24, 2017 (https://variety.com/2017/film/news/justice-league-reshoots-1202502433/).

8. Mission Impossible—Fallout Empire Podcast Spoiler Special Ft. Christopher McQuarrie, Empire, July 31, 2018 (https://www.empireonline.com/movies/news/mission-impossible-fallout-spoiler-special-ft-christopher-mcquarrie-part-1/).

9. Henry Cavill interview, FOX 5 Washington D.C., https://twitter.com/kevinmccarthytv/status/929877220381904897?lang=en.

10. Henry Cavill's Instagram, https://www.instagram.com/p/BTa0j2_FDfB/?utm_source=ig_embed.

11. Henry Cavill's Instagram, https://www.instagram.com/p/BXBJas2FYuP/?utm_source=ig_embed.

12. *Justice League,* Warner Bros., November 2017.

13. AT & T Sets $85.4 Billion Time Warner Deal, CEOs Talk 'Unique' Potential of Combination, *Variety,* October 22, 2016 (https://variety.com/2016/biz/news/att-time-warner-deal-1201897938/).

14. How 'Justice League' Became a 'Frankenstein,' The Wrap, November 29, 2017 (https://www.thewrap.com/justice-league-zack-snyder-batman-v-superman-wonder-woman/).

CHAPTER ELEVEN

1. Author interview with Richard Bullivant, January 21 and February 13, 2020.

2. Justice League's Rotten Tomatoes page (https://www.rottentomatoes.com/m/justice_league_2017).

3. *New York Post* review (https://nypost.com/2017/11/16/justice-league-is-a-stupid-plodding-cgi-spectacle/).

4. *Toronto Star* review (https://www.thestar.com/entertainment/movies/2017/11/15/justice-league-just-isnt-good-review.html).

5. *US Weekly* review (https://www.usmagazine.com/entertainment/news/justice-league-movie-review-mildly-fun-noticeably-flawed/).

6. *The Hollywood Reporter* review (https://www.hollywoodreporter.com/review/justice-league-review-1057114).

7. Author interview with Matthew Criscuolo.

8. Author interview with Fiona Zheng.

9. Author interview with John Aaron Garza.

10. Author interview with Geraldo Cortes.

11. Author interview with the Nerd Queens.

12. Author interview with Joseph Todd.

13. Author interview with Benjamin Hunt.

14. Author interview with Andrea Abbatista, January 22, 2020.

15. Author interview with Zack Snyder.

16. Author interview with Brandon Valenza.

17. Author interview with Sheraz Farooqi, February 19, 2020.

18. Author interview with Giovanni Torres.

19. Warner Bros. Faces A Possible $50M To $100M Loss On 'Justice League,' *Forbes,* Nov. 20, 2017 (https://www.forbes.com/sites/robcain/2017/11/20/warner-bros-faces-a-possible-50m-to-100m-loss-on-justice-league/#1d63b70d5d8b).

20. Author interview with Chris Wong Swenson.

21. Author interview with David McEachrane.

22. Author interview with Lindsey Staton.

23. Fiona Zheng's Vero post, November 2017 (https://imgur.com/XqeAMVP).

24. *The Film Exiles* podcast, November 16, 2019 (https://www.youtube.com/watch?v=QGrhO1YFHgs).

25. *Justice League,* Warner Bros., November 2017.

26. MrJONA's tweet (https://twitter.com/MrJ0NA/status/1217341550457507841).

CHAPTER TWELVE

1. Kneel Before Zack, The Ringer, June 12, 2019 (https://www.theringer.com/movies/2019/6/12/18662603/release-zack-snyder-cut-justice-league-zack).

2. Roberto Mata's Change.org petition (https://www.change.org/p/warner-bros-zack-snyder-s-director-s-and-tom-holkenborg-s-score-for-home-release-e90fef07-11c6-4a9a-9ae8-375c7717dafa).

3. Author interview with Fiona Zheng.

4. Author interview with Alessandro Maniscalco, March 1, 2020.

5. Author interview with Darren Benson.

6. Author interview with Adrienne Marie, April 13, 2020.

7. Author interview with Will Rowlands.

8. Author interview with Matthew Criscuolo.

9. Author interview with Scott McClellan, February 20, 2020.

10. Author interview with Jonathan Nordia, January 6, 2020.

11. Author interview with Sean Maher, January 24, 2020.

12. Why Your Company Needs a Good Tagline, *Forbes* (https://www.forbes.com/sites/theyec/2014/11/03/why-your-company-needs-a-good-tagline/#338f4c696d5b).

13. Jack Waz's tweet (https://twitter.com/jackwaz/status/1240135051288948742).

14. Author interview with Stephen Colbert.

15. Author interview with Justin Lesniewski.

16. Joint Statement on Behalf of the DC Fandom, ComicBookDebate (https://comicbookdebate.com/2018/05/09/joint-statement-on-behalf-of-the-dc-fandom/).

17. *The Film Exiles* podcast, November 16, 2019 (https://www.youtube.com/watch?v=QGrhO1YFHgs).

18. Zack Snyder at SnyderCon on Devin Fuentes' Twitter.

19. Author interview with Devin Fuerte, February 15, 2020.

20. Author interview with the Nerd Queens.

21. Author interview with Ben Wellington.

22. Author interview with Zack Snyder.

CHAPTER THIRTEEN

1. Zack Snyder Vero post (https://vero.co/p/7q-RGHf7qKDvh2dS3J8Jn7xz).

2. Author interview with Zack Snyder, October 2, 2019.

3. Author interview with Deborah Synder, October 2, 2019.

4. This billionaire wants you to sign up to his social network—and promises no ads, CNBC, March 8, 2017 (https://www.cnbc.com/2017/03/08/this-billionaire-wants-you-to-sign-up-to-his-social-network—and-promises-no-adverts.html).

5. Zack Snyder Vero post (https://vero.co/p/F8G-T6fCVG6sJqM1KHff6V19W).

6. Author interview with Giovanni Torres.

7. Zack Snyder Vero post (https://vero.co/p/7j-ZFVm96m9Ht9Khw29RCTKJ).

8. *Justice League,* Warner Bros., November 2017.

9. Zack Snyder Vero post (https://vero.co/p/Tfm-QZ1PbrVMKXrjb8sQxMgm).

10. Zack Snyder Vero post (https://vero.co/p/z-7hJmjCQPfw1H6Zwps4XHQX).

11. Author interview with Carlos Orbegozo.

12. Author interview with Zack Snyder, June 2, 2020.

13. Zack Snyder Vero post (https://vero.co/p/qFRB-GJSXvKNpXxJ2fnDXQ29).

14. Zack Snyder Vero post (https://vero.co/p/z-bMWtwVCzzJ1M8MzSh4m1pg).

15. Zack Snyder Vero post (https://vero.co/p/M9tw-z191V29Gb191WnpTT1g).

16. Zack Snyder Vero post (https://vero.co/p/1nhZ-M761Jzc31DqLFrmwmzN).

17. Author interview with Scott McClellan.

18. Zack Snyder Vero post (https://vero.co/p/qW9B-f23XcHzHcwJvLS6pNwr).

19. Zack Snyder's Justice League teaser trailer, HBO Max (https://twitter.com/ZackSnyder/status/1273646510542974981).

20. Zack Snyder Vero post (https://vero.co/p/Q63-6CgRbbRB9WCvrfHpcMvP).

21. Author interview with Hamad Al-Mansouri.

CHAPTER FOURTEEN

1. Author interview with John Aaron Garza.

2. Author interview with Mick Doyle, May 7, 2020.

3. *The Film Exiles* podcast, November 16, 2019 (https://www.youtube.com/watch?v=QGrhO1YFHgs).

4. Author interview with Robert Gebbia, April 21, 2020.

5. Author interview with Brandon Valenza.

6. Author interview with Brent M. Coffee, June 23, 2020.

7. Author interview with the Nerd Queens.

8. Author interview with Charlie Buda, April 13, 2020.

9. Author interview with Kerry Vanderberg, February 19, 2020.

10. Author interview with Will Rowlands.

11. Author interview with Alessandro Maniscalco.

12. Author interview with Giovanni Torres.

13. RTSC's tweet to Subway (https://twitter.com/RTSnyderCut/status/1202781565996150784).

14. Zack Snyder's Subway tweet (https://twitter.com/ZackSnyder/status/1228455442356957184).

15. Author interview with Victor Ku, March 17, 2020.

16. Zack Snyder's Vero post (https://vero.co/p/BkS-fWRqrcz1BzW2nWGkcKzZ).

17. "It Will Be An Entirely New Thing," *The Hollywood Reporter,* May 20, 2020. (https://www.hollywoodreporter.com/heat-vision/justice-league-snyder-cut-plans-revealed-it-will-be-an-new-thing-1295102).

18. Author interview with Alessandro Maniscalco.

19. Author interview with Darren Benson.

20. "Ben Affleck Says Zack Snyder's Justice League Cut 'Should Be Available,'" CinemaBlend, February 21, 2020. (https://www.cinemablend.com/news/2490644/ben-affleck-says-zack-snyders-justice-league-cut-should-be-available).

21. Zack Snyder's Vero post (https://vero.co/p/R5-PSBkh3DN58CSBqsnXBZGt).

CHAPTER FIFTEEN

1. Author interview with Zack Snyder, June 2, 2020.

2. Ray Fisher on *TheNiceCast* podcast, May 24, 2020 (https://www.youtube.com/watch?v=JuW21muWKeg).

3. Ben Affleck on Fatman on Batman, May 21, 2020 (https://www.youtube.com/watch?v=sQEI0VeARR8).

4. Jason Moma celebrates, May 21, 2020 (https://www.youtube.com/watch?v=ikqMbtRkY44).

5. "Justice League Star Jesse Eisenberg Reacts To Snyder Cut News," Digital Spy, May 26, 2020 (https://www.digitalspy.com/movies/a32668843/justice-league-snyder-cut-jesse-eisenberg/).

6. Jason Momoa's Instagram review of Snyder Cut (https://www.instagram .com/tv/B1U1rmigdlY/?utm_source=ig_embed).

7. Author interview with Megan Loucks, May 25, 2020.

8. Author interview with Sheraz Farooqi, May 21, 2020.

9. Author interview with Carlos Orbegozo, May 24, 2020.

10. Zack Snyder's Justice Con panel, July 25, 2020.

11. Ray Fisher's Justice Con panel, July 25, 2020.

12. Fabian Wagner Justice Con panel, July 26, 2020.

INDEX

INDEX

INDEX